ISBN: 978129036238

Published by:
HardPress Publishing
8345 NW 66TH ST #2561
MIAMI FL 33166-2626

Email: info@hardpress.net
Web: http://www.hardpress.net

Ex Bibl. Dom.
AD S. PATRITIUM,
Quebec. C. SS. R.
Arm.   No.

JOHN M. KELLY LIBRARY

Donated by
**The Redemptorists of
the Toronto Province**
from the Library Collection of
Holy Redeemer College, Windsor

University of
St. Michael's College, Toronto

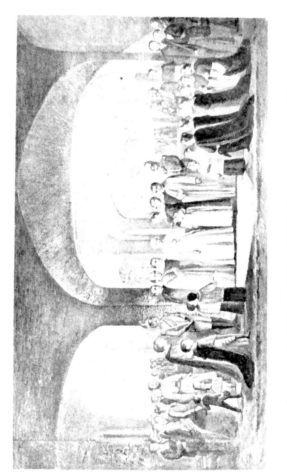

PILGRIMS IN THE SUBTERRANEAN BASILICA OF S. CLEMENT.

SAINT CLEMENT

POPE AND MARTYR

AND

HIS BASILICA IN ROME

BY

REV. JOSEPH MULLOOLY O. P.

> The memory of him shall not
> depart away,
> And his name shall be in request
> from generation to generation.
> (Ecclesiasticus xxxix. 13.)

ROME – 1869
PRINTED BY BENEDICT GUERRA

HOLY REDEEMER LIBRARY, WINDSOR

INTRODUCTION.

In a vineyard about a mile from Rome, the foundation walls of a large villa, the chambers of which are filled up with masses of stucco ornaments and coloured plaster, as indeed the whole soil with bits of Pompeian red, fragments of various and rare marbles, mosaics, glass of so many colours that we wonder at the profusion, pottery from the coarsest to the fine thin polished red clay, and, more rarely, seals, and gold ornaments, attest the mansion of a rich Pagan family. In a corner of the enclosure are ruined columbaria, probably for their dependants, with broken cinerary urns still in their niches; and elsewhere a vast massive round monument of stone for the head of the house, who left to posterity a single sepulchral chamber in the centre. A white marble slab, still preserved, though detached from the building, gives us the title.

<small>A Pagan tomb.</small>

— IV —

> D. M
>
> M. AVRELIVS SYNTOMVS ET
> AVRELIA MARCIANE ÆDIFICIVM
> CVM CEPOTAFIO. ET MEMORIAM
> A SOLO FECERVNT SIBI ET FILIIS
> SVIS AVRELIO LEONTIO ET AVRELI
> Æ FRVCTVOSÆ ET LIB. LIBER.
> POSTERISQVE EORVM.

D. M

« M. Aurelius Syntomus and
« Aurelia Marciana the building
« with garden-tomb and memoria
« made from the foundation for themselves and children
« of theirs, Aurelius Leontius and Aurelia
« Fructuosa, and their freedmen, freedwomen
« and their posterity ».

Its Christian adaptation. Here then we have the whole exterior economy of Roman burial: the *praedium* or farm, and that disposition of the *monumentum* with its area and precincts so sacred, and jealously fenced about by Roman law (1). With this before our eyes we can

---

(1) According to Roman law, land which had been once used for burial purposes was protected by special privileges, one of which was that it was exempted from many of the laws which regulated the tenure and transfer of property. In the technical language of

conceive, were the owner a Christian, how by his licence, or active zeal, the martyr might be safely laid at rest upon his estate ; and history records the names of many noble ladies who thus gave honourable burial to the martyred dead.

The breviary says of S. Andrew that « Maximilla, « dear to Christ, bore the Apostle's body to an excel- « lent place, and buried it with spices » (1). Not long ago several martyrs were found, with the sponges which were used to collect their blood, in the church of S. Pudenziana. In 119, Severina, the wife of Count Aurelian, buried Pope Alexander, Eventius and Theodulus, on her farm seven miles on the Nomentan way, and made a cemetery for them. When the emperor Adrian, in 120, put to death Symphorosa and her seven children at Tivoli, their Acts say : « After this the persecution ceased for a year « and six months, during which time the holy bo- « dies of all the martyrs were deposited with all « care in tombs constructed for them ». The Lucinas were celebrated for this pious work. The first, who buried S. Paul, the sorrowful widow Pomponia

---

the time it became *Religiosus* « Religiosum locum unusquisque sua voluntate facit, dum mortuum infert in locum suum » (Marcian. Digest. 1, 8, 6, §. 4). It was inalienable, and exclusively belonged to the families of those who were buried in it.

(1) Maximilla Christo amabilis tulit corpus Apostoli, optimo loco cum aromatibus sepelivit. Antiph. IV. ad Laudes.

Graecina, as De Rossi thinks ; and, in 251, 252, another Lucina, who buried Pope Cornelius at night, with Cereale and Salustia, and twenty one others on her farm in a crypt next the cemetery of Callixtus on the Appian way. And, even under Diocletian, in 301 , the martyr Restitutus was thus interred. « Justa, a pious and religious matron, with some
« ecclesiastics, a few Christians, and her servants,
« at night, on account of the wickedness of the Pa-
« gans, gathered up his body, went to her house
« towards the *meta sudans,* and there sprinkled it
« with aromatics, and placed it in a snowy winding-
« sheet. Whilst it was yet dark night , she put
« it in her chariot to take it to her grounds on
« the Nomentan way. And whilst she was going
« there , she dispatched a message to the bishop
« (Stephen by name) who lived on the same road ,
« that he might come to meet it with the priests,
« deacons, and other clerks , with the servants of
« God and the sacred virgins. Early in the morn-
« ing they arrived , and with hymns and canticles
« brought the holy body to the sixteenth milestone
« and there worthily interred it ».

But here, on the lands of Aurelius Syntomus, there are no vestiges of the Christian dead, no arenaria, no crypts, and above all no loculi, arcosolia and chapels (1), for the commemoration and *cultus* of the martyr. The first Christian members of the family were obliged to make arrangements for themselves, under the protection of the law, with such decorations as their means and taste afforded. The earlier the conversion of any Roman family the more certainly will their funeral monuments puzzle us by an intermixture of Pagan ornaments. For they had no other at hand, and so long as they were not peculiarly identified with Pagan worship, there was no reason for rejecting them. Whether the convert had to fear a family council upon foreign su-

---

(1) The proper term is *cella*, or *cella memoria*, which was a rectangular chamber cut in the rock, with *loculi*, that is single places for bodies, (sarcophagi being usually on the floor, though in Domitilla's cemetery some loculi were closed with imitations of sarcophagi), and an *arcosolium*, that is an arched recess for the altar-slab over the body. Behind a wall built for concealment in the above mentioned cemetery De Rossi found an arcosolium with marble slabs, and a marble table having two large bronze rings to lift it, beneath which were two bodies, one in cloth of gold, the other in purple with a *terra-cotta* vase at its head. Pope Eutichyan, A. D. 275 283, who was himself a martyr and interred in the cemetery of Callixtus, buried there hundred and sixty two martyrs with his own hands, and forbade the faithful to bury a martyr without a dalmatic, or a purple garment called *colobium*. De Rossi says that the Fathers, especially in Africa, and the Pontifical Book, call such cellae « *cellae memoriae* of the martyrs », to distinguish them from the cellae or chambers in the temples and baths. S. Augustine tells the Manichaean Faustus; « The Christian people celebrate to-
« gether the memories of the martyrs with religious solemnity: both
« to excite imitation, and to be made partakers of their merits,
« and be helped by their prayers. So however, that we sacrifice

perstion, such as sat upon Pomponia Graecina the wife of Aulus Plautius, who conquered Britain under Claudius, or notoriety had provoked imperial edicts, sculpture above ground was not so safe a work as painting below. Pure symbolism must necessarily be the growth of leisure and instruction; and the more exclusively Christian its character the less we should expect to find it among the primitive converts. Hence if we see the vine and vintage (Bacchanalian emblems as classical conceit has christened them) upon the mosaic vault of S. Costanza, or carved on the sarcophagus of her grandmother S. Helen, whilst they may have had an

---

« to none of the martyrs, but to the very God of the martyrs, al-
« though we erect altars at the *memorias* of the martyrs ». And
again: « To our martyrs we build not temples as to gods, but *me-*
« *morias* as to men whose spirits are living with God ». And the
fifth Council of Carthage, Can. XIV, forbids *aedes* to be built for
martyrs except there be on the spot either the body, or some sure
relics, or the origin of some habitation, or of the passion, most
faithfully handed down from the origin. And in his fifth hymn Prudentius describes the tyrant threatening to destroy the bones of Vincentius lest the people of the Lord worship and fix martyrs' titles
over them. The whole technical phraseology is found in the inscription from Caesarea in Mauritania quoted in the Bollettino of
April 1864.

   « Aream at sepulcra cultor verbi contulit
   « Et cellam struxit suis cunctis sumptibus
   « Eclesiae sanctae hanc reliquit memoriam
   « Salvete fratres puro corde et simplici
   « Evelpius vos satos sancto spiritu
« ECLESIA FRATRVVM HVNC RESTITVIT TITVLVM M. A. I. SEVERIANI C. V. »
          Ex ing. Asteri.

indirect reference to the mysteries of faith, it does not follow that they had or were anything more than customary embellishments.

We do not mean that the Christians did not rejoice in images of the vine, but that the earliest converts chose it perhaps as the most easy and least offensive of Pagan ornaments. S. Jerome says « that
« the Syrian tongue naturally lent itself to parable.
« It was one of the mediums which the wisdom of
« our Lord adapted for teaching the people ». The images in the catacombs were scriptural images; and perhaps more familiar to the Christians of Palestine and Africa than to the Romans. S. Asterius of Amasea bitterly inveighs against a singular abuse of them.
« Whenever then they go out dressed, as it were
« depicted among themselves and pointing out with
« their fingers the picture on their garments, they
« follow too at a good distance and keep back not
« indiscreetly ; for there are lions there, panthers,
« bears, bulls, dogs, woods, rocks, and hunters,
« and everything, in short, that exercises the in-
« dustry of painters expressed in imitation of na-
« ture. For as it seems not only walls and houses
« must be so adorned, but their very tunics too
« and the clokes thrown over them. But the men
« and women of those rich folks that are more re-
« ligious give the weavers subjects out of the Gospel
« history: I mean Christ himself with all his di-

« sciples, and every one of the miracles in the
« very way it is told. You will see the marriage
« at Galilee, and the waterpots, the paralitic car-
« rying the bed on his shoulders, the blind man
« who is cured with the clay, the woman who la-
« bours under an issue of blood taking hold of the
« hem, the sinner approaching to the feet of Jesus,
« Lazarus returning to life from the tomb; and
« whilst they do these things, they suppose that
« they are acting piously, and putting on gar-
« ments pleasing to God » (1). It was about the
year 400 that the bishop of Pontus complained of
these walking catacombs.

Classical learning insufficient to elucidate Christian ruins.

Occasion has a large share in funerals as well as in other human actions, and the antiquary who desired to make deductions from a series of coffin-plates, would probably arrive at conclusions very shocking to the respectable deceased. The ancient dead did not undertake to teach theology to remote posterity, and the attempt to reconstruct their tenets from the slabs of their sepulchres, mutilated and dispersed, seems not of the wisest. It is imperfect at best, and hopeless without more enlightened erudition from other sources. If a candid traveller were to examine the magnificent ruined abbey churches of Ireland and England, he might with moderate

---

(1) Sermo de Divit. et Lazar. p. 6.

acumen make out that they were of no sort of use to the practices of the present Establishment; but he could hardly understand the perfection of their purpose without some knowledge of the Catholic Church. He could not mistake that some deplorable flood of ruin had recently swept over the land, and that the variety of sects had not yet repaired its ravages. But he could not learn from the ruins alone that a great living society had never ceased to practise the rites for which those churches were originally designed. But what, if the field of his observations was not for three hundred, but for eighteen hundred years? What, if he would track the footsteps of an Apostle in a country that had literally been ploughed up by waves of ruin again and again for fifteen centuries at least (1). Our traveller upon the waste of the Roman Campagna, even with Murray in his hand and Horace in his head, would find his chances of discrimination rapidly diminished. And if he had been qualified by an Uni-

---

(1) The description of S. Gregory the Great, in the year 600, is well known. « The savage Lombard race drawn out of the sheath « of its dwelling place has been fattened on our necks, and has cut « down and dried up the race of men that in the excess of multi- « tude had risen in this land like a thick cornfield. For the cities « are unpeopled, camps overturned: churches burnt, monasteries of « men and women destroyed, farms made desolate of men and stript « of every cultivator, the earth lying waste in solitude: no owner « inhabits it, beasts have occupied the places hitherto held by a « multitude of men ». Dial. b. 3.

— XII —

versity education to identify the memorabilia of Roman grandeur, to step out on the road to Brundusium, and exhaust the poetry of his affections upon a race whose perishing had been predicted before Moses went up to mount Pisgah (1), he might find it convenient to forget what mould of man founded his « Alma Mater », and politic to decline the distasteful task of grubbing up the soil for Christian ideas. The value of each spadeful of earth would depend less upon the contents than upon his understanding what he found. He might spell out a name upon a bit of leaden pipe, or be very learned upon the marks of the tilemakers; but « cui bono » if he knew nothing of his means and motives for choosing the spot, nothing of his family affections, nothing of his progenitors or descendants: nothing but that once he was and now is not? « Ne sutor ultra crepidam ». Classical literature is not enough for Christian antiquity; and whatever sermons may be found in stones, the monuments of the Catholic Church have a language of their own. Whether they were hastily constructed, or studiously framed to the discipline of the secret; whether stamped on the legend of a royal coin, or printed in the encyclical of the living Pope, they require an initiation and instinct to un-

---

(1) « They shall come in galleys from Italy. They shall overcome they Assyrians, and shall waste the Hebrews, and at the last they themselves also shall perish ». Numbers, ch. 24, v. 24.

derstand them. And we say in no spirit of controversy, but simply as a fact, that no man who is not of the Church can appreciate them. If men will not hearken to the voice of the living Church, how can they catch its echoes in the past?

With the exception of some savages who laid their friends out to dry on little platforms in the open air, or others who eat them at a certain age (1), mankind in general seem to have put their dead out of sight, if not under ground. Whether they burnt and put them in urns, embalmed and packed them in a series of painted cases, or gave them coffins of lead or stone, the actual place of deposit was not usually on the very level of the high-way. Catholics did not burn their dead (2); but restored them to the earth, whence they came; and the practice was not likely to be recommended by the example of the persecutors who did burn them, and scattered the ashes, the Christians venerated to the winds and streams. The learned De Rossi tells us that the Pagans made the same crypts and loculi as those in the Christian cemeteries, but they were only family vaults,

---

(1) The Recognitions of S. Clement notice, « that of the whole « world only the Medes solemnly cast out people still breathing to « be devoured by dogs; that the Indians burn their dead, and the « wives are voluntarily burnt with their husbands: that very many « Germans end their lives with a noose ». Book 9. chap. 25.

(2) Execrantur rogos, et damnant ignium sepulturas. — Minucius Felix. Oct. c. II. 451.

not general, ramifying, well-closed places for worship as well as burial: that among them sarcophagi were in vogue in the days of the Antonines, and that in the fifth century Macrobius writes « urendi cor-« pora defunctorum usus nostro seculo nullus est », « in our age it is not the custom to burn the bo-« dies of the dead ». But from the first the Catholic sleeping places—coemeteria—were meant to preserve the bodies whole, and in most instances singly, and securely, apart from Pagans and heretics, conveniently for the rites of the Church whether at the deposition or commemoration. About Rome the Chrisstians dug into the hill-sides as the Etruscans had done before them; but not so much for private sepulture, as to provide one common place of rest laid out in regular tiers and passages, with economy of space, and choice of strata, where the rich and noble felt it a privilege to be found among the poor, and all yearned to lie not far from the martyrs of Christ. They were not thereby precluded from monuments or chapels above ground (1), and in case of distinguished martyrdom they were sure to construct such *memories*, which when persecution had ceased became basilicas. For if the Catholic Church has one stamp of truth more decisive than another, it is

---

(1) See De Rossi's « Bullettino di Archeologia Cristiana », on the monument of S. Domitilla. December 1865.

that she hallows and consecrates. every legitimate human affection. She honours more the call of God in the vow of the virgin, and the ordination of the priest, but she has set the seal of the sacrament upon the first act of Christian life, baptism, upon the indissolubility of marriage, and the last act of passage to the tomb. The spot where Christian blood was shed for faith, to her was holy ground. She never forgot it; for it was registered by the Church in heaven, and as far as the vicissitudes of time and the malice of the world allowed, she sought to protect, to cherish and make it a monument for ever. Literally « aromatibus sepelivit » (1), she buried with perfumes. She embalmed the memories of those holy dead with the prayers and incense of her daily sacrifice, stupendous monument of love not bound by time or space. Poor Horace had done his best : « Exegi monumentum aere pe-

---

(1) « Aromatibus sepélivit ». This expression seems to have a technical force equivalent to saying, buried as a saint. De Rossi quotes Prudentius : « We will sprinkle both the inscription and the « cold stones ; with liquid perfume », as applicable to the tazze, marble vases, placed upon a short pillar near the tombs of the saints Roma subterranea, pag. 282. Perhaps in the East such pillars, besides holding the balsamic vessel, were inscribed. At least S. Asterius says : « We, disciples of the martyrs, learn to preserve the true « religion even in the extremest dangers by merely looking upon « their sacred *thecae* as pillars inscribed with letters, and accurately « manifesting the agony of their martyrdom ».

— XVI —

« rennius » (1). In the Church the names of the early martyrs will cease to be repeated only with the Eucharistic sacrifice itself, ending with the world and passing triumphantly to the knowledge of the new names in heaven (2). Nor did she neglect the meaner memorials of time. Died they in their house? She set up an altar on the very spot. Witness S. Caecilia, SS. John and Paul, S. Pudentiana, and many more. Was it afar off? Her fondness grew excessive. She begged, she bought, she risked life and limb to get their dear remains, and their possession was made the choice of conquerors and articles of peace (3). She made much of giving a cloth that had touched them, wool soaked with the oil of the lamps that burned before them, mere dust that gathered over them. She rejoiced in distributing their relics to the churches throughout the world, and never did she erect an altar anywhere, that was not enriched with some portion of their blessed remains. Enjoying the sunshine of the Real Presence, she desired that these memorials of His

Relics.

---

(1) Ode XXIV. lib. III.
(2) See Apocalypse ch. 3. v. 12. ch. 2. v. 17. ch. 22. v. 4. And Isaias ch. 65. v. 15. « And you shall leave your name for an exe-
« cration to my elect, and the Lord God shall slay you, and call
« his servants by another name, in which he that is blessed upon
« the earth shall be blessed in God. Amen ».
(3) The holy Cross was recovered from Chosroes in this way. The crown of thorns was chosen by S. Louis.

friends should be found there too. Nay, she became in love with death and treasured up the instruments of agony, and set them, too, like jewels at her shrines. People call it superstition. The Church upon earth, who knows her own mind and her Master's, never grows weary of canonizing the sanctity which He has been pleased to perfect. She loves the saints and martyrs, because they mirrored Him. If she dwells with greater fondness upon the blessed wounds of our Lord, she contemplates with love the sufferings of those who died for Him. She does not forget them, because she knows that He has not forgotten them, and is pleased that they remember her.

The leading idea then in any Catholic church, but more evident in the older historical basilicas, is that we are dead to the world and buried with Christ. On Holy Thursday we literally do bury our Lord in the sepulchre and visit the spot where He is laid. In the Mass we repeat the sacrifice, and represent the circumstances of His cruel death. And if He has deigned to be with us all days, « even to the consummation of the world », His presence may be said to be, in regard to the manifestation of His glorified existence and our inability to bear it and live, even yet swathed and shrouded in the tomb. Man again is a most glorious work of His, and our confraternities by keep-

To bury the dead, a sacred duty.

b

ing up that charity of burying the dead which the angel commended in Tobit, honour the Creator in that slime of the earth which He means to raise again from the tomb. Even the natural instincts of the Pagan Romans granted great legal privileges to burial-clubs. These privileges were confirmed by an edict of Septimius Severus A. D. 200. The burial of those bodies that had been once the temples of the Holy Ghost is for Christians so sacred a duty that in the nervous language of S. Ambrose, « human- « dis fidelium reliquiis vasa Ecclesiae, etiam ini- « tiata, confringere, conflare, vendere, licet ». It is a duty of religion, and not of simple conve-

The Church obliged to pray for the dead.

nience, just as prayers for the dead is a duty for the whole Church, as well as for the survivors. « Lay this body anywhere », said S. Monica to her son Augustine; « let not the care of it any- « way disturb you: this only I request of you that « you remember me at the altar of the Lord where- « ver you be » (1). Intercessory prayer was all the dying mother asked, not some peculiar place of sepulture. And it was to give opportunity for the

---

(1) « She (S. Monica), the day of her dissolution being at hand, « bestowed not a single thought upon having her body sumptuously « swathed.... but only desired a commemoration to be made of her « at the altar, at which she had, without the intermission of a day, « rendered her service, whence she knew was dispensed the holy « Victim, by which the handwriting that was against us is blotted « out ». See S. Augustine, t. I. l. IX. Confess. n. 36. col. 289.

kind of prayer for the dead which she requested that Catholics desired to be buried together, and marked the loculus with a hurried sign or more deliberate inscription.

Now it is not easy, but very difficult, to make those, who think that the reading of the will after the funeral is the chief duty to the deceased, really appreciate the necessities of the Catholic dead. For them to be buried away from the rest was to separate from communion, and withdraw from that jurisdiction which the Pope and bishops exercised over the cemeteries. With the single exception of some Mithric tombs, De Rossi has found in the catacombs no Pagans, or heretics, who intruded themselves among the faithful dead. The notion, after robbing the dead, of dressing up in his clothes, stickling for his name, or of wishing to be buried with him, seems to be almost an idle modern invention. And if that request, which is usually felt to be so urgent, because it comes from dying lips, is to be disregarded as for superstitious uses, because it asks for prayer, how can we understand the language of S. Cyprian ? « To the bodies also
« of those who, although they were not put to tor-
« ture in prison, nevertheless depart by the outlet
« of a glorious death, let a more zealous watch-
« fulness be given ; for neither their resolution nor
« their honour is the less, so as to prevent them

« too from being classed among the blessed mar-
« tyrs. Finally note also the days on which they
« depart that we may celebrate commemorations of
« them also among the memories of the martyrs » (1).
When the cross was a reality, and the roaring lion
physically ready to devour, the heretic was not so
eager to assume the Catholic name. What Maximinus said to S. Tarachus had few attractions to
those without. « I will not merely slay thee that
« they may wrap thy relics in linen cloths, and
« anoint and worship them ». Or again : « Dost
« thou think, most wicked man, that thy body
« after death will be venerated and anointed by silly
« women ? But this also shall be my care that thy
« remains be utterly destroyed ». Nor was the
boast of S. Hilary of Poitiers more inviting. « We
« owe more to your cruelty Nero, Decius, Maxi-
« minus, than to Constantius; for through you we
« have conquered Satan : everywhere was the holy
« blood of the martyrs received, and their vene-
« rable bones are a daily testimony, while evil
« spirits howl at them; while maladies are expelled,
« while wonderful works are seen » (2). The chief
use of the churches then was not to shelter the congregation from the weather, but to provide for the

---

(1) Ep. XXXVII ad Clerum.
(2) S. Hil. lib. II. de Trinit. n. 3. lib. III. adv. Constant. n. 8.
p. 1243. Ed. Ben.

relics, and the commemoration of the dead. The Christians met to pray for the living and the dead; and with greater fervour, because the mortal remains of saints were before their eyes, whose intercessory prayers they knew to be most acceptable to God.

The reason again for the greater honour to the martyrs was not for the illustration of the Church, nor for the romantic circumstances of their deaths. Our Lord himself has pronounced it. « No man hath « greater love than this that he lay down his life « for his friends » (1). They were not merely witnesses of the truth, but of the Author of truth, and especially of His resurrection; that He whom the Jews and Gentiles had conspired together to blot out from the land of the living was nevertheless a living man powerful to protect the Church that had loved Him; and the first martyr looking up steadfastly to heaven deserved to see the glory of God, and to bear witness: « Behold! I see the heavens « opened and the Son of man standing at the right « hand of God ». If love for God was to be the measure of the admiration of the Church, it was found most conspicuously in the martyrs. The charity which worketh love and unites the soul with God, was to be found among all classes, the beg-

Greater honour due to the Martyrs, and why.

---

(1) John, XV. v. 13.

gar and the king, the founders of religious Orders and the hermits, the suffering nun and the active apostle ; and if it were approved by miracles the Church set it before her children as an inheritance and example, (for it is not the Church, but writers in evil days who have said, that the actions of the saints are rather to be admired than imitated); but she gave the first place to that faithful love which was sealed with blood. For that blood was her cement and seed ; and that sanctity contained the special token that the world had striven to destroy it, and striven in vain. She has hardly watched with the shepherds through the night of the Nativity before she celebrates the stoning of Stephen. The cry of the little babe of Bethlehem is upon her ear, and she listens to « Rachael weeping for her children, because they are not ». The mystic gifts are offered by the kings, and she sings :

« Crudelis Herodes, Deum regem venire quid times ?
« Non eripit mortalia, qui regna dat coelestia ».

« Our God, the coming King. why dost thou,
« cruel Herod, dread ?

« He snatches not at mortal things who heavenly
« gives instead ».

She feels that the persecuting malice of the world is an additional wreath for the champions of Christ, whose kingship was mocked and set at nought by the great ones of the earth; a sign of the world's fear, and a prize for those it hates. That little phial in the silent passages of the earth was her ruby jewel. The lips of the martyrs, opened by the Holy Ghost, spoke the truth. Hence the Popes were so solicitous to preserve their Acts that they appointed notaries and deacons for that purpose in the several districts, or regions, of the city, and built so much in the cemeteries, and set ecclesiastics over them (1). Hence when, owing to the desolating persecution of Diocletian, the churches and sacred books had been burnt, and the lands and cemeteries confiscated, we find Marcellus, A. D. 308-310, set twenty five titles, or titular churches, like dioceses within the city for the many Pagan converts, and for the burial of the martyrs, and invited Prisscilla to make another cemetery on the Salarian way. When the suburban cemeteries were ruined by the barbarians, the Popes brought the martyr's bodies

Diocletian's persecution.

---

(1) Pope Zephyrinus, A. D. 202-218, set Callixtus over the cemetery. Of Pope Fabian, 236-250, the breviary says: « Septem diaconis regiones divisit, qui pauperum curam haberent. Totidem subdiaconos creavit, qui res gestas martyrum a septem notariis scriptas colligerent ». « He allotted the regions to seven deacons to have charge of the poor; and created as many subdeacons to collect the Acts of the martyrs written by the seven notaries ».

Pope Cornelius, A. D. 251, 252, testifies that there were forty six priests in Rome, that is with parishes and cemeteries; but there were in the city only twenty five basilicas. In the time of Pope Damasus, A. D. 366-384, every title had two priests, and a recently into the city. When they had repaired the damages in vain, and the cemeteries were no longer safe, they brought them in greater numbers into the basilicas. Even as late as 560-573, John III restored the cemeteries of the holy martyrs, and had Masses and lights supplied every Sunday from S. John Lateran's. It is recorded of Sergius Ist, who lived in the seventh century, that, when he was a priest, he was unwearied in celebrating Mass in the different cemeteries. Gregory III, 731-741, provided a priest to celebrate in the catacombs on the principal martyrs' feasts. It was not only that the martyrs were the earliest saints, but their blood was the seed of the Church, the pledge of fidelity to the last. If she did not honour those chosen instruments of faith, whom should she honour? If

---

discovered inscription in S. Clement's shows that their colleagues were called « *Socii* ». In the following inscription from the cemetery of Domitilla we read the jurisdiction of those priests.

    ALEXIVS ET CAPRIOLA FECERVNT SE VIVI
    IVSSV ARCHELAI ET DVLCITI PRESB.

And in this other from S. Callixtus we find the jurisdiction which the Popes themselves peculiarly exercised over that cemetery. Marcellinus governed the Church from 296 to 304.

    CVBICVLVM DVPLEX CVM ARCISOLIIS ET LVMINARE
    IVSSV PP SVI MARCELLINI DIACONVS ISTE
    SEVERVS FECIT MANSIONEM IN PACE
    SIBI SVISQVE.

☞ We may observe here, once for all, that our notices of the catacombs are chiefly taken from De Rossi's « Roma subterranea » vol. I, and his « Bollettino di Archeologia Sacra ».

she prized chastity, they had died to keep it. If she reverenced old age, her venerable bishops and priests while tortured were admired even by the Pagans. If she needed miracles, the martyrs were miracles. If the Holy Ghost inspired her, the Spirit spoke also by their lips. If generous devotedness could move her, these had indeed given up all. If gratitude became her, she must raise her eyes to heaven and to them. Hence the feeling which moved the learned Benedictine Abbot, Gueranger, to ask leave of Pius IX to renew the celebrations in the catacombs at the grave of S. Caecilia. Hence the joy of the Church at the canonization of the victims of the Calvinists of Gorcum, and the beatification of the martyrs of Japan.

About the year 405, the noble Spanish poet Prudentius come to Rome to satisfy his devotion, and has left graphic passages relating to the catacombs. Two lines of his describe their locality better than a volume.

Prudentius on the catacombs.

« Haud procul extremo culta ad pomeria vallo
« Mersa latebrosis crypta patet foveis ».

« Not far from the last trench *, at the well-kept
« gardens, there lies a crypt buried in darksome pits ».

And he enables us to judge of the decorations of the crypt, and its purpose; for he tells us that in the

* Of the city-walls.

cemetery of S. Cyriaca he saw the body of S. Hyppolitus, with an altar by it at which priests celebrated and distributed the divine mysteries; and that on the walls was a picture of his martyrdom, the faithful gathering his scattered relics, and with cloths and sponges sucking up his blood on the briars and ground. To the confusion of those whose tender piety is scandalized by the sign of the Cross, and much more by the image of the Crucified, who date their new birth from the Holy Ghost, but abhor the emblem of the dove, whose whitewashed walls receive no light from the illumination of the Church, whose dreary devotion denies to Mary the prophetic title « Blessed » ; and who, dating their conversion from the Apostles, neither know nor care to know what became of them when they dispersed to teach the Gentiles, and fear their pictures more than sin, the profusion of paintings with which the early Christians decorated their cemeteries must appear a singular impiety and revolting mistake. After so much devastation enough still remains below ground (without reckoning the peculiar symbols of private graves, doves, anchors, palms, and monograms of Christ) to furnish us with painted ceilings, and pilasters, and altar-tombs, with multiplied effigies of our Lord, the Mother of God, and the saints, the miracles of either Testament, types of the Sacraments and especially of the Eucharist. S. Jerome, who died soon after Prudentius visited Rome, speaks of the inlaid glasses, now preserved in our museums : « *in cucurbitis vasculorum, quas vulgo Sancomarias vocant, solent apostolorum imagines adumbrari* ». « In the bowls of the little vessels commonly called « Sancomarias the images of the apostles are wont « to be shadowed » (1). And wall painting would not be wanting where painted vases were esteemed. But the *cella* above ground, all that art had done in oratories, perished in Diocletian's persecution, and it may be questioned whether Christian decorative art ever recovered that loss. We know that the fine arts, from what cause we cannot say, had so declined in the age of Constantine that the triumphal arch erected by him owes whatever sculptured beauty it possesses to the skill of those who had lived at an earlier age than his own. In the third century there were forty six churches in Rome. What was the style of their decoration ? In the cemeteries, De Rossi thinks that « towards the end of that « century, the arts, which flourished in the times « of Trajan, Adrian and the Antonines, visibly de-

<small>Pictures destroyed by Diocletian.</small>

---

(1) Tertullian, A. D. 195-218, had asked : « Where is the lost sheep sought for by the Lord, and carried back upon His shoulders? « Let the very pictures of your chalices come forth, if even in them « the interpretation of that animal will clearly shine forth, whether « it pourtray the restoration of a sinner that was a Christian or a « Gentile ».

« clined » (1). If this is to be understood of the representation of mere outward natural form, it is probable enough; but it may be questioned whether the decline affected symbolism, and the power of representing Catholic religious feeling; just as while the more celebrated painters of religious subjects since have given the natural with greater truth, they have not always depicted the supernatural, and religious affections, with as much force as other hands inferior to them in the mechanism of art. If Greek art surpassed Roman, and Pagan art declined, neither in fancy nor design did Christian art ever come near it. It is not possible that the obscure sect described by Tacitus could ever get artists of any reputation to paint in the dark; on which account catacombic art, taken by itself, is a fallacious standard. Not possessing the early Church pictures, we can only judge by the mosaics, restored and altered, but not changed in character, that Christian Catholic art by no means declined in elaborate ingenious symbolic ornamentation, and ability to represent what it wanted to inculcate. The drinking fountains of Paris or London, expensive as many of them have been, would not give a fair idea of the appreciation of art either in France or England. Eusebius, A. D. 325, 338, says : « You might see at

---

(1) Roma sott. I. 196. 197.

— XXIX —

« the fountains, in the middle of the market-places, Christian drinking-fountains.
« representations of the good Shepherd well known
« to those acquainted with the divine word, and
« Daniel with the lions, fashioned in brass ». And
speaking of a tablet which the emperor Constantine
placed before the vestibule of his palace to be seen
by all, the same historian says: « The saving sign
« of the Cross is represented as it were resting on
« his head; but that enemy and adverse wild beast,
« which, by means of the tyranny of the ungodly,
« had vexed the Church, he represented under the
« shape of a dragon rushing headlong down ».
And he adds: « I am filled with wonder at the
« powerful understanding of the emperor, who, as
« it were, by a divine inspiration, symbolized those
« things which the words of the Prophet had long
« before proclaimed ». He also says that « the
« house of the woman healed of the issue of blood
« was shown at Caesarea Philippi, and that he had
« himself seen the circumstance represented in brass
« before the door of it. And that it is no won-
« der, for the images of Peter and Paul, and even
« of Christ himself are preserved in paintings » (1).
In the fourth century S. Asterius bishop of Amasea
gives a minute account of a picture of the martyrdom of S. Euphemia. This celebrated virgin martyr

---

(1) Hist. of Euseb. b. 7. c. 18.

A picture at Chalcedon in the 4th century. of Chalcedon is represented with her contemporary S. Catharine of Alexandria, in the niche of the Madonna in our subterranean basilica. S. Asterius says: « Her fellow-citizens and associates in the religion « for which she died, admiring her as a resolute « and holy virgin, reverencing her sepulchre, and « also placing her bier near the temple, pay her « honour, celebrating her anniversary as a common « and crowded festival ». He saw this picture accidently and was affected to tears; and it appears from his description of it, that it must have been an admirable composition. He particularly notices her after sentence of death was pronounced against her. « After this there is a prison, and « again the venerable virgin in her dark robes is « seated alone stretching out her hands to heaven, « and calling on God the helper in trouble : and « there appears to her, whilst in prayer, above « her head, the sign which it is the custom of « Christians both to adore and represent in colours, « a symbol, I think, of the passion which awaited « her. The painter then, a little further on, has « lit up, in another compartment, a vehement fire.... « and has placed her in the midst of it, with her « hands stretched out towards heaven ; her counte- « nance bears on it no sign of sadness; but. on

— XXXI —

« the contrary, is lit up with joy, for that she is
« departing unto a blessed and incorporeal life » (1).

Pope Adrian Ist, in his letter to Charlemagne concerning holy images, quotes Gregory the Great's letter to the hermit of Ravenna. « We have sent
« you two cloths containing the picture of God,
« our Saviour, and of Mary the holy Mother of
« God, and of the blessed apostles Peter and Paul;
« and one Cross: also for a benediction, a key
« which has been applied to the most holy body
« of S. Peter the prince of the apostles, that you
« may remain defended from the enemy ». De Rossi shows distinctly, from the type of the two apostles on the sarcophagi, and from the ancient representation of them, that there was a traditional set of portraits with features peculiar to each. Prudentius, A. D. 405, narrates an incident in his journey to Rome. « I was lying prostrate on a
« tomb which a sacred martyr, Cassian, with his
« body dedicated to God, made beautiful. Whilst
« with tears I was considering within myself my
« wounds, and all the labours and bitter pains of
« life, I turned my face upwards: there was be-
« fore me, painted in dark colours, the image of
« the martyr covered with countless wounds, la-
« cerated in every limb, and with the skin mi-

Other church pictures.

---

(1) Combefis. t. I. Enar. in Martyr. S. Euphem p. 207-210.

« nutely punctured. Around him, oh sad sight!
« there was a countless crowd of boys who with
« their styli pierced the wounded limbs. The keeper
« of the building said in answer to my enquiries,
« ' that which thou seeest, stranger, is no empty
« or idle fable. The picture tells a history. These
« are the circumstances which, expressed in colours,
« have excited thy wonder. This is Cassian's glo-
« ry. If thou hast any just or praiseworthy desire;
« if there be any thing that thou hopest for; if
« thou be inwardly troubled, but whisper it. The
« most glorious martyr, believe me, hears every
« prayer; and those which he sees deserving of
« approval he renders effectual » S. Paulinus of
Nola, who died a year after S. Augustine, in 431,
describes a basilica apparently covered with paintings. He says, expostulating with Severus for placing
his portrait in the baptistery of his basilica beside
S. Martin of Tours : « You did right to have a
« painting of S. Martin in the place where man is
« formed anew : he by a perfect imitation of Christ
« pourtrayed the image of a heavenly being ».
S. Nilus, 448-451, advises his friend, who was
going to build a church in honour of the martyrs,
« to represent in the sanctuary, towards the East,
« one only cross, and cover the building on every
« side with the histories contained in the Old and
« New Testament, done by the hand of most skilful

« painter, in order that they who are not acquainted
« with letters, and are unable to read the divine
« scriptures, may have a remembrancer of the worthy
« actions of those who have nobly served the true
« God ». S. Asterius says boldly : « Were there
« no martyrs, gloomy and gladless would our life
« be ; for what is worthy to be compared with those
« solemn assemblies ! What so venerable and every-
« way beautiful as to behold a whole city pouring
« forth all its citizens, and repairing to the sa-
« cred place to celebrate the pure mysteries of the
« most true religion ! But true religion is both to
« worship and honour those who have so reso-
« lutely endured torments for Him ». This bishop
of Pontus says : « The Gentiles and Eunomian he-
« retics (new Jews, as he calls them) detested
« the honours paid to martyrs and their relics ».
He describes in his own country, precisely what Prudentius saw in Italy, « that on the solemnities of
« particular martyrs, which were kept by the peo-
« ple, all Rome and the neighbouring provinces
« went to adore God at their tombs, kissing their
« relics ». And if we would know how such festivals were kept, in the fourth century, in the East,
we have it in S. Gregory of Nyssa. « Let us view
« the present state of the saints, how very excel-
« lent it is, and how magnificent ! For the soul
« indeed having attained unto its proper inheritance

Festivals of the Martyrs.

S. Gregory of Nyssa's description of the Christian shrine.

rests gladly, and, freed from the body, dwells together with its compeers. Whilst the body, its venerable and spotless instrument, which injured not by its peculiar passions the incorruptibility of the indwelling spirit, deposited with great honour and attention, lies venerably in a sacred place ; reserved as some much honoured valuable possession unto the time of the regeneration, and far removed from any comparison with the bodies which have died by a usual and common death, and this though they are naturally of the same substance. For other relics are to most men even an abomination. Whereas whoso cometh unto some spot like this, where we are this day assembled, where there is a monument of the just and a holy relic, his soul is in the first place gladdened by the magnificence of what he beholds, seeing a house, as God's temple, elaborated most gloriously both in the magnitude of the structure, and the beauty of the surrounding ornaments. There the artificer has fashioned wood into the shape of animals ; and the stonecutter has polished the slabs to the smoothness of silver; and the painter has introduced the flowers of his art, depicting and imaging the constancy of the martyrs, their resistance, their torments, the savage forms of the tyrants, their outrages, the blazing furnace, and the most blessed end of

« the champion : the representation of Christ , in
« human form, presiding over the contest (1); all
« these things, as it were in a book gifted with
« speech, shaping for us by means of colours, has
« he cunningly discoursed to us of the martyr's
« struggles, has made this temple glorious as some
« brilliant fertile mead. For the silent tracery on
« the wall has the art to discourse, and to aid
« most powerfully. And he who has arranged the
« mosaics has made this pavement on which we
« tread equal to a history. And having gratified
« his sight with these sensible works of art he then
« desires to approach the very shrine itself, be-
« lieving that the touching it is a hallowing and
« benediction. And should some one allow him to
« carry away the dust which lies on the surface
« of that resting place, the dust is received as a

---

(1) S. Basil also, A. D. 379, alludes to this same introduction of Christ into the canvass. « Rise up now, I pray you, ye celebrated painters of the good deeds of these wrestlers. Make glorious by your art the mutilated image of their leader. With colours laid on by your cunning make illustrious the crowned martyr by me too feebly pictured. I retire vanquished before you in your painting of the excellencies of the martyr. I rejoice at being this day overcome by such a victory of your bravery. I shall behold the struggle between the fire and the martyrs depicted more accurately by you. I shall see the wrestler depicted more glorious by your representation. Let demons weep at being now also smitten in you by the brave deeds of the martyr. Again let the burning hand be shown them. Let Christ also, who presides over the struggle, be depicted on your canvass ».

« gift, and the earth is treasured up as a valuable
« possession. For to touch the relic itself, if ever
« by so great a good fortune one could obtain leave,
« how very much this is to be desired, and what
« a concession to the most earnest supplication, they
« know who have had experience, and have ac-
« complished this desire. For the beholders, with joy,
« embrace it as if a living and unfading body,
« applying it to eyes, and mouth, and ears, and
« to all the senses; and shedding then a tear of
« veneration and sympathy for the martyr, as though
« he were entire and visible before them, they sup-
« plicate him to intercede, beseeching him as an
« attendant upon God, calling upon him as re-
« ceiving gifts whenever he pleases ». This beautiful passage was written before the year 395.

Although veneration of the martyrs is based upon spiritual relationship and supernatural motives, even in the natural order a rude inhumanity would appear in not treasuring their remains. « We are
« moved », says Atticus to Cicero, « by the very
« places where the footprints of men we admire, or
« love, are present. That very Athens of ours does
« not delight me so much by the magnificent works
« and exquisite arts of the ancients, as by the re-
« membrance of the chiefest men, where one was
« wont to dwell, where to sit, where to argue:
« I studiously contemplate their tombs ».

But our purpose is more with the external mode of honouring than with the sentiment. Granting that Christian art, contrasted with the classical, was never of the highest order, and that (especially in Africa where the cemeteries above ground were more exposed to Diocletian's persecution) it was mercilessly swept away, there is ample evidence that, within fifty years after Constantine gave peace to the Church, able artists had done much to repair the damage. It is very true that religious feeling is often awakened by inferior external forms; but the productions described in such noble language by S. Gregory of Nyssa and S. Asterius could not have been mere daubs. We shall see that the latter speaks of a picture as resembling the style of an artist whose name he gives, and compares it with the old masters. The Vatican bronze medallion of S. Peter and S. Paul, found in S. Domitilla's cemetery, the earliest known representation of these apostles, shows a good style of execution; and if we consider the rank and riches of the noble converts in Rome, it is unlikely that the first Pope, who lived in the palace of a Senator whose daughters were his zealous pupils, or the other apostle who lived in his own hired house, should have failed of competent artists if their portraits were wished for at all. And in the same way, directly the Church had breathing time, whatever the style of the pictures may

Earliest medallion of SS. Peter and Paul.

Profusion of art in the 4th century.

have been, it is evident that the bodies of the martyrs and their pictures were honoured together, and that in the fourth century pictorial art in the churches was public and profuse. Naked form and classical outlines were not to be got, nor probably desired; but it is difficult to believe that the decorations of the Church were deficient in poetry, execution, and effective art.

<small>Disuse of the subterranean cemeteries, and their destruction by the Barbarians.</small>

If the chief motive for Church decorative art was to embellish the places of sepulture and chapels connected with them, and the embellishments themselves, under the pressure of necessity, were confined to symbols, or very simple adaptations of Christian facts, we should expect to find with greater liberty, greater freedom of composition. When the empire became Christian, the sufferings of the martyrs would naturally be chosen for historical religious pictures, and the Roman artist would be no longer doomed to the obscurity of the catacombs, but would enjoy the more favourable light and grander dimensions of the basilicas. The Popes themselves were no longer buried in the subterranean crypts. Melchiades, A. D. 311-314, the first to sit in the Lateran, was the last to be buried under ground : « in coemeterio Callixti in crypta ». Sylvester, A. D. 314-336, was buried in the cemetery of Priscilla in an open-air basilica. Mark, A. D. 336, similarly in the cemetery of Balbina outside the Ardeatine gate, not far from the cemetery of Callixtus on the Appian way. The Constantinian basilicas, S. Lorenzo, S. Agnese, and S. Alexander, even cut away many loculi and crypts to make a level. After the death of Julian the Apostate, in 363, De Rossi says, « that the use of subterranean cemeteries vi- « sibly declined ». In the public distress they were neglected and fell into the hands of private fossors, and, after the year 454, he finds no interment in them at all. The liturgies of the second half of fifth century constantly refer to burials in the basilicas ; and in the sixth century burial was common within the walls of Rome. As for the Pagan emperors, the first direct public attack upon the cemeteries was that by Valerian, in 257, and it only lasted three years ; for his son Gallienus, whose mother, Solinina, was a Christian, recalled it, and ordered the religious places to be restored to the bishops, on which account Dyonisius, bishop of Alexandria, calls him, « more friendly « to God » (1). It is recorded of his contemporary, Pope Dyonisius, that he allotted the churches and cemeteries to priests, and constituted parishes and dioceses. In 303, Diocletian burnt and ravaged every thing. De Rossi thinks that from 370

---

(1) See De Rossi's « Bollettino di Archeologia Sacra » for January 1866, page 6.

to 373 there was again a fashion to be buried near the martyrs. Perhaps the zeal of Damasus for restorations, and his own recorded wish to be laid by the martyrs, had something to do with it. But the invasions of the barbarians were the real destruction of the cemeteries. Alaric marched three times against Rome. The first time he arrived within a few miles of the city, and, as if deterred by some mysterious power, suddenly retreated. But he appeared a second time, in 408, when he besieged the city, and after reducing it to extremeties by famine and pestilence, accepted a ransom of 5000 pounds of gold, 30000 of silver, 4000 vestments of silk, and 3000 dyed furs. On the 24 of August 410 he returned a third time, entered the city through treason at the dead of the night, and the blast of the Gothic trumpet announced to the inhabitants that the barbarian invaders had passed through the Salarian gate. Genseric the Vandal, about the year 460, destroyed all Rome and its suburbs, with the exception of the three principal basilicas. Before the end of the fifth century Ricimer the Suevian Goth besieged and destroyed the doomed city, but was obliged to evacuate it by Belisarius. In the absence of Belisarius, Totila, after taking Fiesola, commenced another siege of Rome in 545. The citizens made a heroic resistance, but suffered cruelly from famine and disease. The Isaurian soldiers, who guarded the Porta Asinaria, no longer able to support the fatigues and privations of a protracted siege, consented to admit the invader by treason, and Totila entered the city in triumph, April 546. He spared the inhabitants for a time, but having learned that the Greeks had defeated the Goths in Lucania, he compelled the entire population to emigrate into the province of Campagna; and thus, as Procopius narrates, « Rome was left absolutely a wilderness of « ruin, and desolated mansions; a city without sound « or tread ; abandoned to the jackal and wolf ». Belisarius retook the city and rebuilt its walls. Totila subsequently returned, but was forced to retire with much slaughter. He besieged the city again in 549, and, as before, entered by the Porta Asinaria. He remained in peaceful possession until 552, when Justinian sent Narses to renew the war in Italy with greater energy. Narses completely defeated the Goths in a general engagement in the passes of the Apennines, and among the slain was Totila himself. Narses then marched to Rome, and the Goths, on his approach to its defenceless walls, retired to the Castle of S. Angelo, which they defended for a short time, but were obliged to capitulate on condition that their lives should be spared by the conqueror. The resting places of the dead were not, of course, spared during those terrible ravages. In 648, 682, the bodies of the martyrs were brought in from the suburban towns, such as Porto and Nomentanum. Astolphus and the Lombards ruined the cemeteries in 760. Paul Ist, who was elected Pope in 757, brought the bodies of the martyrs into the city, because the cemeteries were in decay. Adrian Ist and Leo III tried to restore them. Paschal Ist, in 817, removed the body of S. Cecily with many others. Sergius II and Leo IV brought in some that were still left. Nicholas Ist attempted, in 867, some catacombic restorations, and they were the last.

<small>A religious system cannot be constructed from the catacombs alone.</small>
From these brief notices we may arrive at several general conclusions. 1st That any attempt to construct a religious system from the presence or absence of catacombic data alone, is quite fallacious, owing to the original character and extremely mutilated state of the monuments. 2^d That in so far as art attended upon burial, and that peculiar kind of burial had almost ceased within thirty or forty years after the peace of the Church, we must look elsewhere for it. 3rd We shall find pictorial art still busy about the dead, and the relics of the martyrs removed into the city between 600 and 800, that is in the great basilicas. 4th Whether we look <small>After the peace of the Church, art followed the bodies of the Martyrs transferred into the basilicas.</small> to Christian art for a peculiar class of artistic ideas, or for religious instruction, it is singularly absurd to restrict our enquiries to the more meagre catalogue of the catacombs, and not to go on to the profusion of the basilicas; because if the Christians

— XLIII —

were fond of painting under all the disadvantages of the catacombs, they would certainly develop their school upon the grander scale of the basilicas; and if their thoughts are interesting to us when depicted in the obscurity of difficult times or persecution, we should expect a fuller utterance when they were at peace and free. Hence, on the religious side, the proper test is not whether what we find in the basilicas is different from the little we may know of the catacombs, but whether the basilicas contradict the catacombs. And in this view *even the latest frescoes* in S. Clement have a peculiar interest; because if they were painted when Leo IV was alive, or those relating to S. Nicholas, S. Clement, and S. Cyril, soon after the events they represent, they are a link in religious art, especially as being votive pictures, by which we can trace the ideas which prevailed when the catacombs had fallen into desuetude. Without a single symbol of the catacombs, or a single figure imitated from them, they contain a distinct, formed, and charateristic school of painting. The ideas eliminated from them do not contradict the catacombs. And on the side of art, as compositions, they are superior to any we possess in the catacombs. With all the defects of drawing and perspective, the colouring is pleasing, they tell their story well, and they exhibit a grouping and movement for which

Votive pictures discovered in S. Clement's, bolder in composition than catacombic pictures, and linking Christian art with the early Italian school.

we seek in vain through the catacombs, or indeed in most of the Pagan frescoes which have come down to us. And if some have fixed the age of Charlemagne as the commencement of modern history, these wall-pictures of that age may be taken as forerunners of Cimabue, Giotto, and id genus omne, and the beginning of the modern school of painting.

S. John, in the Apocalypse, saw under the altar the souls of them that were slain for the word of God, and for the testimony they held. The basilicas continued the *cultus* of the dead. The Church brought their bodies in from the Campagna, and placed them more conspicuously beneath her altars. When S. Peter's was ringing with the voices of the tens of thousands giving glory to God for the dogma of the Immaculate Conception, the « Veni Creator Spiritus » intoned by Pius IX, was answered from the Nomentan way. There the ancient Christian basilica was again given to view, the oratory at the cemetery. There appeared the altar-tomb of the martyr Pope Alexander. But if we would venerate his relics, we shall find them with an inscription in the more sumptuous crypt of S. Sabina on the Aventine. The little loculus in the catacombs, with its phial of precious blood and tiny lamp, gave occasion for the oratory, the oratory for the country church; the danger of the sacred deposit of the Church for the securer and grander basilica within

Discovery of S. Alexander's basilica in 1854.

the walls of Rome. There is no lapse or hiatus, any more than there is in the succession and teaching of the Popes. Bosio reckons six cemeteries of the Apostolic age. The first, on the via Cornelia, that of S. Peter's in the Vatican. The Pontifical Book says : « Anacletus memoriam beati Petri construxit, « et loca ubi episcopi conderentur ». If those bishops of Rome did not date from S. Peter, they had no date at all. The ancient Acts of SS. Peter and Paul state that their bodies remained a year and seven months in the catacombs, « quousque « fabricarentur loca, ubi posita sunt in Vaticano et « in via Ostiensi ». The catacombs were crypts at S. Sebastian's to which alone the name of catacomb, for some time, exclusely applied (1). Pope Damasus, in 384, gives us verses upon the spot.

« Hic habitasse prius sanctos cognoscere debes
« Nomina quisque Petri pariter Paulique requiris (2).

« Thou ought'st know that here the saints did dwell the first of all,
« Whoe'r thou art that seek'st the name of Peter and of Paul ».

And of the Vatican cemetery again he writes :

« Cingebant latices montem, teneroque meatu
« Corpora multorum cineres atque ossa rigabant.

---

(1) The names of all the other catacombs, occurring so frequently in the Martyrologies and Lives of the Popes, appear to have been confused with this particular spot; because it always retained its place in the *Libri Indulgentiarum*.

(2) Carmen IX.

« Non tulit hoc Damasus, communi lege sepultos
« Post requiem tristes iterum persolvere poenas.
« Protinus aggressus magnum superare laborem,
« Aggeris immensi dejecit culmina montis.
« Intima sollicite scrutatus viscera terrae
« Siccavit totum quidquid madescerat humor:
« Invenit fontem, praebet qui dona salutis.
« Haec curavit Mercurius levita fidelis » (1).

« The streams the mountain girt, and with their tender rill
« Of many, bodies, ashes, bones, with moisture fill;
« Nor bore this Damasus, by common law who lay
« When once at rest again sad penalties should pay:
« He set to work at once the labour vast surmount,
« Of bulk immense threw down the summit of the mount;
« The inmost bowels of the earth explored with care
« And dried the whole whate'r the moisture wetted there:
« He found the fountain that the gifts of safety lends.
« All this Mercurius the faithful levite tends ».

In this particular instance we have the Pope himself describing his care for the cemeteries. At that date (366-384) it was as easy to ascertain a circumstance relating to the coming to Rome and death of S. Peter, as any now relating to the religious revolution by Henry the eighth. The substructions of S. Peter's conceal the Vatican cemetery. The new basilica of S. Paul shows that the Popes have not yet forgotten the graves of either apostle. But the Basilican churches of Rome were sometimes

(1) Carmen XXXVI. de fontibus Vaticanis.

built upon the martyr's own house, whether interred there as in the case of SS. John and Paul, officers in the army under the Apostate Julian, or not, as in the instance of S. Clement who was martyred in the Crimea. Tradition has always maintained that this church is upon the actual site of his house. When we visit it, we cannot be blind to the inveterate faith with which Catholics venerate the relics of the dead, and the magnificence with which holy Church surrounds the bodies of the saints. For reduced, as this Constantinian basilica may be said to be in its present state, to mere brick and mortar, whilst we admire the beauty of the precious marble pillars, we must replace what was carried up to construct the church above; the noble marble panels of the choir, and especially the two of basket-work - *transennae* - once probably protecting the relics of the saint; the various intricate patterns of the rich opus Alexandrinum of the pavement. If we add frescoes from top to bottom, and from end to end, elegant in their ornamentation, and harmonious in colouring, deficient indeed in perspective and void of classic type, but noble and expressive in telling their story; if we introduce the lights and crowd, and priests at the high altar, we shall conceive no small idea of the Catholic basilica. Nor will it be a hindrance that the frescoes were not all painted at the same time. Their presence, and

Basilica of S. Clement built upon his own house.

Style of its decorations.

the votive character of the most striking, show that the religious spirit which painted the catacombs was not lost with them, and in this respect the pictures in S. Clement's are unique. If we were in possession of those with which S. Damasus adorned his church of S. Lorenzo in Damaso, and which were extant four hundred years afterwards, that is about the year 800, we should have an ascertained series of pictures to supply the link which seems wanting in Catholic decorative art between the catacombs and those church compositions in mosaic, which, if some are of the sixth and seventh, are more generally of the ninth and later centuries. Independently however of any other interest, the frescoes in our basilica of S. Clement go far to fill up the gap; for in them we have the earliest large wall-paintings of church compositions now left to us, certainly in Rome at least: ingenious in their arrangement and replete with piety. They were designed by worshippers who understood that passage of the psalm: « I have loved, o Lord, the beauty of thy house; « and the place where thy glory dwelleth ». If we agree, from the square nimbus about his head, that Leo IV, introduced in the picture of the Assumption of our Lady, was painted before his death, in 855, we can judge in some degree (even without the pictures lost in the interval, and taking no account of the Crucifixion and other earlier frescoes

Its frescoes the earliest Christian compositions now left to us — a peculiarity in their arrangement.

in S Clement's) by comparison with Catholic art of the fourth century, such as the glasses inlaid with gold, and the latest representations in the catacombs, how much has been lost in the lines of drawing, and what progress made in more crowded compositions. If we refer the great picture representing the translation of S. Clement's relics, from the Vatican to his own basilica, to the time of S. Nicholas Ist, who died in 866, we shall not think, even by comparison with the catacombs, that Catholic art had miserably perished. We may find a certain analogy, though a less delicate execution ' between them and the frescoes by Masaccio in the upper church. But our point of comparison is itself inaccurate, that is between simple symbols and historical pictures. It is observable that the bishop of Amasea, S. Asterius, compares the picture of the martyrdom which he saw at Chalcedon between the period of Euphemias' death in 307, and his own about 400, with older productions. « You would « have said it was one of Euphranor's skilful piec- « es; or of one of those old painters who raised « their art to so great an eminence, making their « tables well nigh breathe into life ». Again the composition itself was large, truthful, and forcible; and, as far as mere description goes, not unlike more modern arrangements. « The judge is seated « aloft on his throne looking at the virgin inten-

« sely and fiercely. There are the magistrate's at-
« tendants, and numerous soldiers, and men with
« tablets for their notes, and styles in their hands;
« one of whom has raised his hand from the wax
« and books earnestly at the virgin who is being
« questioned, with his whole countenance bent towards
« her as though bidding her to speak louder. The
« virgin stands there in a dark robe, indicating
« her wisdom by her dress, and is of a beautiful
« countenance as the painter has fancied her, but,
« in my judgement, beautified in mind by her vir-
« tues. Two soldiers force her towards the presi-
« dent, one dragging her forward, and the other
« urging her from behind. One of the soldiers has
« seized the virgin's head and bent it back ; and
« presents her face to the other soldier in a fa-
« vourable posture for punishment, and he standing
« by her has dashed out her teeth. The instru-
« ments of punishment are seen to be a mallet and
« auger. At this I burst into tears, and my feel-
« ings intercept my words. For the painter has
« so plainly depicted the drops of blood that you
« would say they were really flowing from her lips,
« and you would go your way sorrowing ». This
picture seems, like several in S. Clement's, to
have contained three subjects in one. The Saint
then describes the trial and torture, the virgin martyr in prison, and lastly her passion. « A little

« farther on the painter has lit up, in another
« compartment, a blazing fire, and placed her in
« the midst of it with her hands stretched out
« to heaven; her countenance bears on it no sign
« of sadness, but, on the contrary, is lit up
« with joy that she is departing to a blessed and
« incorporeal life ». It may be doubted whether the
notices of our imperial or royal academies supply
more critical description, and whether the religious
pieces of modern painters present more able arrangement and matter for thought. We derive this consolation, at least, from what we can no longer see
and admire, this point of comparison from the early
churches of Asia and Rome, that upon the largest
scale, and with all the available resources of art
the memories of the sainted dead were perpetuated
for public reverence. The peace of the Church brought
with it the fruits of peace, public joy, and hope,
and regard for those who fought the good fight.
That puritanical iconoclastic mania, which, like every dereliction from truth, dries up the heart and impoverishes the understanding, never had any place in the bosom of the Catholic Church. When the iconoclastic emperor Leo, in 813, threatened the bishops in his palace, the bishop of Sardes replied:
« For these eight hundred years past since the
« coming of Christ there have always been pic-
« tures of Him, and He has been honoured in them.

The iconoclastic mania.

— LII —

<small>Christian affection for Martyrs, from S. Stephen downwards, illustrated by the pictures found in S. Clement's.</small>

« Who shall now have the boldness to abolish so ancient a tradition? » It is not without reason that the Acts tell us, when the great persecution at Jerusalem dispersed all, except the apostles, that devout men took care of Stephen and made great mourning over him. The same affection for the saints distinguished the noble Roman matrons in the first three centuries. The very same urged S. Cyril to bring S. Clement's relics to Rome, and Methodius to desire that his brother should repose beside them. The very same sent no less a Pope than Gregory the Great to preach in S. Clement's over the corpse of the poor cripple Servulus, who used to lie in its porch. The same affection had carried thither also what remained of the bones of S. Ignatius ground by the teeth of lions in the Coliseum to become the pure bread of Christ. The same laid under the high altar the body of the martyr-consul Clement. The same depicted on the walls the crucifixion of S. Peter, the death of S. Alexius, and the tomb of S. Clement. And what men learned to love and praise, what eloquence extolled and piety revered, the spirit of martyrdom, the actions of the martyrs and their remains, were felt to be no disgrace to the hand of the artist, and no unseemly memorial in the house of God.

LIFE OF S. CLEMENT
POPE AND MARTYR.

CHAPTER I.

S. Peter in Rome — His preaching in that city — Lineage of S. Clement — His birth-place — His conversion by S. Peter.

« The providence of the universal Ruler », says Eusebius, « led as it were by the hand to Rome, « against that sad destroyer of the human race *(Si-* « *mon Magus)*, S. Peter, that strong and great one « of the Apostles, and on account of his virtue the « leader of all the rest, who as some noble gene- « ral of God armed with heavenly weapons brought « the precious merchandise of intellectual light from « the East to the dwellers in the West » (1). In Rome itself the home of Pagan superstition, and mistress of error, (for she welcomed to her hearths

---

(1) H. E. l. II. c. 14. p. 63-4.

and temples the gods and creeds of every race) and central seat of military power, the prince of the apostles determined to fix his See. In that great metropolis of the world he decided on founding the fortress of faith, to attack Satan in the stronghold of his tyranny, to light up the dark valley of the shadow of death, and, thence by diffusing the gospel, facilitate the conquest of the rest of the world to the kingdom of Jesus Christ. Rome was to the Gentiles what it has been to the Catholic world, no insulated or merely national capital city, but the focus of thought, of civilization, and the most authoritative power. With no theories to suit the imperial mind, with no schemes drawn from family ambition and masked by an hypocritical life, S. Peter, directed by the spirit of God, left Antioch, and, single-handed, entered the Babylon of human power to preach Christ crucified to its licentious, proud, and fanatically idol-worshipping inhabitants. From the Jewish quarter to that inhabited by the Gentiles the mystery of the Cross spread through the city (1). The burning zeal and inspired eloquence

---

(1) The learned Dominican Ciacónius, author of the lives of the Popes, says in his biography of S. Peter that « he sojourned for some « time among the Jews, who, as Philo and Martial narrate, lived « in the Trastevere, before he began to preach to the Gentiles : but, « when the fame of his preaching became known, Pudens, believing « in Christ, received and treated him hospitably in his own palace ».

of the Galilean fisherman were so irresistably impressive that all regarded him as a man mighty in word and work. He was only fulfilling the promise of his Lord: « I will give you a mouth and « wisdom, which all your adversaries will not be « able to resist and contradict (1) ».

Much as has been written about the conversion of Rome a great deal more requires to be added to it. We read indeed in the acts of the martyrs how the rich and noble were victims of their faith: most touching the simple innocence with which youthful and delicate virgins, whose names and memories are yet household words among their fellow citizens, gave up all that the world prizes: most admirable the courage with which illustrious men and noble matrons devoted life and fortune to the assertion of truth, and the burial of the martyred dead: but the rapidity with which the leaven hid in the three measures of meal leavened the whole mass, the jealousy of their political power which animated the emperors of those days and whetted the rancour of their prefects, and the divine power by which tender souls were changed at once and strengthened to bear the worst persecutions of the state, can only be understood from an intimate acquaintance with the genealogy and connexions of the Patrician families.

---

(1) Luke XXI. 15.

« Men cry out », says Tertullian A. D. 195-218, « that the state is beset, that the Christians are « in their fields, in their forts, in their islands : « they mourn as for a loss that every sex, age, « condition, and now even rank, is going over to « this sect » (1). We cannot open the acts of the early martyrs without perceiving that their rank and estates were aimed at as in much more modern religious proscriptions.

Crowds then from every quarter rushed to listen to S. Peter. If miracles also bespoke the presence of an apostle, we must not forget that the sudden conversion of multitudes upon hearing of his words was one of the greatest, and that it had been foretold. The infidels who try to account for the reception of Christianity by natural causes alone, and believers who ascribe it to the miracles of healing which strike the sense of sight, seem to have overlooked that grace given to speech, which penetrates and makes the soul captive to faith, without striking eloquence, without learned disquisition, without merely human motives and passion, with a simplicity apparently inadequate to its marvellous effects — a phenomenon in the lives of many of the saints. Among those who had ears to hear was the noble youth Clement. Zazera

---

(1) Apol. n. 1. p. 2.

thinks-that he belonged to the Octavian family (1).
To the Claudian as Hesychius Salonitanus asserts (2).
To the Senatorial and Caesarean family, as Ciaconius, Sianda, Burius, Boscus, Audisius and many others maintain on the authority of the celebrated letter of S. Eucherius bishop of Lyons to his kinsman Valerian A. D. 427 (3). Also the Recognitions (falsely attributed to S. Clement) published in Greek in the beginning of the second century and translated into Latin by Rufinus priest of Aquileia towards the end of the fourth, represent Clement as related to the Caesars. « Peter says, no one in truth
« is superior to thee in race. I replied there are
« indeed many powerful men come of Caesar's stock
« .(prosapia). For to my father, as to his relation
« and brought up with him, he gave a wife of an
« equally noble family by whom he had twin sons
« before myself » (4). In this no doubt tradition was followed. De Rossi remarks that if we were to read in the lives of the saints that christianity, almost at the death of S. Peter and S. Paul, was so nigh to the im-

---

(1) See notes of Oldoinus in Vita S. Clementis.
(2) Paternum illi genus ex antiquissima Claudiae gentis Neronum familia.
(3) Ciaconius, Vitae et res gestae Pontificum Romanorum, in S. Clemente. Sianda, Breviar. Hist. Burius Rom. Pont. Brevis not. pag. 7. Bosco, Vita dei Sommi Pontefici, in S. Clemente. Audisius, Storia dei Papi, in S. Clemente.
(4) Recogn. lib. VII.

perial throne that the cousin and niece of Domitian were not only Christians, but suffered exile and death for the faith, the incredulous would laugh, and yet he proves it from profane authors alone. He distinguishes Marcus Arecinus Clemens twice consul, first A. D. 73, and next under Domitian who had him put to death, from the martyr consul. Titus Flavius Clemens son of Vespasian's eldest brother Titus Flavius Sabinus many years praefect of Rome; and he conjectures that pope Clement was the child of an older son of Sabinus and consequently nephew to the martyr. We can only refer to this learned, ingenious and interesting account (1). Others, from a phrase in S. Clement's epistle to the Corinthians, set aside unvarying tradition, and will have him to be a Jew. The arguments adduced by Tillemont, Cellier, Baillet, Galliciolli, and others to make him out a Jew or a Greek are so feeble as to excite surprise. They say he calls Jacob « our father » (2), and therefore he must have been a Jew. But these critics should have reflected that when Abraham was constituted « a father of many nations » (3), all those who were converted to the faith had a right to call

---

(1) De Rossi, Bullettino di Archeol. Crist. Roma. Marzo 1865.
(2) « Through envy our father Jacob fled from the face of Esau « his brother ».
(3) Gen. XVII. 4.

Abraham and Isaac their fathers, and to consider themselves fellow-citizens with Judith, the Machabees, and other confessors of the old law. Nor because the priest is of the order of Melchisedech, who was not a Jew, is he therefore according to the flesh of the stock of that royal priest. The alliance between God and Abraham was spiritual « Know ye therefore », says S. Paul, « that they who are of the faith the same « are the children of Abraham » (1). With the same acumen by which Tillemont makes him a Jew, Hesel maintains that he was a Greek and Philippian, because he assisted S. Paul in his evangelical labours among that people. If he travelled with that apostle in Greece, S. Luke of Antioch did the same, and was martyred in Achaia. The faith could not be pent up within the narrow limits of Judaea, and independently of the facilities for travelling in the more settled parts of the empire, many Scripture personages fled from the persecutions of the Jews to Rome and Gaul without having been born there. We believe that S. Clement was a Roman, and a noble Roman citizen.

Passing from the question of S. Clement's country to that of his parentage, we find it generally admitted that his father's name was Faustinus, or

---

(1) Gal. III. 7.

. Faustinianus, or Faustus (1), and his mother's Matidia, or Macidiana, of the most noble family of the Anicii (2): and that he was born on the first of July, in the consulship of Sextus Elius, and Cajus Sentius Saturninus, the very day on which Tiberius was adopted by Augustus (3). We read that he had two brothers Faustinus and Faustus. S. Zosimus, one of the most illustrious occupants of the pontifical throne, informs us that the noble youth Clement was so affected by the words which fell from the lips of S. Peter that, without any deliberation, he submitted to the sweet yoke of the gospel, and was regenerated in the waters of baptism. Considering his noble ancestry and accomplished education, « a man replete with all know-
« ledge and most skilful in the liberal arts » (4), we are not surprised that he was very dear to S. Peter, and also to S. Paul who calls him one of his fellow-labourers in the mystic vineyard of the Lord, « whose names are in the book of life » (5). Origen, S. Jerome, S. Epiphanius, Eusebius, Rufinus,

---

(1) See Rondinini, de S. Clemente ejusque Basilica, lib. 1. cap. 1. §. 4.
(2) « Maternum illi genus e gente Anicia ». Hesych. Salonitanus.
(3) « Clemens natus Romae Kalendis Julii, ipso die quo Tiberium
« Augustus adoptavit, Sexto Aelio et Sentio Saturnino Coss. »
(4) « Omni scientia refertus, omniumque liberalium artium peri-
« tissimus ». S. Hieron. Comment. ep. ad Philip. IV. 3.
(5) S. Paul to the Philippians, IV. 3.

and many other ancient and modern historians do not hesitate to affirm that the Clement mentioned here by the apostle was the successor of S. Peter in the apostolic chair (1): and also the Church, as Martini, the learned archbishop of Florence, observes, seems to favour this opinion by ordering a part of that epistle to be read at the altar on the festival of S. Clement (2). Therefore, concludes Rondinini (3), little or no attention ought to be paid to Oldoinus and a few others who endeavour to controvert and contradict it.

But although we willingly adhere to the opinions of the abovenamed holy Fathers and celebrated writers, who make S. Clement the companion and fellow-labourer of S. Paul in his apostolic missions, we cannot admit that he was a Canon Regular or a Carmelite, or that he was the first bishop of Velletri, or of Cagliari in Sardinia, or of Sardis in Lydia. As for the abovementioned religious orders which are anxious to add this rare and precious gem to their treasures, it is certain that they have not authentic titles for doing so, and that the former, as Rondinini observes, has attempted it

---

(1) See Calmet's Commentaries on S. Paul to the Philippians. IV. 3. Also Cave, Baillet, Ladvocat, Cesarotti, Rohrbacher's universal history, vol. IV, book 26. Audisius, etc. etc.
(2) See notes by Martini on S. Paul to the Philippians.
(3) Rondinini, de S. Clemente, lib. 1. cap. 1. §. 4.

« *inani prorsus conatu* », and the latter « *levi pariter traditione* » (1). With regard to those who assert that S. Clement was the first bishop of Velletri the capital of the Volsci, Oldoinus, quoted by Rondinini, says: « Those writers who enumerate « S. Clement among the bishops of Velletri must have « been deceived either by a similitude of name, or « by a love of country, for I cannot, as well as « I recollect, find that statement affirmed by any « ancient historian » (2). And to this similitude of name may also be ascribed the mistake of those who, with Phara in the first book of his history of Sardinia, assert that S. Clement was sent by the apostles, a short time before he was elevated to the Popedom, to govern the church of Cagliari. Or perhaps the mistake arose from the passage which Godfrey Heinschenius quotes from cardinal Sirletti, « *Clemens qui ex gentibus conversus factus est Epi-* « *scopus Sardorum* », and of which he says in his acts of Apelles, Lucius and Clement, « here men- « tion is made of the Sardi the inhabitants of Sardis « the metropolis of Lydia under Croesus, according to « the Poet: « *Quid Croesi regia Sardis* » (3). And

---

(1) Oldoinus' annotations on Ciaconius, and his book on the Clements.
(2) Rondinini, de S. Clemente, lib. 1. cap. 1. §. 18.
(3) Horace, book 1. ep. 11.

the same learned critic in his remarks on these words which he quotes from another very ancient calendar, « *Clemens primus ex gentibus credens episcopus Sardicae* », says « that some writers have erronously asserted that Clement here mentioned was afterwards raised to the pontifical chair » (1). But we have dwelt long enough on this subject, and our limits do not permit us to proceed with investigations which, if not devoid of some shadow of truth, require much stronger evidence before the inference drawn from them can be applied to the subject of our enquiries. For the same reason we omit the extracts given by Ughelli in the sixth book of his « Italia Sacra », from a Greek menology of the tenth century preserved in the Vatican library, in which he confounds the person and martyrdom of Clement of Ancyra with the person and martyrdom of Clement of Rome.

---

(1) One of the writers here alluded to is evidently Raphael of Volterra who in the 19th book of his Commentaries says « Clemens Praesul Sardicensis, postea Pontifex, primus ex gentibus Christianus ».

CHAPTER II.

S. Clement consecrated bishop by S. Peter, and appointed his coadjutor in the apostolic ministry — Chronological order of succession of the three first Popes who governed the Church after Peter — Opinions of ancient writers on this subject — Opinions of modern writers — The Ebionite and Marcotian heresies condemned by S. Clement.

We now come to facts connected with the life of our Saint, which can be more satisfactorily proved, and are more interesting to the reader. Ciaconius, on the authority of the epistle of the martyr Ignatius to the Trallians, tells us that S. Clement was baptized by S. Peter, and afterwards on account of his rare merits ordained deacon for the purpose of assisting him in his sacred ministrations (1). He made great and rapid progress in the path of virtue, and converted many souls to Christ by the persuasive powers of his preaching, and the silent eloquence of his example. The prince of the apostles

---

(1) « A Beato Petro baptizatus Clemens, et diaconus sibi assi-« stens, ut Ignatius tradit ». Ciaconius in Vita S. Clementis. De Rossi asserts that out of the seven Roman deacons each Pope chose an archdeacon whose office was very much such as that of the cardinal Vicar now.

observing the excellent qualities of his deacon Clement, ordained him priest, and shortly after raised him to the dignity of the episcopacy and made him his own coadjutor in the apostolic ministry. So earnestly and zealously did Clement labour in his vocation that Rufinus calls him an apostolic man, nay almost an apostle (1). Clement Alexandrinus styles him an apostle (2), a distinction accorded to him by all antiquity, as Isaac Vossius, Godfrey Vendolinus, and many other renowned writers most satisfactorily prove (3).

It has not escaped our attention that some historians assert that Clement preached the gospel to the inhabitants of Metz, and afterwards became the first bishop of that city, then one of the most important and populous in France. Even Audisius, frequently quoted by us, refers in his life of our Saint to the origin of this tradition, and says « that Cle-
« ment preached the gospel in France is evident
« from the acts of Metz, which formed the subject
« of a work by Paul the deacon a distinguished
« writer of the middle ages ». Oldoinus also adverts to this in his commentary on the ides (15th) of October of the Gallican Martyrology. But he says

---

(1) Rufinus, de adulteratione librorum Origenis.
(2) Clemens Alexandrinus Stromat. lib. IV.
(3) Vossius, Judicium de Barnaba.

that the Clement here mentioned is not our Saint, but his uncle of the same name and the companion of the prince of the apostles during his travels (1).

Writers of the most remote antiquity are loud in their praise of our holy Pontiff, in whatever sphere of action they regard him. But of all the virtuous qualities with which he was adorned we may say: *velut inter ignes Luna minores* (2), that virginal purity shone the brightest. If the « book of Recognitions » be styled apocryphal, that only means that the name of its compiler is uncertain, and that those who ascribe it to Clement do so without sufficient proof. It is however generally admitted that it is a production of the second century (3), when there still were living eye and ear witnesses of the words and writings of our venerable Pontiff. In the first page of that work we read: « I Clement born in the city of Rome, from « my earliest age cultivated chastity, whilst the « natural inclination of mind kept me bound as it

---

(1) Tres invenio Clementes Apostolorum temporibus apud probatae fidei scriptores. Tertius hujus nominis Romani Pontificis patruus ab ipsomet Apostolorum Principe, cujus fuerat in itineribus comes, Metensis episcopus ordinatus est, et ad Gallos missus.

(2) Horace, lib. 1. Od. 11.

(3) Eosdem libros sacculo secundo in lucem prodiisse ferunt. Rondinini, de S. Clemente lib. 1. cap. 11. §. 6. Origen also mentions them.

« were with certain chains of anxiety and grief » (1). Words which are almost literally repeated in the Clementine homilies. « Be it known to you, my Lord, « that I Clement who am a Roman citizen and have « wished to pass the first age of life with modes- « ty and moderation, when I had taken to heart « a thought which had crept in upon me I know « not whence, and begat for me frequent musings « upon death, I was living with labour and anxie- « ty » (2). And in that part of the letter to the Philadelphians attributed to S. Ignatius martyr, but interpolated by some very early unknown hand, in which mention is made of those who were extolled for having preserved intact the flower of their virginity, we read: « Would that I might enjoy your « sanctity, like that of Elias, of Josue, of Mel- « chisedec, of Elisaeus, of Jeremias, of John the « Baptist, of the belovèd disciple, of Timothy, of « Titus, of Evodius, of Clement » (3). And since,

---

(1) « Ego Clemens in Urbe Roma natus ex prima aetate pudici-
« tiae studium gessi, dum me animi intentio velut vinculis qui-
« busdam solicitudinis et moeroris innexum teneret ».

(2) « Notum sit tibi, Domine mi, quod ego Clemens, qui Civis
« Romanus sum, et primam vitae aetatem pudice ac moderate transi-
« gere volui, quum animo percepissem cogitationem, quae nescio
« unde irrepserat, crebrasque mihi de morte meditationes pariebat,
« cum laboribus et anxietatibus vivebam ».

(3) Utinam fruar vestra sanctimonia ut Eliae, ut Josue filii Na-
vae, ut Melchisedeci, ut Elisaei, ut Hieremiae, ut Baptistae Joannis, ut Dilecti Discipuli, ut Timothei, ut Titi, ut Evodii, ut Clementis, qui in castitate e vita excesserunt.

as Adelmus, a writer of the middle ages, remarks: « S. Clement, even before his conversion, led a pure « and chaste life, how much more, and to what a « greater extent, must those virtues have become the « cherished objects of his life after he was rege- « nerated with the waters of baptism, and began « to practice evangelical perfection, by imitating the « example set him by the apostles, and recom- « mended by our Divine Saviour himself » (1).

We now come to the question, – who was the immediate successor of S. Peter ? which has occupied the attention of some of the most eminent ecclesiastical historians. Peter, Linus, Cletus, Clement : such is the order of the succession of the Popes, as asserted by the tradition and offices of the Church. Linus of Volterra, Cletus and Clement of Rome, and all three consecrated bishops by Peter. It is said that Clement was instituted by Peter to be his immediate successor (2). If we could admit that S. Peter had no inspiration of the Holy Spirit, and that so vital a matter as the form of the succession of the Vicars of Christ was left to chance, that the Papacy instead of becoming an elective (and elective with the special assistance of the Holy Ghost) was on the point of being a delegated power, we

---

(1) See Adelmus.
(2) See Clement's letter to S. James bishop of Jerusalem.

might admit that S. Peter did ordain Clement to be the second Pope ; and that his prudence and modesty declined the honour , upon the death of his patron, until after the martyrdom of the two other bishops. We believe , however , that S. Peter did no such thing. If he expressed a hope , a preference, a conviction of his disciple's future elevation to the Pontificate , that has not been a rare foresight or inspiration. If he ordained him bishop, many Popes have done the like. But what is perplexing is that scarcely two authors agree about the precise chronological order of the four first Popes. There are many Sees which can trace their bishops with more or less precision from the first induction by an apostle. At Smyrna, for instance , S. Polycarp ordained by S. John. S. Ignatius of Antioch, who succeeded Peter there after the death of Evodius , was a disciple of S. John. S. Irenaeus of Lyons says of Polycarp : « that he not only had
« been instructed by apostles , and had conversed
« with many who had seen the Lord , but was also
« appointed by the apostles bishop of Smyrna in
« Asia ; that he had seen him (1) , and that he

---

(1) « I can tell you the very place where the bishop Polycarp sat
« as he discoursed; and his goings out and his comings in, and the
« character of his life and his bodily appearance, and the discourses
« which he addressed to the multitude, and how he narrated his
« daily intercourse with John and with others who had seen the

« came to Rome under Pope Anicetus ». The visit would have been about a hundred years after the martyrdom of S. Peter. S. Irenaeus was made bishop a very few years later, viz, A. D. 177. He was a man remarkably zealous for apostolical tradition, active in the affairs of the Church at Lyons, to which Rome and Roman information were easily accessible, very near to the facts themselves; one would suppose that of all men he should know the list of the Popes. « The blessed apostles », says he, « having founded and built up that Church,
« conferred the public office of the episcopacy upon
« Linus, of whom Paul makes mention in his e-
« pistle to Timothy. To whom succeeded Anacletus,
« and after him the third from the apostles who
« obtained that episcopacy was Clement, who had
« seen and conferred with the blessed apostles, and
« who still had before his eyes the familiar teaching
« and tradition of the apostles; and not he only,
« for many were then still alive who had been in-

« Lord; and how he commemorated their discourses, and what were
« the things which he had heard from them concerning the Lord,
« and concerning his miracles and his doctrine; how Polycarp having
« received them from those who had seen the Word of Life narrated
« the whole in consonance with the Scriptures. These things did I,
« at that time, hearken to eagerly, though the mercy of God then
« shown me, making remembrance of them, not on paper, but in
« my breast, and by the grace of God I ever revolve them in my
« mind ».

« structed by the apostles. But to this Clement suc-
« ceeded Evaristus, and to Evaristus Alexander.
« Next to him, thus the sixth from the apostles,
« Sixtus was appointed, and after him Telesphorus
« who suffered a glorious martyrdom; next Hyginus,
« then Pius, after whom was Anicetus. To Ani-
« cetus succeeded Soter, and to him, the twelfth
« in succession from the apostles, succeeded Eleu-
« therius who now holds the episcopate. By this
« same order and succession both that tradition which
« is in the Church from the apostles, and the preach-
« ing of the truth have come down to us ». The
singularity is that Cletus is suppressed altogether,
and Anacletus, whom the breviary places after Clement, comes after Cletus. Tertullian, who was of
the same age as Irenaeus, seems to introduce another confusion and to insinuate, though he does
not expressly say, that Clement was next to Peter.
« Let them make known the origin of their church-
« es, let them unroll the line of their bishops,
« so coming down by succession from the begin-
« ing that their first bishop had for his author and
« predecessor some of the apostles, or of apostolic
« men, so he were one that continued steadfast with
« the apostles. For in this manner do the apostolic
« churches bring down their rolls; as the church of
« the Smyrnians recounts that Polycarp was placed
« there by John, as that of the Romans does that

« Clement was in like manner ordained by Peter, just
« as also the rest show those whom being appointed
« by the apostles to the episcopate they have as
« transmitters of apostolic seed ». Another source
of confusion (and worse, because it palms off an
account of Clement's appointment to succeed S. Peter
as if given by Clement himself) occurs directly after the time of Irenaeus and Tertullian in the pretended epistle of S. Clement to S. James. The very
language is sufficient to convict it of forgery. It
is contained in the Clementina, which, according
to Gallandius, was written A. D. 230, whereas Irenaeus died A. D. 202, and Tertullian twenty years
after him. The Clementine Recognitions again were
written in the second century, and the Apostolic
Constitutions may be set down as of the middle of
the third century. Eusebius, who was made bishop
of Caesarea, in 314, says : « Linus was the first
« after Peter to obtain the episcopate of Rome.....
« but in the progress of this work, in its proper
« place according to the order of time, the suc-
« cession from the apostles to us will be noticed ».
And accordingly in book III, c. XI, he says :
« Anacletus after having occupied the See of Rome
« for twelve years consigned it to S. Clement » (1).

---

(1) « In Urbe vero Roma duodecim Anacletus annis in episcopatu
« exactis, Sacerdotii sedem Clementi tradidit ». Butler says in his

So-far the oldest authorities, giving the order of succession of the Popes professedly, set S. Clement in the third place after S. Peter. S. Irenaeus' work has come down to us in a very fragmentary state: whether a copyist conceived Cletus and Anacletus to be one and the same person, and so wrote Anacletus instead of Cletus, or Anacletus, by an error of transcription, was left out after Clement, we are unable to determine. As far as the place occupied by S. Clement in the series is concerned, S. Irenaeus supports tradition and the breviary. With regard to Tertullian the difficulty is less; because he was not treating of the collocation of the Popes, but of the apostolicity of churches. He was saying what S. Clement himself says in his first epistle to the Corinthians, « preaching through countries and « cities, they appointed their first fruits, having « proved them by the spirit, bishops and deacons « of those who were about to believe ». Or as the Presbyter of Africa says, more in detail, in the middle of the sixth century : « For it is ini-

---

life of Cletus, April 26th, « that Eusebius a Greek easily made mis-
« takes in similar Latin names, and confounded Cletus with Ana-
« cletus, Novatus with Novatian, Pope Marcellus with Marcellinus.
« But the Latins who had authentic records by them, especially the
« author of the first part of the Liberian Calendar, which appears
« in most particulars to be copied from the registers of the Roman
« Church, could not be mistaken : which authorities make it appear
« that Cletus sat the third and Anacletus the sixth bishop of Rome ».

« quity to break unity, rending, as it were, the
« garment of Christ, and tearing the nets, as it
« were, of the fishermen the apostles, from whose
« fellowship all heretics are strangers; who having
« abandoned the peace of communion and of the
« one bread of God and the apostles, preach in
« their not churches but squares, and do not com-
« municate with their memories, separated from the
« whole; assume for themselves the name of catho-
« lic. Whereas in Jerusalem James, and Stephen
« the first martyr; at Ephesus John; Andrew and
« others in various parts of Asia ; in the city of
« Rome the apostles Peter and Paul, delivering to
« their posterity the church of the Gentiles, at peace
« and unity, in which they taught the doctrine of
« Christ our Lord, hallowed it with their blood ».
For Tertullian's argument was that on points of doctrine only apostolic churches deserve to be heard.
« On this principle therefore we shape our rule of
« prescription, that if the Lord Jesus Christ sent
« the apostles to preach, no others are to be re-
« ceived as preachers but those whom Christ ap-
« pointed; ' for no man knoweth the Father save
« the Son and he to whom the Son hath revealed
« Him ' (1). Neither does the Son seem to have
« revealed Him to any other than to the apostles,

---

(1) Mathew XI.

« whom he sent to preach, to wit, that which he
« revealed unto them. Now what they did preach,
« that is what Christ revealed unto them, I will
« here also rule, must be proved in no other way
« than by those same churches which the apostles
« themselves founded, by preaching to them as well
« *viva voce,* as men say, as afterwards by epistles. »
Again he says: « but if any heresies dare to place
« themselves in the midst of the apostolic age, (that
« they may therefore seem to have been handed
« down from the apostles because they existed un-
« der the apostles) we may say : let them make
« known the origin of their churches, let them un-
« roll the line of their bishops etc. » (1). It is
simply by implication caused by his mentioning the
notorious fact that Polycarp ordained by John was
the first bishop of Smyrna, and that *in like manner*
Clement was ordained by S. Peter; whereas dealing
not with the regular order of succession, but with
the ordination, it would have served equally to say
that Linus or Cletus was so ordained, but the argument is carried incidentally over a longer space of
time by mentioning the ordination of Clement who
was the most distinguished of the three. And that
such was the scope, and not the order of succession of the Popes, appears from what he says af-

---

(1) Tertullian, de Praescript. haeret. No. 21. 209.

terwards. « Come now, thou that wilt exercise thy
« curiosity to better purpose in the business of thy
« salvation, run over the apostolic churches in which
« the very chairs of the apostles to this very day
« preside over their own places, in which their own
« authentic writings are read echoing the voice and
« making the face of each present. Is Achaja near
« to thee, thou hast Corinth. If thou art not far
« from Macedonia, thou hast Philippi, thou hast
« the Thessalonians. If thou canst travel into Asia,
« thou hast Ephesus. But if thou art near Italy,
« thou hast Rome, whence we also have an au-
« thority at hand. That church, how happy! on
« which the apostles poured out all their doctrine
« and their blood; where Peter had a like passion
« with the Lord; where Paul was crowned with an
« end like the Baptist's; where the apostle John
« was plunged into boiling oil and suffered nothing,
« and was afterwards banished to an island; let us
« see what she hath learned, what she hath taught,
« what fellowship she hath had with the African
« churches likewise ». In short Tertullian was speaking of the uninterrupted episcopal succession in all
the apostolic churches (1), and not of the primacy

---

(1) « Clear it is that no one has founded churches throughout the
« whole of Italy, the Gauls, Spain, Africa and Sicily, and the in-
« terjacent islands, except those whom the venerable Apostle Peter
« or his successors appointed priests ». Pope S. Innocent I. epist. 25
ad Decentium, A. D. 417.

or the succession of Popes. He was not saying that Linus did not succeed S. Peter, but that the succession in Clement was unbroken.

The aprochryphal Clementine writings were sure to create fresh difficulties. Eusebius of Caesarea in Palestine must first have felt their influence. Then A. D. 384, died Optatus bishop of Milevis in Numidia who agrees with Irenaeus and Eusebius in making Linus the first; but where Irenaeus has set Anacletus he puts Clement. « Peter therefore first « filled that individual chair which is the first of « the gifts of the Church; to him succeeded Li- « nus, to Linus Clement, to Clement Anacletus ». Here Cletus again is doomed to disappear from the roll of the early Popes. A. D. 403, S. Epiphanius bishop of Salamis died in the island of Cyprus. He, like Irenaeus, places Clement in the third place. « In Rome Peter and Paul were the first both a- « postles and bishops; then came Linus, then Cle- « tus, then Clement the contemporary of Peter and « Paul, of whom Paul makes mention in his e- « pistle to the Philippians. And let no one won- « der that, though he was the contemporary of Peter « and Paul, for he lived at the same time with « them, others received that episcopate from the « apostles. Whether it was that while the apostles « were still living he received the imposition of « hands of the episcopate from Peter, and having

« declined that office he remained unemployed.....
« or whether after the death of the apostles he was
« appointed by bishop Cletus, we do not clearly
« know..... However the succession of the bishops
« of Rome was in the following order: Peter and
« Paul, and Cletus, Clement, Evaristus, Alexan-
« der, Sixtus, Telesphorus, Hyginus, Pius, Ani-
« cetus ». Here two points are to be noticed, that treating expressly, like Irenaeus, of the order of S. Peter's successors, he gives Clement the third place as Irenaeus did. He leaves out Anacletus, and refers cursorily to Clement's episcopal consecration by S. Peter, but without any nomination as successor. Through the mistake of a transcriber Linus has been left out in the order of the succession, although Epiphanius had named him before as next to the apostles.

The next author, Rufinus priest of Aquilaeia died in Sicily about A. D. 410. He published and relied upon the Clementines *in extenso*. S. Augustine died A. D. 430. To prove that no Donatist bishop appears in the Roman succession he begins it: « To « Peter succeeded Linus, to Linus Clement ». Here again Cletus disappears. It is worth noticing that both African bishops Optatus and Augustine agree with Irenaeus, Eusebius, and Epiphanius in making Linus the immediate successor of S. Peter; and it is a fair inference that either they did not take their countryman Tertullian to mean that Clement was that successor, or that they rejected his opinion. So far we have given almost all the ancient authorities we know of. But as we are more concerned to fix some place in the series of Popes for Clement, than to distinguish between Cletus and Anacletus, and as S. Irenaeus and S. Epiphanius were both writing upon the actual Roman succession, and their Sees were nearer to Rome, we prefer their argument which makes S. Clement the third in succession from S. Peter. Peter, Linus, Cletus (or Anacletus), Clement. The same opinion is adopted by S. Jerome (1).

We shall now say something of modern authors, and their dealings with Linus and Cletus as sitting before Clement. If the Apostolic Constitutions, and Clement's letter to S. James of Jerusalem were not apocryphal, those who give the second place after Peter to Clement would have more weight; but the older authority of S. Irenaeus would still be against them, and the two oldest authorities after those apocryphal writings, viz: Eusebius and Optatus, whilst they agree with the Apostolic Constitutions and Irenaeus by giving Linus the first place, flatly contradict the letter to S. James, which pretends that Peter gave the keys to Clement. The

---

(1) Lib. de Script. Eccl. cap. XV.

Apostolic Constitutions A. D. 270, say that « Linus « the son of Claudia was ordained first bishop of « the church of the Romans, by Paul, but, af- « ter the death of Linus, Clement was ordained se- « cond bishop by Peter » (1). Rufinus' version of the adulterated letter to James says: « Be it known unto « thee, my Lord, that Simon, who on account of « his true faith and the most secure basis of his « doctrine, was appointed to be the foundation of « the Church, (and who on this very account had « his name, by the mouth of Jesus, which de- « ceives not, changed into that of Peter, the first « fruits of our Lord, the first of the apostles, to « whom the Father revealed the Son, whom Christ « justly proclaimed blessed....). At the time that « Peter was about to close his career, when the « brethern were assembled, suddenly taking hold « of my hand, he arose and thus addressed the « Church.... I ordain this Clement your bishop to « whom I entrust this my chair of instruction.... « wherefore I communicate to him the power of bind- « ing and of loosing in order that in respect to « whatever he shall ordain on earth it may be de- « creed in heaven. For he will bind what ought « to be bound, as one who knows the rule of the

---

(1) « Linum Claudiae filium Ecclesiae Romanorum Episcopum primum a Paulo ordinatum, post mortem vero Lini Clementem quem ego Petrus secundum ordinavi ». Lib. VIII. c. 47.

« Church. Him therefore hear ye, knowing that he
« who grieves the teacher of the truth sins against
« Christ and angers God the Father of all: there-
« fore shall he not live. But it behoves him who
« is appointed over the rest to hold the place of
« a physician, and not to be stirred up with the
« rage of a wild beast » (1). On this impudent
attempt to lecture the Popes to be doctors and not
brutes criticism would be wasted.

Butler learnedly demonstrates that the Apostolic
Constitutions cannot be ascribed to Clement, nor to
any apostle, and Rondinini quotes Epiphanius to

---

(1) « Notum tibi facio, Domine, quia Simon Petrus, qui verae
« fidei merito et integrae praedicationis obtentu, fundamentum esse
« Ecclesiae definitus est, qua de causa etiam Domini ore cognomi-
« natus est Petrus, qui fuit primitiae electionis Domini. Aposto-
« lorum primus, cui et primo Deus Pater Filium revelavit, cui et
« competenter beatitudinem contulit... In ipsis autem diebus (quibus
« vitae finem sibi imminere praesensit) in conventu fratrum positus,
« apprehensa manu mea repente consurgens, in auribus totius Ec-
« clesiae haec protulit verba....... Clementem hunc Episcopum vobis
« ordino, cui soli meae praedicationis et doctrinae cathedram trado....
« Propter quod ipsi trado a Domino mihi traditam potestatem ligan-
« di et solvendi, ut de omnibus quibuscumque decreverit in terris,
« hoc decretum sit et in coelis. Ligabit enim quod oportet ligari,
« et solvet quod expedit solvi, tanquam qui ad liquidum Ecclesiae
« regulam noverit. Ipsum ergo audite, scientes, quia quicumque
« contristaverit doctorem veritatis, peccat in Christum, et Patrem
« omnium exacerbat Deum, propter quod et vita carebit. Ipsum au-
« tem qui praeest caeteris, oportet medici vicem agere, et non fe-
« rae bestiae furore commoveri ». Epist. I Clementis ad Jacobum
fratrem Domini, pag. 133.

prove that the heretics misinterpreted them, as is also declared by the third oecumenical council of Constantinople (1). For the letter to S. James some quote the epistle of S. Ignatius to the Trallians; but no stress can be laid upon it, because the best critics prove that it also has been interpolated. We have explained before that Tertullian in his book of prescription (c. 32) was speaking of the certainty of Clement's consecration by S. Peter, and not of his place in the list of Popes. And that if Rufinus in his preface to the apocryphal book of the Recognitions, which he dedicated to Gaudentius bishop of Brescia, does certainly place Clement before Linus, just as certainly did he rely upon the forgery he was editing. That able schismatic Photius A. D. 878, who, if we are to believe Nicetus, was a good hand at forgeries himself, says : « Some « suppose that Clement was the second bishop of « the city of Rome after Peter ; but others the « fourth, for that Linus and Anacletus intervened « as Pontiffs between them » (2). Archbishop Rabanus Maurus of Mentz, a learned monk who lived in the middle of the ninth century, adopted the o-

---

(1) « Aliqua in eis haeretici nequiter interpretati sunt. Ab eisdem « multa fuere corrupta ».
(2) « Clementem secundum post Petrum Urbis Romae episcopum « fuisse quidam autumant, alii vero quartum; Linum enim et Ana- « cletum inter utrumque Pontifices intercessisse ». Codex CXIII.

pinion of Rufinus, but with some modifications, as we read in his treatise on choral bishops, which Labbè inserts in his collection of the councils. « In « the epistle to James you will find in what way « the Church was committed to Clement by blessed « Peter, therefore Linus and Cletus will not be en-« rolled before him, because they were ordained by « the Prince of the Apostles himself to show forth « the sacerdotal ministry » (1). He concludes again « that Linus and Cletus performed the ordinations « of priests » (which is now the office of the cardinal Vicar and the bishop Vicegerent of Rome) « and that after the martyrdom of Peter not they but « Clement succeeded to the honour of the chair » (2). The whole if this seems to be mere guesswork mixed up with heretical opinion. Isidore Mercator, who lived towards the end of the ninth century, agrees in some respects with Rufinus and Rabanus Mauro. In the first letter of his Collections he adheres to the apocryphal letter to S. James. In the letter he is said to have addressed to Pope John III (3), he says: « But if Peter the prince of the apostles adopted « Linus and Cletus his assistants, nevertheless he « did not formally deliver to them the pontifical « power either of binding or loosing; but to his suc-

---

(1) Vol. VIII. p. 1853.
(2) Ibidem.
(3) N. 559-72.

« cessor S. Clement, who deserved to hold the a-
« postolic See and pontifical power after him by de-
« livery of blessed Peter. Linus and Cletus indeed
« administered outer matters, but the prince of the
« apostles Peter was earnest in word and prayer.
« For nowhere do we read that Linus and Cletus
« ever discharged any function of the pontifical mi-
« nistry as Ordinaries, but only used to do as much
« as was enjoined upon them by blessed Peter ».
This again is obviously special pleading borrowed
from the account in the acts of the first institution
of deacons : neither they nor Clement could exercise any pontifical powers in Peter's lifetime except
by direct delegation. Rabanus and Mercator rest e-
vidently upon the apocryphal letter to S. James. Nor
are solid reasons wanting to refute their assertions
that Linus and Cletus were choral bishops; on which
subject we refer the reader to the learned work of
Peter Coustant in his preface to the epistles of the
Roman Pontiffs (1). At the close of the tenth century, Aymon, a monk of Fleury, says in his third
book « *de Christianorum memoria :* » « Some who
« have investigated the chair of the sovereign Pon-
« tiffs to whom in his lifetime blessed Peter en-
« trusted a dispensation of things ecclesiastical, but
« himself spent the time only in prayer and preach-

---

1) N. 7.

« ing. » Whence as ordained by him with so great
« authority they deserved to be placed in the cata-
« logue of sovereign Pontiffs. But blessed Peter him-
« self constituted Clement as his own successor, as
« seems besides to agree with the Canons and the
« epistle of Clement to James. But Clement, who was
« flourishing in becoming manners so as to be a-
« greeable to Jews and Gentiles, and all the Christian
« people, had the poor of each of the regions written
« down by name, and those whom he had cleansed by
« the sanctification of baptism he did not allow to be-
« come subject to public mendicity ». As our answer
to this is already given, we need not here repeat it.

Taking S. Peter as the root, it is certain that Linus came next to him and then Cletus; for in fixing this order of succession all the Calendars of the Roman and Italian churches agree, as well as the pictures in S. Paul's on the Ostian way, the Calendars preserved in other churches, the testimony of ancient writers, the Canon of the mass, uninterrupted universal tradition, and by the dearth of facts and arguments, or even probable conjecture to the contrary. In like manner the authorities which assign the third place to Clement are so grave and satisfactory that little or no doubt can remain regarding it. If Pagi (1), Vendelinus (2), Hensche-

---

(1) Franc. Pagi ad an. Christi c.
(2) Vendelinus, Comment. in epistolam Clementis.

nius (1), Bianchini (2), Orsi (3), Muratori (4), and others of less celebrity, rely upon the Liberian Calendar, and the opinions of S. Optatus Melivitanus and S. Augustine to give the second place to Clement instead of Cletus, weighty and respectable writers though they be, they cannot counterbalance a host of others. The Liberian Calendar is the only one which puts Clement in the second, Cletus in the third, and Anacletus in the fourth place. « *Clemens annis IX, mensibus XI, diebus XII. Cletus annis VI, mensibus XI, diebus X. Anacletus annis XII, mensibus X, diebus III* ». Ancient and valuable as this Calendar is it need not be preferred to the agreement of almost all the early writers who have learnedly discussed this subject. If the authority of a Calendar, a document, or an individual, however ancient and respectable, is to be preferred to the great consent of Calendars, documents and historians, how can the supporters of the Liberian Calendar refute the author of the *Carmen* against Marcian, who maintains that Cletus took up the government of the Church after Linus, after him Anacletus, and then Clement. As Coustant remarks in his life of Cletus: « the mere antiquity of the

---

(1) Henschenius, Apparat. ad Chronol. Pontif. exercit. 5.
(2) Bianchini Not. Chronolog. in Pontificat. S. Clementis et S. Cleti.
(3) Orsi, Stor. Ecclesiast.
(4) Muratori, Annal. d'Italia. an. 66 67.

« Liberian Calendar should affect no one, since it
« contains many patent errors regarding facts in
« the early ages ». We have already remarked
upon S. Optatus and S. Augustine, and preferred to
them S. Irenaeus and S. Epiphanius, and we may
add S. Jerome (1). Rondinini asserts that « the old
« authors of ecclesiastical matters bear witness una-
« nimously that Clement succeeded Cletus » (2). Burius however says: « *Disputat hic mundus sit quar-
tus, sitne secundus* » (3): or taking Peter as the
root, whether he was the third or first. In our opinion the whole may be traced to the apocryphal letter to S. James, the eagerness and veneration with
which such documents were received, and the im-
pression, in the absence of decisive authority, which
they naturally produced upon the later writers that
there must be some ground of truth in them. « *Nihil
est tam incredibile, quod non dicendo fiat probabile* » (4).
It may have been through this veneration with which
S. Clement's writings were received next after the
scriptures that S. Jerome, without stopping to distinguish the spurious from the true, remarks: « most
« of the Latins suppose Clement to have been the

---

(1) Irenaeus adversus haeres. lib. III. c. 3. — Epiphanius, Tom. I, adv. haeres. (27) p. 107. — Eusebius, Hist. Eccl. lib. III. c. 13. — Hieronymus, de Script. Eccl. c. XV.
(2) Rondinini, lib. 1. c. 1. §. 2.
(3) Burius, Elench. not. Roman. Pontif. See c. XXX.
(4) Cicero.

« second after the apostle Peter » (1), that is before Cletus. There are many who although convinced by tradition that Clement held the fourth place and not the second, did not like to contradict S. Jerome. We do not allude to Henry Hammond who thought that Linus, Cletus, and Clement governed the Church together: the two first the Gentile converts, and the latter the Jews, and, after the death of his colleagues, both together, an hypothesis by which he tried to defend the Episcopalians against the Presbyterians, but which by no means pleased his own colleague John Pearson, who repudiates it in his posthumous works (2), as contrary to the discipline by which only one bishop should preside over the same diocese (3). But we allude to the opinion of Baronius (4), which others maintain, and among them Coteler (5), and the Bollandists (6), who affirm that Peter consecrated Clement bishop of Rome, and nominated Linus his successor. Clement, however, for reasons not assigned, (perhaps because they never existed, though merely

---

(1) Hieronymus, de viris illustribus, c. XXV. We adhere to the opinion expressed by S. Jerome in his work on Ecclesiastical writers. Ch. 15.
(2) Pages 180 181.
(3) Tillemont, not. sur S. Clément.
(4) An. 69. n. 43.
(5) Const. Apost. p. 31.
(6) Pont. p. 15.

alluded to by S. Epiphanius) (1), resigned the pontifical chair to Linus, who was succeeded by Cletus, after whose death he assumed the government of the universal Church.

Linus suffered martyrdom on the 23rd of September A. D. 82, and Cletus glorified God with his blood in the year 92 or 93, and was buried in the Vatican near S. Linus, where his relics are still preserved (2). After his death Clement had no excuse for not accepting the government of the Church. The Latin and Greek fathers unanimously attest with what zeal and assiduity he laboured for the salvation of souls. He was adorned with every public and private virtue, and all antiquity is loud in his praise. It is not our scope to describe in what heroic degree he practiced each virtue, but we cannot refrain from some notice of his writings which constitute his peculiar characteristic. He laboured strenuously to preserve intact and inviolate the sacred deposit of faith, to condemn heresy, and root out vice. S. Epiphanius, writing against the Ebionites, says: « There are other books too which they use,

---

(1) Adversus haeres. XXVII. n. 6.
(2) The beginning of S. Clement's pontificate dates, according to different writers, from 90 to 93. Butler says that Cletus governed the Church from 76 to 89. Ciaconius, in his life of Cletus, relates that he was crowned with martyrdom on the 26th of April 92. Natalis Alexander ad soec. pr. records the same. Baronius, ad an. I. says in 93.

« as the Itinerary of Peter compiled by Clement,
« in which book, with the exception of a few words,
« they have made the rest supposititious; as Cle-
« ment himself rebukes them in those circular epistles
« which, written by him, are read in the very ho-
« ly churches; from which it is certain that his
« faith and speech are very far abhorrent from the
« things which in those Itineraries under his name
« have an adulterated existence » (1). He also points
out two of these discrepancies. « Clement teaches
« the observance of virginity, they reject it. He
« recommends Elias, David, Samuel, and all the
« prophets, they detest them » (2). Nor were Clement's learning and authority confined to the vindication of the orthodox doctrine of virginity against
the Ebionites (3), and the harmony which results

---

(1) « Sunt et alii libri, quibus utuntur, velut Petri circuitus a Clemente conscripti, quo in libro paucis verbis relictis caetera supposuerunt, quemadmodum Clemens ipse omnibus illos modis redarguit iis epistolis circulatoribus, quae ab eo scriptae in Sacrosanctis Ecclesiis leguntur. Ex quibus constat longe ab iis, quae in circuitibus illis sub ejus nomine adulterina existant, illius fidem ac sermonem abhorruisse ». S. Epiphanius adv. haeres. XXX. p. 15.

(2) « Etenim virginitatem Clemens edocet, isti repudiant: ille Eliam, Davidem, et Samuelem, omnesque Prophetas commendat. Ebionitae detestantur ». S. Epiphanius, ibidem.

(3) Epiphanius says that S. John went into Asia by the special direction of the Holy Ghost to oppose the heresies of Ebion and Cerinthus. Ebion seems to have been the father of the Unitarians. After the destruction of Jerusalem he taught the Christian refugees at Pella that Christ was the greatest of the Prophets, but a mere man, the natural son of Joseph and Mary; an error which he bor-

— 39 —

from the legal, prophetic and christian economy as in contradiction to the dreams of the Cerinthians (1). He likewise condemned the Marcotian heresies. Praedestinatus, who lived in the sixth century, tells us in his first book on heresy, par. 14th : « The four-
« teenth heresy was invented by one Mark, who,
« denying the resurrection of the flesh, endeavoured
« to build up that Christ did not suffer truly, but
« by supposition. Him S. Clement bishop of Rome
« and most worthy of Christ, confuting by irre-
« fragable assertions, and convicting in the Church
« before all the people, punished with eternal damna-
« tion ; teaching that our Lord Jesus Christ was
« truly born and suffered, summing up that by Him
« nothing was done under a phantastic form; and
« evidently showing that truth, the enemy of false-
« hood, could have nothing whatever in itself that
« was false, just as neither could light have dark-

---

rowed from the sect of the Nazarenes. He mutilated S. Matthew's gospel, pretended that the legal ceremonies were indispensable, and permitted divorces.

(1) Cerinthus added his share to Ebion's impieties. He defended the obligation of circumcision, and of rejecting the use of unclean meats. He extolled the angels as the authors of nature, pretending that the world was not created by God, but without his knowledge by some distinct virtue; that the God of the Jews was a mere man preeminent for his virtue and wisdom, pointed out by the dove at baptism, and proceeding to manifest his father hitherto unknown to the world. He seems to have invented the myth that Christ fled away at his passion, and Jesus alone suffered and arose again.

« ness in itself, nor blessing malediction, nor sweetness
« bitterness : and if those might be mingled toge-
« ther, yet did he teach that it is impossible for
« God to be mixed up with a lie ».

As Tertullian says in defending S. Luke's gospel and the Apocalypse against Marcion : « Wasps
« build nests: Marcionites too build churches ». To trace the architects of these churches, or builders of those nests, is not always easy. But we do not know upon what principle Peter Coustant attempted (1) to deprive Clement of the merit of having anathematized the idealism of the Gnostics, and vindicated the scandal of the Cross, and the resurrection of the flesh. S. Irenaeus says: « Before
« Valentinus there were no Valentinians, nor Mar-
« cionites before Marcian ; nor in fact any of the
« other malignant sentiments enumerated above, be-
« fore there arose inventors and beginners of each
« perverse opinion. But the sect called Gnostics,
« who derive their origin, as we have shown, from
« Menander, Simon's disciple, each of them of that o-
« pinion which he adopted, of it he was seen to be the
« parent and high-priest » (2). He says, however, that before Marcian, Cerdon taught similar errors under Pope Hyginus, A. D. 139-42. Valentinian at

---

(1) Epist. Romanor. Pont. pag. 6.
(2) S. Irenaeus adv. haeres. lib. III. c. 4.

the same date revived those of Simon Magus. Menander had done it before him. It does not follow that any of these men were the disciples of Simon directly, but only his followers and imitators. And as Simon practised magic, so Irenaeus mentions that even in Lyons Mark and his followers used love philters, permitted women to consecrate, and made the chalice seem filled with a red liquor which he called blood. Evidently this Mark was later than Clement; but it does not follow that a previous Mark and Gnostic principles were not condemned by him. The same remark applies to Eusebius, who says that Mark was living when Valentinian came to Rome under Hyginus, and remained there under Anicetus (1). S. Paul and S. John, S. Ignatius and S. Polycarp encountered similar heresiarchs long before Hyginus. Even without the authority of Praedestinatus it would be very odd if they had given Clement a truce. In his preface that writer says: « In the detection
« therefore of falsehood, and in the defence of truth,
« we have followed the footsteps of Catholics, and
« we have done it that in the first book the an-
« cient superstition of heresy may be thorougly laid
« open. Clement then the Roman bishop, S. Peter's
« disciple, most worthy martyr of Christ, fully
« explained the heresy of Simon vanquished with

---

(1) Eusebius, Hist. Eccl. lib. IV. c. XI.

« Simon himself by the apostle S. Peter. Him fol-
« lowed five holy orthodox men, and each of them
« in his own time wrote down the rise and con-
« flict and issue of each several heresy in many
« books and many thousands of lines, which we,
« by God's assistance, have epitomized in this little
« book » (1). As the deposit of faith contains within itself every dogma before it becomes necessary to ascertain it by precise definition, so every heresy like some fungus contains within itself the seed which it scatters to generate its kind. S. Clement was not likely to forget the warning of S. Paul.
« Men shall be lovers of themselves, covetous, haugh-
« ty, proud, blasphemers, disobedient to parents,
« ungrateful, wicked. Traitors, stubborn, puffed up,
« and lovers of pleasures more than of God; hav-
« ving an appearance of godliness but denying the
« power thereof. Now these avoid. For of these sort
« are they who creep into houses, and lead cap-
« tive silly women loaden with sins, who are led
« away with divers desires: ever learning and ne-
« ver attaining to the knowledge of truth » (2). Nor was the apostolic man who wrote to the Corinthians:
« Do ye therefore who laid the foundation of this
« sedition submit yourselves to the priests, and be
« instructed into repentance, bending the knees of

---

(1) Apologet. 5.
(2) II Epist. to Timothy, chapter III. v. 2. 4. 5. 6. 7.

« your hearts learn to be subject, laying aside all
« proud and arrogant boastings of your tongues ;
« for it is better for you to be found in the sheep-
« fold of Christ little and approved than thinking
« yourselves above others to be cast out of his hope »;
likely, when sitting in the chair of Peter to refrain from anathematizing a rebel, whether his name was Mark, Marcian or Legion. Seeing the licentious impieties of one Mark at Lyons no long time after Clement's death, and of that other Manichaean Mark who afterwards went into Spain and seems, by instituting the Priscillianists, to have anticipated the Mormons and Agapemone, it is not unlikely that there may have been Marks enough before them, who preferred the flesh to the spirit, and deserved the excommunication of the Church.

CHAPTER III.

S. Clement's solicitude to hand down to posterity the Acts of the Martyrs — He divides the fourteen regions of the city into seven districts, and appoints seven notaries over them, whence he is said to be the founder of the Prothonotaries called Participantes *— Roman Martyrology — Its author — Liturgy of the Mass.*

To the indefatigable solicitude with which Clement fed the flock and extirpated heresy, we must add his anxiety to preserve and hand down to posterity the exploits of the champions of Christ. He governed the Church under the reign of Domitian, who was for cruelty, as Tertullian says, « a piece of Nero » (1). « Domitian », says Eusebius, « grew « through all the grades of crime to dare by edicts « of a most cruel persecution, published everywhere, « to pluck up Christ's Church greatly strenghtened « in the whole world » (2). In his persecution, the second against the Church, it was that S. John, after having come miraculously out of the caldron of boiling oil at the Latin gate, was exiled to Patmos, where he had those visions which he recorded in the Apocalypse. « Like Herod the emperor feared « the advent of the Messiah, and had the descen- « dants of the house of David searched out and put « to death » (3). But what most exasperated him was to see the number of the Christians, in spite of his sanguinary edicts, daily increasing in Rome, nay in his own family and palace. He had no respect for dignity of position or nobility of birth : not even for those of his own kindred. And here we may quote from the Prophet (4) : « For there

---

(1) « Portio Neronis de crudelitate ». (Apologet. 5).
(2) « Per omnes scelerum gradus crevit, ut confirmatissimam toto « orbe Christi Ecclesiam, datis ubique crudelissimae persecutionis « edictis, convellere auderet ». (Oros. VIII. 10).
(3) Eusebius, Hist. Eccl. III. 19.
(4) Osee, chapter IV. v. 1. 2.

« is no truth, and there is no mercy, and there
« is no knowlegde of God in the land, cursing,
« and lying, and killing, and theft, and adultery
« have overflowed, and blood hath touched blood ».
Domitian beheaded his cousin german the consul Flavius Clement, and banished, to Pandatereia (1), his wife Flavia Domitilla (2) whose sons (3) he had adopted and destined for his successors; and his niece Flavia Domitilla, for having embraced the christian faith, he transported to the island of Ponza. The persecution spread like a fire throughout the empire, and torrents of noble and innocent blood were poured out to slake the insatiable thirst of that imperial monster. Examples of the most heroic fortitude daily presented themselves to the Christians who were to be immolated, and to the Pagans who ridiculed and scoffed at their madness, and in their scoffing were sometimes converted to the faith by the patience of the martyrs, and condemned to perish by their side. No age, sex, or condition could escape the sword of the ruthless tyrant. Imagine what sweet incense of confession rose up to the throne of God from the lips of those devoted

---

(1) Pandatereia is an island opposite the gulph of Gaeta half-way between Ponza and Ischia, now known by the name of S^a Maria.

(2) This Flavia Domitilla was Domitian's sister.

(3) Vespasian junior, and Domitian junior who had for their tutor the famous Quintilian.

victims, questioned about their faith, tempted by the most deceitful promises, racked by demoniacal tortures. But the most cruel punishments seemed light to them, believing as they did in the promise of their Divine Saviour : « Fear not them that kill the
« body, and are not able to kill the soul.... every
« one therefore that shall confess me before men,
« I will also confess him before my Father, who
« is in heaven » (1). That these confessions of the faith, so consolatory to the christian heart, so dear to God, might not be lost, Clement divided the fourteen regions of the city into seven districts over which he appointed as many ecclesiastics distinguished for learning and piety. Their duty, as Baronius tells us (2), was not alone to collect the Acts of the Martyrs and the records of their sufferings, but also, to register the answers they made to their persecutors, when arrested or put on trial, or condemned to death. In them we possess the most luminous practical proof of Catholic truth, for in them the gospel was put in practice before a raging world.
« Why have the Gentiles raged, and the people de-
« vised vain things ? The kings of the earth stood
« up, and the princes met together against the Lord
« and against his Christ » (3). In venerating them

---

(1) Matthew, X chap. v. 28-32
(2) An. 238.
(3) Psalm. II. verse 1. 2.

we bow our heads to the God of the martyrs, humbled, but consoled to see how frail nature was elevated by grace, how the prophetic words of Christ were fulfilled, how his children, of whom the world is not worthy, preserved to the last the priceless treasure of their faith, how their triumphs eclipsed and have survived the triumphs of the Capitol by how much the nearer they were made like to Calvary. O how true is the exclamation of S. Eusebius bishop of Lyons! « The minds of the children are set in arms
« whilst the triumphs of their fathers are rehearsed;
« for from them we understand how much that life
« eternal should be longed for, which we see sought
« for through torments, through wounds, through in-
« -supportable toils; which we know to have been pur-
« chased with the price of blood » (1). Rondinini says of these seven Clementine notaries that « their
« name, and office partly, passed formerly into the
« seven Prothonotaries whom they call *Participantes* »; and they, increased by Sixtus V, to the number of twelve, were enriched with very notable privileges, in that especially that before others they have the power to confer the degree of Doctor, just as have the illustrious universities of the world, refer their origin to S. Clement as their author, and in the pendent seal which they annex to the doctoral diploma,

---

(1) Homily of S. Eucherius on S. Peter and S. Paul.

are used to print an image of S. Clement with the epigraph *S. Clemens Collegii Prot. Part. Fundator*.

Whereas the principal origin of the most ancient Martyrologies is only an epitome of the acts of the martyrs collected by those clerical notaries, S. Clement is called by many writers the author of the Roman Martyrology. Bencini in his notes to the life of S. Clement, published by Anastasius, says: « Out « of these acts related in the churches the oldest mar- « tyrologies and lessons are made up » (1). And to them may be traced the origin of other martyrologies which even yet deserve to be studied by the learned. Hence Boldetti says: « Those notaries diligently re- « gistered in the ecclesiastical Tables the days that « were called Fasti, from which were compiled the « Martyrologies, out of which were read, on the day « before, the names of the martyrs whose festivals « occurred the next day, in order that the memory « of their triumph might be celebrated with greater « spiritual solemnity on the anniversary of their mar- « tyrdom which was called their birth day » (2). In the choirs of monastic Orders the same is done to this day. The acts were not collected for entertaining historical reading, but that as far as possible the Church upon earth might join on the very day with

---

(1) Acta Martyrum, pag. 541.
(2) Boldetti, Osservazioni sui Cimiterii de' Martiri, lib. I. c. XI.

the Church triumphant in heaven, where are the souls of them that were slain for the word of God, and for the testimony which they held (1).

In addition to the other works which distinguished our Saint, we must not omit the liturgy of the Mass, of which, according to Baronius, Proclus, Usher, and others, he was the author. Baronius writes: « Moreover there is a tradition that Clement left in « writing the rite of offering the sacrifice which he « had received from S. Peter, to wit the Mass itself « of the Roman church ». To which tradition Proclus « adheres in these words: « Many other divine pastors « too who succeeded to the apostles, and ancient « churches, explaining the reason of the sacred mys- « teries of that heavenly Mass, have delivered the « order of the Church in writing: amongst whom « first and foremost blessed Clement, disciple and suc- « cessor of that sovereign prince of the apostles, who « published those most holy mysteries revealed to him « by the sainted apostles ». So says Proclus, bishop « of Constantinople (in 447), of Clement, with whom « others of the Greeks who have written commenta- « ries upon the sacred rites equally agree; though « some have supposed that by the liturgy of Clement « we must understand what are held as written by « him of the same most holy sacrifice in the seventh

---

(1) S. Cyprianus, Epist. ad Clerum, XXXVII. pag. 114.

« book of the Constitutions (1), and in the eighth (2).
« But the form of holy Mass which is prescribed to
« the Latins and whole Western Church, some things
« excepted which were added or changed not only by
« Clement himself but by the prince of the apostles
« Peter himself, ancient tradition vindicates to itself,
« since there is nothing else to point out its begin-
« ning and origin » (3).

The consent of authors is sufficient to show that Clement had a true zeal to provide for the worship and religious decorum of the Catholic Church, whether he actually committed anything regarding the sacred liturgy to writing or not; nor does it seem more inconvenient that the chief part should be preserved as a standard in some authentic roll than that the epistles and gospels should be copied. On which account it is not worth while to examine the opinion of Peter Le Brun who maintains « that no liturgy « was published either in Greek or Latin before the « sixth century » (4). If this means publication for general circulation it may be likely enough; for the Christians had seen so many of their volumes committed to the flames, so many scattered to the winds, and had smarted so severely for bringing out the

---

(1) C. XXV. XXVI. XXVII.
(2) C. XV. et seq.
(3) Baronius, An. CII. 23.
(4) Disputatio liturgica, vol. III.

treasures of the Church, that common prudence would warn them, even upon the peace of the Church, to be chary of diffusing the mysteries. And again if it means that nothing was written down, it would be contrary to human nature among so many literary bishops and priests, with the utmost religious veneration for secrecy, that no notes or manuscripts should ever be made, and contrary, we may say, to the very necessity of the case, so prolonged was the initiation of the Church in comparison with modern times. Usher says: « In the Arabic catalogue of Chaldaean « and Syrian liturgies, which belonged to Ignatius the « late Patriarch of Antioch, is reckoned (1) one of « Pope S. Clement composed in Greek, which one Tho- « mas Harchalanus translated into Chaldaic 407 years « after the Nativity of our Lord ; and another of « S. Ignatius composed in Greek at Antioch twenty « seven years after our Lord's Ascension, which James « bishop of Rehanus did into Chaldaic. And Clement « is reckoned by the Patriarch Proclus among the first « who delivered a written exposition of the liturgy to « the Church. Bessarion in his book of the Sacra- « ment of the Eucharist thus replies to the Greeks « urging his (Clement's) authority : ' Though these « words of Clement be usually enumerated among « apocryphal writings, yet we are agreeable to as-

---

(1) See Cornelius Schulting, Biblioth. Theolog. tom. III. p. 1.

« sent to them as true in present circumstances ; but « that liturgy is a certain part of the eighth book « of those which in some *Codices* bear the title « Διδασκαλιας of doctrine, in others of Διαταγών, or of « 'Apostolic Constitutions written by Clement » (1). It is obvious however in reference to Proclus who did not write before the middle of the sixth century, that he has given a merely imaginary account of the long chanted prayers with which the apostles celebrated the mystic sacrifice, and probably he had no authority for saying that the apostles themselves dictated the Roman liturgy to S. Clement ; though he may have been correct in saying that S. Basil and S. Chrysostom, to meet the degeneracy of the times, abridged the one they used. Pope S. Innonocent I, who held the See at the beginning of that (5th) century, declared that the Roman liturgy is of apostolic origin, which, it may well be, whether oral or written. Waterworth says in his extracts from the fathers of the first five centuries, that from the testimony of several of the fathers there

---

(1) Usserius, de Ignatii Martyr. epist. Consult also, Liturgia Orientalis by Eusebius Renaudat, book 3. page 186. Les anciens liturg. by John Grancolas, page 96. Bibliotheca Orientalis by Simon Assemanni, tom. 1. ex codice Vitriensi III. Liturgical codex of the whole Church by Lewis Assemanni, book 4. p. 2. In the 4 vol. part 1. p. 137, he (Assemanni) and Muratori in his dissertation de rebus liturgicis, completely demolish the assertion of Le Brun.

is reason to believe that no public liturgy of any church was written earlier than the middle of the fourth century, and that the Clementine is no exception; for as compiled in the Constitutions it is not known to have been used in any church service whatever (1). But Oldoinus in his notes to Ciacconius' life of S. Clement enumerates a number of liturgical observances as enforced by S. Clement, and Moroni repeats the same in his erudite ecclesiastical dictionary. It is also said that he was the first to introduce into the liturgy of the Mass the salutation *Dominus vobiscum*, and the *Orate Fratres* (2). *Non nobis tantas componere lites.* All we wish to show from their disputes is that Pope Clement has a traditional claim to zeal for liturgical observance.

---

(1) See the specimens he gives of all the liturgies, referring them to three sources, to wit, that of S. James, S. Mark and S. Peter, besides the Gothic fragments of Spain and Gallia Narbonensis published by Mabillon in 1685.
(2) See Gem. lib. I. cap. 87.

CHAPTER IV.

Zeal of S. Clement to diffuse the gospel of Christ — Missionaries sent by him to France, Spain, and elsewhere — His letters to the Corinthians, and to Virgins — The Book of Recognitions — The Clementine Homilies, and Epistle to S. James — The Apostolic Canons.

Not alone did S. Clement provide with unwearied vigilance for the unity of the faith and for the decorum of public worship, but like one who heard his Master's words ringing in his ear: « And other « sheep I have that are not of this fold, them also « must I bring, and they shall hear my voice, and « there shall be one fold and one shepherd » (1). He spared no pains to maintain uninterrupted the succession of the hierarchy, and propagate the Kingdom of Christ. We read in the pontifical book that he held two consecrations in the month of December in which he ordained ten priests, two deacons, and fifteen bishops. He baptized the son of Tarquinius a Roman (2), initiated him in holy orders, and sent him to France with S. Denys, S. Ursenius, S. Gratianus, S. Saturninus, and S. Nicotius. Some modern writers have

---

(1) John c. 10. v. 16.
(2) See Roman Martyrology, 11 of August.

disputed the authenticity of these facts, but, as Rondinini observes (1), they cannot succeed in subverting the more ancient authorities. We read in the chronological manuscript of S. Ivo, quoted by Patrick Young, that Clement sent Pothinus to Lyons, Paul to Narbonne, Gratian to Tours, and Julian to Mans. Bernard Guidoni cited by cardinal Mai in his Specilegium attests the same. « He also sent « many bishops to different regions : Pothinus to « Lyons, Paul to Narbonne, Gratian to Tours, « Denys the Areopagite to Paris where he suffered « martyrdom by decapitation, together with his com- « panions on the ninth of October in the ninetieth « year of his age » (2). The Maurist Fathers follow the same opinion. « No matter what modern « writers may say it is very probable that the mis- « sion of the first bishops into Gaul, such as S. Tro- « phinus of Arles, S. Gratian of Tours, S. Denys « of Paris, S. Paul of Narbonne, S. Austromonius « of Clermont, and S. Martial of Limoges, is due to « Clement and not to S. Fabian ». Nor is it likely that these were all he sent, or to Gaul only. Oldoinus and other writers say that « he consecra- « ted Eugenius first bishop of Toledo, and that in « the second year of his Pontificate, when blessed

---

(1) Book 1. ch. 1. §. 5.
(2) See Cardinal Mai's Specilegium, vol. 6. p. 13.

« Mark of Atina had borne the palm of martyr-
« dom by orders of the president Maximus, he made
« Fulgentius bishop of the same city who presided
« over the church of Atina thirty one years, seven
« months and twenty eight days » (1). Atina was
then a flourishing city near the Pontine Marshes.

If S. Clement earnestly laboured to diffuse gospel truth, he knew that it was essential to preserve it pure and undefiled, and that that could only be done by submission to a divinely constituted authority. A scandalous schism broke out among the Christians at Corinth, in which some of the laity rebelled against the priests, and carried their sacrilegious violence to the point of preventing them from exercising the functions of their ministry. Fortunatus, who is mentioned by S. Paul (2), was sent to Rome to lay the whole matter before the Pope. Clement bitterly deplored the ruin impending over that portion of his flock, and addressed to them, in the name of the Roman Church, a very pathetic and instructive epistle. Writing with the effusion of the paternal heart he does not forget the firmness without which dignity becomes a bauble, and the authority, which is meant to check, a provocation to fresh aggressions. Eusebius styled it

---

(1) See Oldoinus, ad vitam S. Clementis per Ciacconium.
(2) Corinth, XVI. v. 17.

« an admirable work » (1), and all the Fathers of the first four centuries spoke of it with admiration. It may give an idea of the difficulty of ecclesiastical researches, since the vast destruction of original documents, that this epistle, which was read in the churches next to the Scriptures, was entirely lost. For several centuries not a trace of it could be found. Baronius deeply deplored its loss, and collected all the extracts he could find of it from the works of Irenaeus, Dionysius bishop of Corinth, and Eusebius of Caesarea. Fortunately, however, to the great delight of the learned, it was discovered at the end of a very ancient Alexandrian manuscript of the Bible written, about the time of the first council of Nice, by an Egyptian woman named Thecla. Cyril Lucarius the schismatical patriarch of Constantinople brought it from Alexandria and presented it to James Ist of England. The royal librarian Patrick Young published a copy of it at Oxford in 1633. Pages 58, 59, 60 are still wanting. It begins: « The Church of God which is at Rome to that of « Corinth, to those who have been called and sancti- « fied by the will of God in our Lord Jesus Christ, « may the grace and peace of Almighty God be « increased by Christ Jesus in every one of you ». He reminds them of their former peace. « At that

---

(1) Hist. Ecclesiast. lib. 3. c. 16.

« time your virtues, piety and zeal, your invio-
« lable attachment to the law of God, were the
« admiration of all who knew you. You were then
« submissive to your Pastors, you respected your
« superiors : you set an example of sobriety and
« modesty to your children, you established and
« maintained good order within your own families.
« More ready to obey than command, more eager
« to give than to receive, you cherished the sen-
« timents of moderation and humility in your hearts.
« Content with the common gifts of Providence for
« your support in life, you turned your thoughts
« to God and studied the observance of His holy
« law. Thus you enjoyed the sweetest tranquillity
« and peace of mind. Being animated with the
« purest charity you felt a warm desire and seized
« every opportunity of doing good. Full of con-
« fidence and zeal you never ceased lifting up your
« hands to the throne of mercy, humbly begging
« forgiveness for the sins of frail mortality. Day
« and night you poured forth your prayers for the
« salvation and happiness of your brethren in Jesus
« Christ that the number of the elect might be
« speedily filled up. You were then void of ma-
« lice, your conduct was sincere and blameless.
« You held in abhorrence the very name of con-
« tention and discord. You pitied your deluded
« neighbour, and bewailed his faulty oversights

« as your own. But how sadly has this prospect
« changed since then ! How clouded and how dis-
« mal the view which was once so bright and de-
« lightful ! In place of content and harmony, jea-
« lousy and disunion prevail among you ». He
puts his hand at once upon the root of the evil,
speaks with just indignation of their disgrace, and
exhorts the refractory to more generous and cha-
ritable sentiments. « Wherefore are these conten-
« tions and swellings and dissentions, and wars a-
« mongst you ? Have we not one God and one
« Christ, and one Spirit of Grace poured out upon
« us, and one calling in Christ ? Wherefore do
« we rend and tear in pieces the members of Christ,
« and raise a sedition against our own body, and
« come to such a height of folly as to forget that
« we are members one of another. Remember the
« words of our Lord Jesus, how he said: ' Woe
« to that man by whom scandal cometh ; it were
« better for him that he had never been born than
« to scandalize one of my elect: it were better for
« him that a millstone should be hanged about his
« neck, and that he should be cast into the sea, than
« that he should scandalize one of my little ones. '
« Your schism hath perverted many, hath cast ma-
« ny into dejection, many into doubt, and all of
« us into grief; and yet your sedition continues.....
« Take up the epistle of the blessed Paul the a-

« postle. What did he first write to you at the
« beginning of the gospel? Verily he did by the
« spirit admonish you both concerning himself and
« Cephas and Apollo; because that even then you had
« formed particularities amongst yourselves, though
« that your particularity had led you into less sin,
« for you were partial to tried apostles and to ano-
« ther who had been approved by them. But now
« consider who they are who have led you astray,
« and have lessened the majesty of your much spoken
« brotherly love. It is shameful, my beloved, it
« is most shameful and unworthy your Christian
« profession that it should be heard that the most
« firm and most ancient church of the Corinthians,
« on account of one or two persons, is in a se-
« dition against the priests..... « Who then amongst
« you is generous, who that is compassionate, who
« that is filled with charity? Let him say : ' If
« sedition and strife and schism be through me,
« I will go and depart whithersoever you please, and
« do whatever is appointed by the multitude, only
« let the flock of Christ be at peace with the consti-
« tuted priests' ». He exhorts them by the example
of God himself to be patient and long suffering and
to acknowledge his benefits to all : each in his degree. « Behold the Creator of the world, and think
« how patient and gentle he is towards his whole
« creation. The heavens, the earth, the oceans and

« worlds beyond them, are governed by the com-
« mand of this great Master. Let every one be
« subject to another according to the order in which
« he is placed by God. Let not the strong man
« neglect the care of the weak, let the weak see
« that he reverence the strong, let the rich man
« contribute to the necessities of the poor, and let
« the poor bless God who hath given him one to
« supply his wants. Let the wise man show forth
« his wisdom not in words but in good works. Let
« him that is humble never speak of himself, nor
« make show of his actions. Let him that is pure
« in flesh not grow proud of it, knowing that he
« received the gift of continence from another. In
« our body the head without the feet is nothing,
« nor the feet without the head, and the smallest
« members of our body are yet useful and neces-
« sary for the whole ». Not content to appeal to
the necessary harmony of parts, he warns the ring-
leaders to make a voluntary submission and not to
incur excommunication. « Do you therefore who laid
« the foundation of this sedition submit yourselves
« to the priests, and be instructed unto repentance.
« Bending the knees of your hearts learn to be sub-
« ject laying aside all proud and arrogant boast-
« ing of your tongues : for it is better for you to
« be found in the sheepfold of Christ little and ap-

« proved, than thinking yourselves above others to
« be cast out of His hope ».

He points out to them the source of Catholic and Episcopal power, and that disputes for prelacy and precedence were foreseen and provided against; and he insists upon the strictness of ritual observance. The apostles have preached to us from the Lord Jesus Christ, Jesus Christ from God. Christ then was sent by God, and the apostles by Christ.... Preaching therefore through countries and cities they appointed their first fruits (having proved them by the spirit), bishops and deacons of those who were about to believe. Nor was this a new thing, seeing that it had been written long before concerning bishops and deacons. « I will appoint their bishops in righteousness and their deacons in faith » (1).
« And what wonder if they to whom in Christ such
« a work was committed by God, appointed such
« as we have mentioned when even that blessed and
« faithful servant in all his house, Moses, notified
« in the sacred books all things that had been com-
« manded him..... Our apostles knew through our
« Lord Jesus Christ that contentions would arise
« upon the name of the episcopacy, and for this
« cause, having a perfect foreknowledge, they ap-
« pointed the aforesaid and then gave directions in

---

(1) Is. IX. 17.

« what manner, when they should die, others should
« succeed them in their public ministry. Wherefore
« we account that they who have been appointed
« by them or afterwards by other eminent men,
« the whole Church consenting, and who have mi-
« nistered blamelessly to the flock of Christ with
« humility, peacefully, and not illiberally, and who
« also for a long time have been approved by all;
« that such are not to be without injustice thrown
« out of the ministry. For it would be no small
« sin in us, if we should cast off from the episco-
« pacy those who offer up the gifts blamelessly and
« holily ». Refusing to sacrifice any bishop to popular clamour or secret prejudice, he speaks of the
due order of Church functions. « As these things
« are manifest to us, it behoves us looking into
« the depths of the divine knowledge to do all things
« in order whatsoever the Lord hath commanded to
« be done; at stated times to perform both the obla-
« tions and the liturgies; and not at random and
« disorderly hath He commanded this to be done',
« but at determined times and hours. And He him-
« self hath ordained by His supreme will both where
« and by what persons He wills them to be per-
« formed; that all things being holily done, unto
« all well pleasing, they may be acceptable unto
« His will. They therefore that make their obla-
« tions at the appointed times, are at once ac-

« cepted and blessed, because that following the
« institutes of the Lord, they sin not. For there
« are proper liturgies delivered to the chief priest,
« and a proper place assigned to the priests; and
« there are proper ministrations incumbent on Le-
« vites, and the layman is adjudged to the appoint-
« ment of laymen. Let every one of you, brethren,
« give thanks to God, in his proper station with
« a good conscience, with gravity, not going beyond
« the prescribed canon of his liturgy ». He desires them to send back his legates to acquaint him
of the restoration of peace. « Those that have been
« sent to you by us, Claudius, Ephetus, Vale-
« rius, Vitone together with Fortunatus also, send
« back to us again with all speed, in peace and
« in joy; that they may the sooner acquaint us
« of your peace and unanimity so much prayed
« for and desired by us. So that we may speedily
« rejoice at your good order ».

The authenticity of this epistle is generally acknowledged; but assuming for a moment that it is
a forgery, it is by its adaptation to circumstances,
by the moderation and elevation of its language one
of the most skilful literary forgeries ever penned.
It is pregnant with the spirit of papal power. And
viewing it from the ground of Catholic principles,
it would be no small compliment to Clement that so
weighty, reasonable, and eloquent a document could

be attributed to no less a man. The soul of the priest responsible for the souls of others, the heart of the Christian man, the mind of the Vicar of Christ laying his obligations at the foot of the altar of his Lord ; the spirit of the prelate commanding in the place of the apostles, the peaceful order of the ecclesiastic consecrated for his office, are conspicuous in every line of it. It is a pleasure to believe it produced the desired effect. The holy Pontiff's prayers were heard, all dissensions ceased, the laity became submissive to their pastors, and peace and concord reigned again in the church of Corinth.

A very considerable fragment of a second letter to the Corinthians was found in the same Alexandrian manuscript. S. Dionysius of Corinth tells us (1) that it was read in that church, but was not so celebrated among the ancients as the first. It recommends the faithful to despise the world and its allurements, to subdue their passions, and to keep their minds always fixed on heaven.

In addition to those two letters to the Corinthians our Saint addressed two others to Virgins. Westein, a Lutheran, found them in a Syrian manuscript of the new Testament, in 1752, and published them the same year at Amsterdam with a Latin translation, and again in 1757. The authenticity of these

---

(1) L. 1. c. Jovinian. ch. 7.

letters was impugned by Henry Venema, a German Lutheran, but his objections, as we read in the Acts of Leipsic, for January 1756, were refuted by Westein, who also acknowledges that Clement differed much in his opinion of celibacy from Martin Luther. « But it has not been proved », says the Protestant writer, « that his opinion has been wrong ». « For, if any one denies himself what it is allowed « him to enjoy, that he may the better, and the « more freely apply himself to the care of the Church, « why ought he not hope to receive a great re- « compense in the life to come? » S. Jerome alludes to these letters in his book against Jovinian (1): « In these epistles which S. Clement, the successor « of the apostle Peter, wrote to them, that is to « certain eunuchs, almost his whole discourse turns « upon the excellency of virginity ». Butler remarks that they are not unworthy of the great dissciple of S. Peter. They expound the counsels of S. Paul regarding celibacy and virginity, the practise of which they recommend without diminishing the respect due to the holy state of matrimony.

Many other works have been attributed to, and circulated under, the name of Clement, but the universal consent of almost all writers regards them as either apocryphal, or supposititious. These, as well

---

(1) C. 7. p. 527.

as the genuine works of our Saint, were collected and published by Coteler at Paris in 1672. We have alluded already to the Book of Recognitions, as a production of the second century. The Clementine Homilies and the Epistle to S. James were got up about the year 230 by some learned and clever unknown writers. Gallendius thinks that the Apostolical Constitutions should be referred to the year 230. They are quoted by S. Epiphanius (1), and are a compilation of ancient pastoral regulations. Bzovius translated them from Greek into Latin in 1603. Turrianus illustrated them, and Servius and Burius inserted them in their collection of the Councils. They have been erroneously ascribed to Clement, as Pagi, Baronius, Natalis Alexander, Coteler, and almost all modern writers, except Whiston, satisfactorily prove. They comprise eight books, and contain much valuable information, regarding the liturgy, discipline, and practices of the primitive Church, although neither the precise time when they were written, nor by whom, can be ascertained.

The Apostolical Canons were thought by some really to have been written by the apostles. Others referred them to the close of the fifth century. They are a compilation from various synods, and are now

---

(1) Hom. 45. 35.

generally supposed to be not later than the beginning of the third century. They were 85 in all and were all received by the Greeks in the sixth century. The Latins received only the first 50, and even these with some reserve, particularly Canons, 7, 46, 47, rejecting altogether the last 35. Turrianus, a writer of the 16th century, strains every nerve in defence of the whole. Bellarminus (1), Baronius (2), and Bassenius in his « Apparatus sacer » think the first fifty to be authentic. Burius (3) admits all but 65 and 84. Natalis Alexander (4) explodes them all together. It is certain that not a single Father, except S. John Damascene, has placed them among the canonical writings. They are not quoted by Eusebius, Jerome, Athanasius, Epiphanius, or any of the early Fathers in their vindication of the discipline of the primitive Church. Of some of them, however, the antiquity cannot be denied, for they were quoted at the Council of Nice ; but it is admitted that they were adulterated at a very early period, and that their number was increased to 85 in the ninth century. Whether any of the Canons drawn up by Clement is comprised or not in these compilations no one can say. We are content to

---

(1) De script. eccl. in Clemente.
(2) Ann. in an. 102.
(3) Vol. I. Concil.
(4) Hist. eccl. saeculi primi.

rest his reputation as an author upon his Epistle to the Corinthians, and his character as a prelate, upon the general approbation of antiquity: registered in the Book of life, an apostolic man, a martyr Pope. The petty disputes of critics about uncertain writings may obscure but not elucidate his career.

CHAPTER V.

Morality of Roman emperors in the days of S. Clement — S. Ignatius of Antioch condemned to death by Trajan — His journey to Rome, and martyrdom in the Coliseum — S. Clement exiled to the Chersonesus by orders of Trajan — Condition of the Christians in that penal settlement — Fruits of his Apostolic labours among its inhabitants — His martyrdom — Miraculous recovery of his body by S. Cyril who brought it to Rome, and deposited it in the Basilica dedicated to him at the foot of the Coelian Hill.

It is the fashion of writers led away by classical enthusiasm, or rather by their indifference to true religion, to speak of the pagan despots, who one after the other possessed the imperial throne of Rome, sometimes with apology, sometimes with praise. The epithets, *just, humane, and virtuous,* are bestowed upon men who, in the recesses of their dwellings probably led no more decent lives than the rest of the idolatrous aristocracy, who have left obscene pictures upon their walls, their statues, and mythology, to justify the reproaches which the martyrs cast upon the infamous vices of the heroes and gods they cherished and adored. True, that the Roman eagle hovered over that cunning, lust, and cruelty, from which at various periods even Christian emperors have not been free, as well as over the reigns of princes less base ; and that as in more modern times, between emperor and king, flatterers could be found, by winking at their vices, by dissembling their hypocrisy, by shutting their eyes to everything but the external glitter of their rule, to prate of justice, benevolence and freedom, and of two usurpers to choose between. But glory based upon a lie cannot endure. To men liable at any moment to be seized and transported to unhealthy exile, through imperial fear, to have their homes suddenly invaded, their subsistence seized, and confiscated at the pleasure of the prince, if not to be burnt alive in villages by the commander of his troops, to be burnt and flayed before the tribunal of the judge, to be hooted and hunted, and branded as useless members of society, reviled and execrated as adverse to civil government; superstitious wretches who, of either sex, deserved no mercy but to be driven forth to beg — for them indeed, between Pilate and Herod, between Octavius who seated himself upon the ruins of the Republic and thought to number the whole world , or Nero who drove his vile mistresses in the imperial chariot, blaspheming the Christians the while , and contriving the destruction of S. Peter , and whose victorious march into Greece was marked by the degradation and death of nobles, the confiscation of estates and plundering of temples ; between Domitian who debauched his own niece , and , as Suetonius and Eusebius say , took the titles of Lord and God , who varied his amusement of impaling flies by the delight with which he beheld the most barbarous executions: or Nerva, whose philosophic indolance gave the Christians a respite of fifteen months, and his successor Trajan ; men who suffered always might learn that between emperor and emperor there were gradations of vice and brutal power. Nero was a man of taste, loved music and songs, and theatres and their accompaniments , did not disdain races , and driving himself dressed like a charioteer ; if he did not write pamphlets and memoirs , he composed poetry ; he had an extravagant passion to make a new Rome which should be built in a more sumptuous manner ; he wanted room in particular to enlarge his own palace, which after the destruction of the quarters of the city adjacent to it, he immediately rebuilt of an immense extent and adorned with whatever the world afforded that was rich and curious, and no doubt with sumptuous quarters for his imperial guard. Of course he had no love for Christians. He permitted his satellites to defame them as much as they pleased, though his hypocrisy could not escape the satire of the public; and the legal officers he let loose upon them rather excited compassion for their sufferings, than respect for themselves or their chief. He was the first that made a general indiscriminate persecution of religion, and thought perhaps that by cutting off the Pope and his fellow-martyr S. Paul to put an end to what he considered a farce and obstacle to his own arbitrary power. He miserably ended his days by committing suicide. How S. Clement escaped him, how he got through the first ten years of Domitian's reign, and especially the next five years after he sat in the Apostolic Chair, history does not record. A prince was coming who had some literary pretensions and more ambition : before printing was invented he had his own way of inscribing his name and actions, and got the nickname of « wall-dauber » for his advertisements : he had his eye upon the East, and promoted foreign expeditions. He lived in incest with his sister. Like Vespasian and Domitian he ordered all who were of the race of David to be put to death; and, accused of this as well as of being a Christian, the bishop of Jerusalem,

S. Simon, who was over his hundredth year, was tortured for several days and then crucified. He originated the third, as Domitian did the second general persecution. As usual, there have not been wantting men to style him « a just and virtuous prince », and he affected moderation. From the beginning of his reign he prohibited the assemblies of Christians; but he directed his Prefects to punish them only who were legally convicted, and not to go out of their way to arraign them for supposed criminality. He punished informers as well as the accused. Thus he seems not to have adopted espionage, and he rejected anonymous charges as repugnant to the equity of his government, and required for the conviction of those to whom the guilt of criminality was imputed the positive evidence of an open accuser. Mahomedanism was not yet invented, but Trajan especially after he had marched towards the Danube and achieved victories over the Dacii and Scythians, who may be taken as ancestors of the Russians, shewed his native superstition and policy, out of gratitude to his imaginary deities. The next year, A. D. 106, the ninth of his reign, he set out for the East on an expedition against the Parthians and entered Antioch with the pomp of a triumph. What compliments he paid and received from the chiefs and tribes, what respect the Caesar showed for their polygamy and polytheism, we know not. His first concern was about the affair of religion, and the worship of the gods. And for this purpose he resolved to compel the Christians either to own their divinity and to sacrifice, or to suffer death. Of the way in which this « *excellent and equitable Prince* » presided at trials, we have a specimen in the Acts of S. Ignatius the Martyr bishop of Antioch. « Who « art thou, wicked demon, that dust transgress « my commands and persuade others to perish? » Ignatius mildly answered: « No one calls Theophorus « a wicked demon ». Trajan said: « Who is Theo- « phorus? » « He who carrieth Christ in his breast ». « And do we not seem to bear the gods in our « breast whom we have assisting us against our « enemies ? » Ignatius answered : « You err in « calling them gods who are no better than devils, « for there is only one God who made heaven and « earth and all things that are in them, and one « Jesus Christ his only Son into whose kingdom « I earnestly desire to be admitted ». Trajan asked: « Do you not mean him who was crucified under « Pontius Pilate ? » « The very same : who by « his death has crucified sin with its author, over- « came the malice of the devils, and has enabled « those who have Him in their breasts to trample « on them. Yes, for it is written: ' I will dwell « and walk in them ' ». Trajan then dictated the sentence. « It is our will that Ignatius who saith

« that he carrieth the crucified man within himself
« be bound and conducted to Rome, to be de-
« voured by wild beasts for the entertainment of the
« people ». The holy martyr, having heard the sentence pronounced against him, cried out with a heart full of joy: « I thank Thee, oh Lord! for having
« vouchsafed to honour me with this pledge of per-
« fect love for Thee, and to be bound with chains
« of iron in imitation of the apostle Paul, for Thy
« sake ». He was then put in chains and consigned to a troop of savage soldiers to be conducted to Rome. On arriving at Smyrna he had an interview with S. Pylicarp, the disciple of S. John the Evangelist, and addressed most affecting and instructive letters to the churches of Ephesus, of Magnesia, of the Trallians, and to the Christians of Rome. He then implored S. Polycarp and others to unite their prayers with his, that the ferocity of the lions might soon present him to Christ; and with this view he also wrote to the faithful at Rome, beseeching them not to deprive him of his crown by praying to God that the beasts might spare him, as they did other martyrs. « I fear your charity », he says, « least it prejudice me. For it is easy
« for you to do what you please, but it will be
« difficult for me to obtain God if you spare me.
« I shall never have such an opportunity of enjoy-
« ing God, nor can you, if ye shall now be silent,

« ever be entitled to the honour of a better work.
« For if ye be silent in my behalf, I shall be made
« partaker of God, but if ye love my body, I
« shall have my course to run out. Therefore a
« greater kindness you cannot do me, than to suf-
« fer me te be sacrificed unto God; whilst the altar
« is now ready, that, so becoming a choir in love,
« in your hymns ye may give thanks to the Father,
« by Jesus Christ, that God has vouchsafed to bring
« me the bishop of Syria, from the East into the
« West to pass out of the world into God, that
« I may rise again unto Him. Ye have never en-
« vied any one. Ye have taught others. I desire
« therefore, that you will firmly observe, that which
« in your instructions you have prescribed to others.
« Only pray for me that God may deign to give
« me both inward and outward strength that I may
« not only say, but do, that I may be not only
« called a Christian, but be found one ; for if I
« shall be found a Christian, I may then deservedly
« be called one, and be thought faithful when I
« shall no longer appear to the world. Nothing is
« good that is seen. A Christian is not a work of
« opinion, but of greatness, when he is hated by
« the world. I write to the churches and signify
« to them all that I am ready to die for God,
« unless you hinder me. I beseech you that you
« show not an unreasonable good will towards me.

Suffer me to be the food of wild beasts, that I may be found the pure bread of Christ, whereby I may attain unto God. Rather entice the beasts to my sepulchre that they may leave nothing of my body, that being dead I may not be troublesome to any one. Then shall I be a true disciple of Jesus Christ when the world shall not see so much as my body. Pray to Christ for me that in this I may become a sacrifice to God. I do not, as Peter and Paul, command you; they were apostles, I am an inconsiderable person; they were free, I am even yet a slave; but if I suffer, I shall then become the freeman of Jesus Christ, and shall arise a freeman in Him. Now I am in bonds for Him, I learn to have no wordly or vain desires. From Syria, even unto Rome, I fight wild beasts both by sea and by land, both night and day, bound to ten leopards, that is to say a band of soldiers, who are the worse for kind treatment. But I am the more instructed by their injuries, yet I am not therefore justified. I earnestly wish for the wild beasts that are prepared for me, which I heartily desire may soon dispatch me, and whom I will entice to devour me entirely and suddenly, and not serve me as they have done some whom they have been afraid to touch; but if they are unwilling to meddle, I will even compel them to it.

Pardon me this matter, I know what is good for me. Now I begin to be a disciple, so that I have no desire after anything visible or invisible, that I may attain to Jesus Christ. Let fire or the cross, or the concourse of wild beasts, let cutting or tearing of the flesh, let breaking of bones or cutting off limbs, let the shattering in pieces of my whole body, and the wicked torments of the devil come upon me, so I may but attain to Jesus Christ. All the compass of the earth, and the kingdoms of this world will profit me nothing. It is better for me to die for the sake of Jesus Christ than to rule unto the ends of the earth. Him I seek who died for us. Him I desire who arose again for us. Pardon me, brethren, be not my hindrance in attaining to life, for Jesus Christ is the life of the faithful; whilst I desire to belong to God, do not ye yield me back to the world. Suffer me to partake of the true light. When I shall be there, I shall be a man of God. Permit me to imitate the passion of Christ my Lord. If any one has Him within himself, let him consider what I desire, and let him have compassion on me, as knowing how I am straitened. The prince of the world endeavours to snatch me away, and to change the desire with which I desire, with which I burn, of being united to God. Let none

« of you who are present, attempt to succour me.
« Be rather on my side, that is on God's. En-
« tertain no desire of the world, having Jesus Christ
« in your mouths. Let no envy find place in your
« hearts. Even were I myself to entreat you when
« present, do not obey me, but rather believe what
« I now signify to you by letter. Though I am
« alive while writing this, yet my desire is to die.
« My love is crucified, the fire that is within me
« does not crave any water, but being alive and
« springing within says : Come to the Father. I
« take no pleasure in the food of corruption, nor
« in the enjoyment of this life. I desire the bread
« of God which is the flesh of Jesus Christ, and
« for drink His blood which is incorruptible cha-
« rity. I desire to live no longer according to men,
« and this shall be if you are willing. Be then
« willing, that you may be accepted by God. Pray
« for me, that I may possess God. If I shall suf-
« fer, ye have loved me. If I shall be rejected,
« ye have hated me. Remember in your prayers
« the church of Syria, which now enjoys God for
« its shepherd instead of me. I am ashamed to be
« called of their number, for I am not worthy,
« being the last of them, and an abortive, but
« through mercy I have obtained that I shall be
« something, if I enjoy God ». The holy martyr arrived in Rome on the 20th of December, and was

immediately sent to the amphitheatre where he was devoured by lions « *for the entertainment of the people* ». Thus it is ever. Whether a S. Ignatius of Antioch, a S. John Chrysostom, a S. Thomas of Canterbury, a Gregory VII, or any exiled bishop of the nineteenth century, is to be persecuted, and, if possible, doomed to suffer death, the pretext of crowned tyrants is ever, the well-being, and « *the entertainment of the people* ». The Christians, to the lions! was the shout of the popular diversion then — then as now war upon Catholic priests and prelates was the maxim of men whom God, who waiteth patiently to repay, permitted for his own wise purposes to disgrace for a while the thrones of the earth. — S. Ignatius, as we have said, was instantly devoured by the lions that were let loose upon him, and nothing of his body remained but the larger bones, which, as S. John Chrysostom relates, were religiously taken up and « carried in « triumph on the shoulders of all the cities between « Rome and Antioch » where they were laid in a marble urn as an inestimable treasure. Evaristus writes (1) that « at first they were deposited outside « the Daphnitic gate, but in the reign of Theodo- « sius the Younger were translated with extraordina- « ry pomp to a church in the city, which had been

---

(1) Hist. eccl. lib. 1. cap. 16.

« a temple of Fortune, and which has ever since
« borne his name ». They are now in our church
of S. Clement in Rome, whither they were translated
when, in 637, Antioch fell into the power of the
Saracens.

To the bishop of Rome the head of the state adopted that policy of grinding exile which more petty kings, since then, have used, lacking the courage to consummate a greater crime ; whilst their works point out the bent of their will. He could not bear the Christian Prelate in his own capital; he could not suffer him in Bologna, or Naples, or in any of the great Italian towns. That he had succeeded in planting military colonies in various places, won some victories over men brave, but not numerous enough to defend themselves effectually, and gained fresh cities, was not enough so long as there was a bishop with the soul of a freeman, and whom the consciences of men voluntarily obeyed. The greater the virtues, talent and holiness of such a man the more obnoxious to the prince by reason of the contrast of his character with his own: the warmer the affection in which he was held by the moderate and good, the more jealous the suspicion with which he was watched by the magistrates and their master. Clement was accused of being the leader of what then was called a new sect, and the organizer of their meetings. Accordingly he was cited before Mamertinus the Prefect of the city. As was not unusual with persons of noble birth, he was treated with a certain degree of urbanity. He had only to do what many persons nobly born had found it convenient to do, to betray his Sovereign, to renounce his faith, to prostrate body and soul before the ideas and will of the Caesar. He had only not to know Christ the King, to give up what he was assured was superstitious excess, and offer incense to the gods, the protectors of the empire. His common sense ought to show him that the stronger were the best judges, and that his private opinions, even if he were consecrated to herald them to the world, ought not to be pushed too far in opposition to the material interests and wishes of so well-judging a prince (1). But Clement was the Bishop of bishops, and he assented not to such suggestions. A report of the trial was submitted to the em-

---

(1) We have in the martyrdom of S. Chrysogonus which the Church celebrates on the day after the feast of S. Clement, an example of this method. He was shut up in Rome for two years, and his wants supplied by Anastasia. Diocletian ordered all the Christian prisoners to be put to death, but Chrysogonus to be sent to him to Aquileia. « I sent for you » said the emperor « to increase you « with honours, if you will bring your mind to worship the gods ». « I do venerate » was the answer « with mind and prayer Him who « is truly God; but the gods who are nothing else but images of « devils I detest and execrate ». The emperor had him beheaded. It has been well said that there are more ways than one of sacrificing to the infernal deities; and modern iniquity has not been at a loss for victims to the prejudice, passion and injustice, of which those deities are the authors.

peror, who ordered him to be banished to Cherson beyond the Euxine sea. Under an escort of soldiers he set out on his long and dreary journey. If we would know how such prisoners were treated, history furnishes us with many examples, and among them that of S. Ignatius already referred to, that of S. John Chrysostom from Constantinople to Comana Pontica in Cappadocia, that of Pius VI from Rome to Valence. If we would know how an imperial jailor can treat his victims, we can read it in Napoleon the First bullying Pius VII at Fontainebleau. And if we would estimate the limits which such men put upon moral and religious authority, we find it where that emperor tells his agent to treat the Pope as a power of a hundred thousand bayonets. S. Helena was the only fit comment. The power and the stones of ancient Rome were literally cemented with blood. When the sentimental traveller visits the Coliseum by moonlight, or deplores the wreck of marble columns, he seldom thinks with what agonies, and deaths, of slaves those masses were quarried and set up. At that great day when the just will stand with confidence against their oppressors, to Caesar will be given the things that are Caesar's, the dross of the metals he coveted for his filthy pleasures, the armour of his legions, the stones ransacked from every quarter of the world for his buildings and his statues. Perhaps the last of those fallen columns which has been set up again in

Papal Rome to bear aloft the image of the Mother of Christ, that pure and immaculate creation who never knew a stain of sin, was hewn and polished and consecrated by the toil and misery of Christian men. Clement found two thousand Christians doomed to hopeless slavery in the marble quarries of the Chersonese. What a consolation commingled with feelings of the deepest grief, must it not have been to those martyrs of Christ to see the Supreme Pastor descend into those gloomy prisons! He taught them to bear with fortitude the trials they were subjected to, reminding them that they were not better than their Master, who suffered the direst persecutions, and shed His blood for their redemption; and that if they would imitate His example, they would share His glory. His admonitions produced the desired effect. They submitted to the tyranny of their masters, to the severity of their labours, and to the gloom of their prisons, with Christian meekness and fortitude. They were obliged to carry water from a long distance under a parching sun; like another Moses, Clement caused a limpid stream to gush from a rock that was miraculously pointed out to him. This fact is best explained by the Antiphons of Lauds, which are read in the Office for his feast, on the 23 of November.

1st « Whilst Clement was in prayer, there appeared to him the Lamb of God ».

2nd « Not by my merits; the Lord has sent me to you to be partaker of your crowns ».

3rd « I saw upon the mountain the Lamb standing, from underneath whose feet is welling out a living fountain »,

4th « From underneath whose feet flows forth the living fountain; the gushing of the stream makes glad the city of God ».

5th « All the people around believed in Christ the Lord ».

The fame of this supernatural event spread throughout that entire region, and the result was that most of its pagan inhabitants embraced the Christian faith, broke their idols, razed, to the ground, the temples in which they were enshrined, and upon their ruins built no less than seventy five churches. When Trajan was informed of the miracles wrought by S. Clement, and the innumerable conversions made by his preaching, he became so incensed that he despatched his prefect Auphidianus armed with full powers to take proceedings against the Christians, and punish their temerity in violating the laws of the empire and insulting the gods, its protectors. Auphidianus on arriving at Cherson caused numbers of its inhabitants to be put to death by various kinds of torture. But seeing that, owing to the persuasive and inspired eloquence of Clement, they met their fate with cheerful resignation, he ordered the Pontiff to be thrown into the sea with an anchor fastened to his neck The sentence was executed in the presence of an immense crowd. The Christians being grieved that they could not recover his relics, were advised by his disciples, Cornelius and Phoebus, to have recourse to God by prayer, and humbly implore of Him to indicate to them the spot where the holy martyr's body lay. As their prayers ascended to heaven, the sea miraculously retired from the shore: they followed the receding waters, and having gone to the distance of about three miles, they found, to their astonishment, and inexpressible consolation, a marble temple, and within it an urn containing the holy Pontiff's body. while near it lay the anchor, the instrument of his martyrdom. Falling on their knees they returned thanks to God for having recovered so priceless a treasure. For more than two hundred years the sea used to retire on the anniversary of S. Clement's martyrdom. leaving a dry path to the faithful for visiting his tomb, which remained accessible for the seven following days, when it was again covered by the waters, as is recorded by S. Ephraim, the martyr bishop of Cherson, by S. Gregory of Tours, Peter de Natalibus. and many other trust-worthy authors. Trajan thought to disperse the sheep by striking the Shepherd, but he little knew that « the blood of martyrs is the seed « of the Church ». The miracles wrought by S. Clement during his exile, and after his martyrdom, had such an effect on the inhabitants of Cherson that they all embraced the Christian faith, so that, as Bosco informs us, neither Jew, nor Pagan, nor heretic, nor schismatic, was to be found in any part of that country; and the penal settlement of the Christians became a nursery of Saints. As we stated above, the miraculous reflux of the sea continued for more than two hundred years; but owing to the frequent incursions of the barbarians, the primitive inhabitants were gradually eradicated, so that, before the ninth century, the whole of that region was repeopled by a new race of men, and even the very spot, where once stood the celebrated temple of S. Clement, was forgotten, and of the sacred treasures it contained nothing was known until they were miraculously discovered by S. Cyril.

Not as Pope wrote, in his « Moral Essay ».

« Where London's column pointing at the skies
« Like a tall bully, lifts the head and lies »;

do the two great sculptured columns of pagan Rome reflect upon the victims of persecution. The Antonine column records the rain in answer to the prayers of the Christian soldiers who saved the army of Marcus Aurelius from perishing by thirst. Where tier upon tier the sculptured marble gives the exploits of Trajan in minute detail, we see nought to remind us of his vindictive cruelty against the Christian martyrs; but we miss the anchor there. Generally speaking, when the pagan Romans had slain men, they let them be buried: they did not root out their ashes; they did not destroy their sepulchres; to purify, they did not burn down their temples; they did not take much pains to blacken their reputation after death. It was done sometimes, but not for long. Neither Nero nor the senate built a column to record that the Christians set fire to Rome. Perhaps though they tortured men, they did not wish to boast of it. They did not think their power was built on that. We gaze indeed upon that proud monument of Trajan's triumphs, but the figure which crowns it is that of an Apostle. We look upon the shattered granite pillars of his forum, where Constantine proclaimed the empire Christian. We smile at the impotent conventions of emperors and kings, and bless the providence of God.

We have seen something of one of the first of S. Peter's disciples, a Roman, a Pope, and a Martyr. That first Christian century began with the stoning of Stephen, it ended with S. Clement's exile, and the second commenced with his having been hurled into the sea. We must pass over seven centuries to find him again. The ninth century was one of great men, and of great events. It began with a great Catholic emperor, Charlemagne, it ended with a greater Catholic king, Alfred the Great. Both were self-taught men, and both were full of Catholic instincts. Sir Henry Spelman (1) thus panegyrizes the character of the Monarch of England: « O, Alfred, the wonder and astonishment of all « ages! If we reflect on his piety and religion, « it would seem that he had always lived in a « cloister; if on his warlike exploits, that he had « never been out of camps; if on his learning and « writings, that he had spent his whole life in a « college; if on his wholsome laws and wise ad-« ministration, that these had been his whole stu-« dy and employment ».

The monarch of France was active in war and in peace, constant at Mass, a linguist and a legislator, who began too old even to write well, yet the friend of Alcuin. He restored the States of the Church, and, in 800, was crowned at Rome, by Leo III, emperor of the West. It is possible that Alfred stood before the fresco of our Lady's Assumption in S. Clement's; at least if Leo IV, who is painted beside it, was, as is, with the greatest probability, supposed, painted in his lifetime; for twice Alfred was brought, by his pious father Ethelwulph, to Rome, and Leo adopted him for his son, and anointed him for future king.

---

(1) Con. Brit.

This is no place to dwell on the glories of his reign, but no greater king ever graced the English throne. If he appears less conspicuously on the behalf of the Popes, it was for no want of will. He thought Peter's pence no detriment to the realm, and we have recorded the names of the noblemen who carried his presents to Rome (1). Nor was the ninth century without its missionary Saints. Charlemagne had subdued the Sclavonians by his arms, S. Cyril won them to Christ in the warfare of the faith. It is not uncommon in the lives of the Saints that the child is marked, as it were, by the finger of God, and pointed out for future sanctity; perhaps that when death crowns the work, men may remember that it was one of patience and love and not of man's doing. Thus Peregrina, the pious mother of the great bishop of Fiesoli, S. Andrew Corsini, dreamt that she gave birth to a wolf which ran into a church and was turned into a lamb; and the young rake actually did retire to the Carmelite church which he did not leave until he had put on the habit of that Order. Thus the Blessed Jane of Aza, the mother of S. Dominic, dreamt that she brought forth a whelp with a lighted torch in his mouth, which set the whole world on fire;

---

(1) See Asserius, William of Walmsbury, and Mathew of Westminster.

and that is the arms of the Order to this day. From his early youth Constantine Cyril of Thessalonica, the son of a senatorial Roman family, was called the Philosopher from his rare talents and aptitude for learning. Happier than others who had the same title, he dedicated the education he received at Constantinople to God's service in the priesthood. It was not a mean one. He knew Greek, Latin, and the Sclavonian languages, and he learned the Turcic spoken by the Huns, Chazari, and Tartars, that he might become the Apostle of their country. In 848, the Chazari, the descendants of the Huns of European Scythia, then settled on the Danube, sent to the emperor Michael 3rd and his pious mother Theodora, an embassy unlike modern embassies, for it was for priests to teach them the faith of Christ. The empress sent for the patriarch S. Ignatius, and, by his advice, Cyril was charged with this important mission. Recommending his undertaking to God, he set out, and in a short time after entering the field of his missionary labours, he instructed and baptized the Cham together with his whole nation. He then committed his church to the care of pious and zealous pastors, and returned to Constantinople, absolutely refusing to accept the rich presents which the new convert and his people wished to bestow on him; while he assured them that he valued, more than all the gifts they could give him, a promise that they would emancipate their Christian slaves, which they accordingly did (1).

Cyril's second mission was to the Bulgarians, in which he was assisted by his brother Methodius (2). Perhaps the circumstance which led to the conversion of Boigoris their king, had something to do with the previous embassy; for his sister had long been a hostage in the court of the empress Theodora, and became a Christian there. Her prayers, doubtless, ascended night and day to the throne of God for the conversion of her brother, which is said to have been effected, like many others in our own day, by a picture. Methodius was an artist monk; and when Boigoris asked the emperor for a painter to adorn his new palace, Methodius was selected. The king ordered him to execute a subject which would strike terror into all who saw it, and the good monk thinking nothing more awful than the last judgement, executed it in the most lively colours. The terrors of the scene and the explanation of it had

---

(1) Illi (Chazari) plurimi exhilarati et in fide catholica roborati gratias referebant, offerentes philosopho maxima munera, qui illa omnia respuens rogavit eos, quatenus pro muneribus quotquot captivos haberent Christianos servituti deditos, dimitterent liberos; quod protinus est adimpletum. Quo facto philosophus reversus est Constantinopolim. MS. Blauber.

(2) Egressus igitur (cum Methodio germano suo) prius venit ad Bulgaros quos gratia cooperante sua predicatione convertit ad fidem. MS. Blauber.

so powerful an effect on Boigoris that he instantly desired to be baptized, and took the name of Michael. His subjects hearing of his conversion rose in arms against him and marched to attack his palace; but he put himself at the head of his army and defeated them. The rebels thus checked returned to their allegiance, and shortly afterwards followed the example of their sovereign by embracing the Christian faith. A thorough convert, this prince sent letters and ambassadors to Nicolas Ist begging his Holiness to let him know what more he should do (1). The Pope gave him the instructions he desired, and sent Legates, in 867, to congratulate him on his conversion to the faith. He also answered many difficulties that were proposed to him, and declared baptism administered, in case of necessity, by laymen, and even by infidels, to be good and valid (2). Boigoris Michael renounced his crown in 880, and, putting on a monastic habit, led an evangelical life on earth. The year of his death is unknown. From Bulgaria Cyril and Methodius passed into Moravia, by invitation of king Rastices, whom they baptized with most of his people. Augustine, in his catalogue of the bishops of Ulmutz (3), and Dubravius (4) assert that S. Cy-

---

(1) Anastas. Bibl. in Nicolao I, et ipse Nicolaus ep. 70. Hincmar etc.
(2) See his response ad consulta Bulgarorum. Conc. t. 7. p. 1542.
(3) Inter rerum Bohemiae scriptores. Hannoviae 1632.
(4) Hist. Behemiae, lib. 4.

ril was the first bishop of the Moravians. Also, the Bohemians, under God, owe their faith to our Apostolic monks. Dubravius writes that Borivorius, or Boriway, duke of Bohemia, was converted to the faith by hearing the holy missionaries preach, and being baptized by Methodius he invited him to Prague where he instructed his wife Ludimilla, their children, and many of his subjects, and regenerated them with the waters of baptism. Methodius also built at Prague the church of our Lady and several others. Stredowski, in his « *Sacra Moraviae historia* », styles SS. Cyril and Methodius the apostles of Moravia, upper Bohemia, Silesia, Cazaria, Croatia, Circassia, Bulgaria, Bohemia, Russia, Poland, Dalmatia, Pannonia, Dacia, Carinthia, Carniola, and of almost all the kingdoms in which the Sclavonian language is spoken. Pope John VIII, in 879, in his letters to count Spentopulf, writes that the Sclavonian alphabet was invented by S. Cyril. « The Sclavonian letters or alphabet invented by Constantine the philosopher that the praises of God may be sung, we justly commend » (1). The brothers also translated the liturgy and Mass into that tongue. In 1631, the Sclavonian missal was revised by Urban VIII, and his approbation of it was confirmed by Benedict XIV. It was not until after S. Cyril's death that Methodius, who was made archbishop

---

(1) Ep. 247 ad Spendopulchrum comitem.

of Moravia, obtained from John VII permission to use the Sclavonian language in the Mass. Both brothers came to Rome by invitation of Pope Nicolas Ist. Cyril died there and was buried in the church of S. Clement.

It is necessary to know what we may style the family affections of the Church in Rome even in unhappy times; what brotherly rejoicing in the canonization of a saint, what devotion in united prayers, what interest the good take even in the trifles of their father, to appreciate the eagerness with which the Roman people received the news of the arrival of the missionary saint, bringing with him the relics of S. Clement. The contemporary bishop of Velletri, Gaudentius, has given us an account of the translation of the relics of S. Clement which he witnessed; and Rondinini thinks that he may have had the account of their discovery from S. Cyril himself. When Constantine Cyril went to Pontus, the present Crimea, to study the Turcic for his mission to the Chazari, he tried in vain to learn something about S. Clement's relics. The people, who were not the tribes of Clement's day, but others who had come in since then, could give no information about them; and, for more than five centuries, the miraculous receding of the sea had ceased. He applied to George, the bishop of the diocese, and they agreed to search what they supposed to be the original spot. « Taking ship on « a calm day, under the guidance of Christ, they

« took their way, to wit, the aforesaid Philosopher,
« with the bishop, George by name, and the re-
« verend clergy , and some of the people as well.
« Sailing then with great devotion and confidence,
« hymning and praying, they reached the island in
« which they supposed the holy martyr's body to
« be. Getting round about it then, and searching,
« with great brilliancy of lights, they began, more
« and more earnest in their holy prayers , very
« anxiously, and without intermission, to dig in that
« mound where so great a treasure was suspected
« to rest. After working there for some time, and
« with much holy desire, on a sudden, as if God
« gave some brilliant star, one of the precious mar-
« tyr's ribs shone forth. At which spectacle all filled
« with immense exultation, and, not now without some
« excitement, vying with each other to dig out the
« earth more and more, his holy head also in due
« course appeared. And then behold after a little
« while again, as it were out of some parcels of
« holy relics, by degrees, and at moderate inter-
« vals, the whole was found. And last of all there
« appeared the anchor with which he had been cast
« into the deep. After the celebration, by the bi-
« shop, of the sacred mysteries upon the spot, the
« holy man lifting the chest of the sacred relics
« upon his own head, bore them to the ship; then

« transported the *glory* (1) to the metropolis. On the
« following morning the entire population of the ci-
« ty getting together, and taking up the chest of
« sacred relics, went round the town with much
« thanksgiving, and coming to the greater basilica
« honorably placed them in it ». If any one should
suppose that this account is fabulous and incredi-
ble, he would betray his ignorance of Church history. When S. Helen recovered the true Cross,
it was distinguished, from the other two which lay
beside it, by a miracle of healing. S. Ambrose relates how he himself recovered the relics of SS. Gervasius and Protasius. « Whilst I was dedicating
« the basilica, many began, as with one voice, to
« call upon me saying: ' Let this be dedicated as
« was the Roman basilica. ' I will do so, if I can
« find martyr's relics; and instantly there came upon
« me an ardour which presaged something. What
« need of many words? The Lord granted the fa-
« vour. And though even the clerics were alarmed,
« I ordered the ground to be dug up before the gates
« of SS. Felix and Nabor. I met with suitable in-
« dications. We found two men of wonderful sta-
« ture. All the bones entire and much blood. The
« crowd was great throughout the whole of the two

---

(1) Deinde *Gloriam* metropolim transportavit. Rondinini thinks
it should be *Georgiam*. See Rondinini, lib. I. §. III.

« days. In a word, we translated them when the
« evening was near at hand to the basilica of Fau-
« stus, and on the following day to the basilica
« which they call the Ambrosian. Whilst we were
« translating them, a blind man was restored to
« sight ». In the three instances here mentioned,
search was made at a particular spot, where the
relics were suspected to be. The relics of S. Cecily were found, by Pope Paschal Ist, in the catacombs, through a dream in which the saint appeared
to him after he had actually abandoned the search
as useless. The recovery of the relics of the protomartyr, the deacon S. Stephen, was still more
extraordinary. In the year 415, while Lucian, a
venerable priest who was attached to a church in
the small town of Caphargamala, about twenty miles
from Jerusalem, whilst sleeping in a room near the
sacristy where he lived in order to guard the sacred vessels, he dreamt that a tall comely old man
appeared to him clad in a white garment edged with
small plates of gold and decorated with crosses, and
holding a golden wand in his hand. Approaching
Lucian, and calling him three times by name, he ordered him to go to Jerusalem and tell bishop John
to come and open the tombs in which his remains
and those of other servants of Christ lay ; Lucian
asked his name, and he replied : « I am Gama-

— 99 —

« liel (1) who instructed Paul in the law, and on
« the east side lieth Stephen who was stoned to
« death by the Jews outside the north gate. His
« body was left there exposed one day and one
« night, but was not touched by birds or beasts.
« I exhorted the faithful to carry it away during
« the night, and had it secretly brought to my
« house in the country, where I celebrated his ob-
« sequies for forty days, and then buried him in
« my own tomb. Nicodemus who came to Jesus
« by night, lies in another sarcophagus. He was
« expelled the synagogue for following Christ, and
« then banished from Jerusalem, whereupon he came
« to my house, where I kept him till his death
« and buried him near S. Stephen. I also buried
« there my son Abibas : his body is in a coffin
« higher up in which I myself was also interred ».
Lucian, unable to understand the vision, begged of
God that if it came from Him, he might be fa-

---

(1) Gamaliel was of the sect of the Pharisees, and a legal doctor of high reputation in his day at Jerusalem. We read in the acts of the apostles, ch. 22. n. 3, that S. Paul recommended himself to the Jews by saying that he had been his scholar. When the Jews were contriving to put the apostle to death, Gamaliel dissuaded them by proving that the christian religion was the work of God. And this he did with such prudence that he did not incur the least suspicion of favouring the Nazarenes, as the Christians were then called. He was not then a Christian, but S. John Chrysostom assures us that he embraced the faith before S. Paul. See Acts of the apostles ch. V. v. 34. Hom. 20. S. Joannis Chrys. in Joan. Hom. 14 in Act.

voured with it a second and a third time. And so it was, Gamaliel appeared to him in a dream a second and a third time, in the same dress as before, and commanded him to obey. Lucian communicated his vision to the bishop of Jerusalem. The search was made, the coffins were found, one of which was higher than the others, and in it lay the bodies of an old and a young man, and one in each of the other sarcophagi. On the lid of the highest coffin, or sarcophagus, were engraved in large letters *Gamaliel, Abibas.* On the second *Cheliel,* the Syriac name of *Stephen*, or *crowned;* and on the third *Nasuam*, which in Syriac means Nicodemus, or *victory of the people.* Lucian immediately sent messengers to communicate the discovery to bishop John, who was at the time assisting at the council of Diospolis. The good tidings filled the heart of the holy old man with joy; and forthwith he set out accompanied by Eutonius, bishop of Sebaste, and Eleutherius, bishop of Jerico, to visit the place where the relics were found. On opening the coffin of S. Stephen, the earth shock, a balmy perfume was diffused, such as no one there present ever smelt before, and no less than seventy three persons afflicted with various maladies were cured on the spot. The history of this miraculous discovery written by Lucian, and translated into Latin by Aritus, a Spanish priest and an intimate friend of

S. Jerome, is published by the Benedictine monks in the appendix to the seventh volume of the works of S. Augustine. The same is attested by Chrysippus, a learned and holy priest of Jerusalem, as well as by Idatius, Marcellinus, Basil bishop of Seleucia, by S. Augustine, Bede, and several other Fathers and historians of the early Church. S. Augustine says that the place where the martyrs of Milan lay hid, was discovered to S. Ambrose by a vision. « I was there, « I was at Milan. I know the miracles wrought. « A blind man, very well known to the whole city, « recovered his sight. He ran. (He caused him- « self to be led to touch the bier with his hand- « kerchief). He came back without a guide. We « have not yet heard that he is dead : perhaps he « is still living. He dedicated himself to serve « during his whole life in that basilica of theirs, « where their bodies are ». Paulinus says, in his life of S. Ambrose : « To this very day, he (the « blind man) lives as a religious in the same ba- « silica which is called the Ambrosian, whither the « bodies of the martyrs were removed ». The very energy of Augustine's language shows his belief in what he says. But the festival which the Church keeps on the 3rd of August for the finding, in 415, of S. Stephen's relics is still more remarkable — they were discovered entirely by a dream several times repeated, and more than ordinary mi-

racles confirmed its truth in divers places. Augustine's friend Evodius, bishop of Uzalis, published two books recording the miracles. In his own church were preserved two phials of the martyr's blood, and some fragments of his bones, by which several miracles were performed, a list of which he had publicly read, and as the name of the person cured was called out, he was desired to go up to the apse that he might be seen by the people. So that here is a case notorious enough, in which, not satisfied with observing the martyrdom on the 26th of December, the Church has a special festival to celebrate a dream and its results. If, as S. Gregory Nazianzen energetically says, « such is the vene-
« ration of truth, that a little dust, or some small
« relic of old bones, or portions of hair, or shreds
« of a rag, or a stain of blood, are enough to have
« the same honour as the whole body », the Church does not shirk the marvellous in the discovery of relics ; but celebrates together the dream vouchsafed from God to do honour to His saint, and to bring blessings on His people in the gifts of healing which followed upon the finding of the relics. « *Magna et in exigua sanctorum pulvere virtus* ».

Cyril, after having deposited the chest containing S. Clement's relics in the metropolitan church of Pontus, set out for his mission to the Chazari, and, after having converted that people, he returned to

Constantinople. On his way he passed again through Pontus, and obtained from the bishop S. Clement's relics, which he always carried about on his missions, and finally brought them to Rome when called thither together with his brother Methodius by Nicholas Ist. Nicholas died before they arrived, and was succeeded by Adrian II, who being informed that they were not far distant from the city and had brought with them the relics of S. Clement, went out to meet them together with the Roman clergy and people (1). Gaudentius, who assisted at their deposition by the Pope's orders in S. Clement's church (2), says that they were the instruments of many miracles (3). In a short time after, Cyril died in Rome, and the Pope had him interred in the Vatican, with pontifical honours, in the

---

(1) Papa Hadrianus exhilaratus valde cum clero et populo procedens illis obviam honorifice eos cum sacris suscepit reliquiis. MS. Blaub.

(2) Sepelierunt autem corpus sanctum in ecclesia quae in nomine ejus diu antea fuit constructa. MS. Blaub.

(3) Caeperunt itaque ad praesentiam sanctarum reliquiarum per virtutem omnipotentis Dei sanitates mirabiles fieri, ita ut quovis languore quivis oppressus fuisset, adoratis pretiosis martyris reliquiis sacrosanctis, protinus salvaretur. Quapropter tam venerabilis apostolicus, quam et totius Romani populi universitas, gratias et laudes Deo maximas referentes, gaudebant et jucundabantur in ipso qui iis post tam prolixi temporis spatio concesserit in diebus illis sanctum et apostolicum virum, et ipsius Apostolorum principis Petri successorem in sede sua recipere, et non solum urbem totam, sed et orbem quoque totum Romani imperii signis ejus ac virtutibus illustrari. See Gaudentius in Rondinini, pag. 49.

marble sarcophagus he had prepared for himself, and sealed it with his own ring. The two brothers before setting out on their mission to the Bulgarians, had promised their pious mother that if either should die, the survivor would bring his remains to the monastery and there bury them with suitable honours (1). Methodius, mindful of this promise, begged of Adrian to allow him to take back his brother's remains to his native country. The sequel we give from the Duchesne manuscript : « Although it seemed some-
« what grievous to himself, the Pope did not see
« fit to refuse a petition and desire of that kind,
« but having closed the body carefully in a mar-
« ble chest which he sealed with his own ring,
« and after seven days gave him leave to return.
« The Roman clergy taking counsel with the bi-
« shops and cardinals and nobles of the city, came
« together to the Pope and said: ' Venerable Fa-
« ther and Lord, it seems to us very unworthy that
« so great and magnificent a man, through whom
« our city and church has had the fortune to re-
« cover so precious a treasure, and whom God has
« designed of his gratuitous compassion to bring to
« us out of such distant foreign regions, and even

---

(1) Mater cum multis lacrymis obtestata est, ut si aliquem ex nobis antequam reverteremur obiisse contingerit, defunctum fratrem frater vivus ad monasterium eum reduceret, et ibidem illum digno et competenti honore sepeliret. **MS. Blaub.**

« to take to His kingdom from this place, should
« be allowed by us to be translated to other parts;
« but here rather would we have him honorably in-
« terred.' Then Methodius prayed that he might
« be laid in the church of blessed Clement, whose
« body found again by his great labour and zeal
« he had brought thither. The most holy Pontiff
« assented to this petition, and, with a great con-
« course of the clergy and people, with great glad-
« ness and much reverence, they laid him, together
« with the marble chest in which the Pope had
« placed him before, in a marble monument, pur-
« posely prepared in the basilica of S. Clement, on
« the right side of the altar » (1). That pious of-

---

(1) Tunc supradictus frater ejus Methodius accedens ad Sanctum Pontificem, (scilicet Hadrianum II), et procidens ad vestigia ejus petiit sacrum corpus....... Non est visum apostolico, quamvis grave sibi aliquantulum videretur, petitioni et voluntati hujusmodi refragari; sed clausum diligenter defuncti corpus in locello marmoreo et proprio insuper sigillo signatum, post septem dies dat ei licentiam redeundi. Tunc Romanus clerus simul cum episcopis, cardinalibus et nobilibus urbis, consilio habito, convenientis ad Apostolicum coeperunt dicere: Indignum nobis valde videtur, Venerabilis Pater et Domine, ut tantum tamque magnificum virum per quem tam pretiosum thesaurum urbs et ecclesia nostra recuperare promeruit, et quem Deus ex tam longinquis regionibus et exteris ad nos ex sua gratuita pietate perducere, et adhuc etiam ex hoc loco ad sua regna est dignatus assumere, qualibet interveniente occasione, in alias patiamini partes transferri, sed hic potius placet honorifice tumuletur....... Tunc Methodius oravit ut in ecclesia Beati Clementis cujus corpus multo suo labore ac studio repertum huc detulit recondetur.

fice having been performed, Methodius, with a heart laden with grief, set out alone from Rome and returned to Moravia to attend to the duties of his ministry. Having incurred the displeasure of the archbishops of Saltzburg and Metz, by celebrating Mass in the Sclavonian tongue, they, conjointly with their suffragans, addressed two letters to Pope John VIII, which are still extant, complaining of the novelty introduced by Methodius. The Pope, in 878, called Methodius, whom he styles archbishop, to Rome. He obeyed and gave ample satisfaction to his Holiness, who confirmed him in all the privileges of the archiepiscopal See of Moravia, exempted him from the jurisdiction of Saltzburg, and approved of the Sclavonian language in the liturgy and office of the Church, as it continues to be to this day. He lived to an advanced age, but the year of his death is uncertain. Dubravius affirms that he died in Rome and was buried with his brother in the church of S. Clement, where his relics wrought many miracles. The same is mentioned by Baronius in his notes on the Roman Mar-

---

Annuit hujusmodi petitioni Praesul sanctissimus, et concurrente cleri et populi maxima frequentia cum ingenti laetitia et reverentia multa, simul cum locello marmoreo, in quo pridem praedictus Papa condiderat, posuerunt in monumento ad id praeparato in basilica Beati Clementis ad dexteram partem altaris ipsius. MS. Duches.

tyrology, by Panciroli in his « *thesauris absconditis Almae Urbis* », and by Heinschenius, who, moreover, adds, that some portion of his relics were sent to Moravia and enshrined in the collegiate church of Brunne.

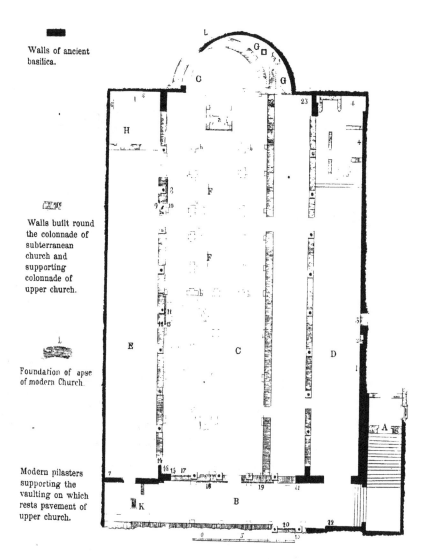

GROUND PLAN OF SUBTERRANEAN BASILICA.

A. Entrance to the subterranean basilica. B. Narthex. C. Nave. D. North aisle. E. South aisle. FF. Site of ambones and marble enclosure of choir. GGG. Apse of subterranean basilica H. Supposed tomb of S. Cyril. II. Passage leading to the walls of the imperial, republican, and kingly periods. a. Altar. bbbb. Modern pilasters from which spring vaults supporting the pavement of modern church. 1. Fresco of the martyrdom of S. Catharine of Alexandria. 2. Niche of the Madonna. 3. Council-painting. 4. Mutilated figure of our Saviour. 5. Martyrdom of S. Peter. 6. Baptism by S. Cyril. 7. Miracle of Libertinus. 8. Installation of Clement by S. Peter. S. Clement celebrating mass, and Miracle of Sisinius. 9. 10. S. Antoninus. Daniel in the lions' den. 11. Life, death, and recognition of S. Alexius. 12. 13. S. Giles. S. Blaze. 14. S. Prosper. 15. Crucifixion. 16. The Marys at the Sepulchre, descent into Limbo, and marriage feast at Cana. 17. Assumption of the B. Virgin. 18. Translation of S. Clement's relics from the Vatican to his own church. 19. Miracle at the tomb of S. Clement. 20. Our Saviour blessing according to the Greek rite. 21. 22. Heads of unknown personages. 23. Our Saviour delivering Adam from Limbo. K. Altar of Mithras.

SUBTERRANEAN BASILICA
OF S. CLEMENT.

CHAPTER I.

Basilica — Its meaning and purpose — Christian churches called basilicas, and why? — Pagan basilicas converted into churches — Basilican-design carried out in S. Clement's — Oratory of S. Clement replaced by a basilica in the 4th *century — Diocletian's doings in Nicomedia — Churches restored to the Christians by Licinius and Constantine —* Memoria, *technical meaning of —* Memoria *of S. Clement.*

The Greek word Βασιλική – Basilica – means a royal hall, and in this sense it is used at the end of the Recognitions of S. Clement, where it is stated that Theophilus, the first citizen of Antioch, « domus suae ingentem basilicam ecclesiae no- « mine consecravit », for the reception of S. Peter's chair ». It was a covered building, not like the forum, an open place surrounded by covered porticoes. The first great basilica in Rome was built, A. U. C. 568, by Cato the elder (Marcus Portius), whence it was called Portia; the second was called Opimia; the third, that of Paulus, built at so great expense, and with such magnificence, that it was called Regia Pauli. Julius Caesar built, under the direction of Vitruvius, the basilica Julia, which served not only for the hearing of causes, but also for the audience and reception of foreign ambassadors. It was supported by one hundred marble columns in four rows, and enriched with decorations of gold and precious stones. Pagan Rome contained many other basilicas also, such as the Emilian, the Ulpian, the Constantinian, etc. Ecclesiastical writers generally use the word to signify a church of great magnificence, and in that sense it is frequently employed by S. Ambrose, S. Augustine, S. Jerome, Sidonius Apollinaris, and several other writers of the fourth and fifth centuries. Some, with the learned Jesuit Alexander Donati, and Rondinini, assert that the ancient churches were called basilicas from their having been built in the style of the Roman halls, while others maintain that those halls were given to the Church for the celebration of Christian rites, as may be collected from that passage in Ausonius, where he tells the emperor Gratian: « The basilicas, which

« heretofore were wont to be filled with men of
« business, are now thronged with votaries praying
« for your safety ». These words clearly indicate
that at least some of the Roman basilicas were converted into Christian churches. The design of the
basilica was simple and grand : oblong in form,
with a nave and two aisles, separated by lines of
columns from which, in many instances, sprung
arches to support the walls that sustained the roof.
At the extreme end opposite the door was a raised
platform for the tribune, and the apse in which it
stood was often ornamented with mosaics. The main
entrance to the building was through a portico supported by five or seven columns according to the
size of the structure. All these arrangements are still
preserved in the modern basilica of S. Clement, the
style of which, we presume, was borrowed from the
ancient one. Bottari (1), Agincourt (2), Raoul Rochette (3) and Father Marchi (4) have maintained that
the style of the Christian basilica was borrowed from
the chapels in the catacombs. But these chapels were
rather modelled after the plan of the ancient Roman
basilica, as it was natural for the Christians to adopt
the designs to which they were accustomed.

---

(1) In his Roma Sotterranea, 6. 3. pag. 75.
(2) Histoire de l'art par les monuments, liv. I. pag. 25.
(3) Tableau des catacombes.
(4) Monum. delle arti primitive, architettura.

History (1), as well as tradition, informs us that Clement, shortly after his conversion, erected an oratory in his own palace at the foot of the Coelian Hill, to which the catechumens and Christian neophytes used to repair for instruction in the mysteries of the faith, to assist at the celebration of the sacred rites, and eat of the bread of life. How long this oratory existed after the exile and martyrdom of its founder there is no historical proof; but judging from the veneration in which the primitive Christians held the abodes of the martyrs, there is every reason to believe that it witnessed and withstood all the persecutions which assailed the Church from Nero to Diocletian, and that it was replaced by a basilica of great size and magnificence in the beginning of the fourth century. The first act of Diocletian's sweeping persecution, in 302, was to level to the ground the lofty Christian church of Nicomedia, whilst he and Galerius looked on from a balcony of the palace. The pretence was that certain just men hindered the oracles of Apollo; and the emperor Constantine records this in an edict issued by him which is preserved by Eusebius. « Thee
« I call to witness, most high God. Thou knowest
« how I being then very young, heard the empe-

---

(1) See Ciacconius, in Vita S. Clementis. Pompeo Ugoni, Sacre Stazioni, Chiesa di S. Clemente. Rondinini, lib. II. c. 1. Panciroli, Tesori nascosti dell'alma Città. Baronius, etc.

« ror Diocletian enquiring of his officers who these
« just men were, when one of his priests made
« answer that they were the Christians; which an-
« swer moved Diocletian to draw his bloody sword,
« not to punish the guilty, but to exterminate the
« righteous whose innocence stood confessed by the
« divinities he adored ». Lactantius says: « When
« they are sacrificing to their gods, if there stand
« by one who has his forehead *signed* (that is with
« the sign of the Cross), they cannot proceed with
« their sacrifices. *Nec responsa potest consultus red-*
« *dere vates*. And this has been often the chief
« cause why wicked kings have persecuted righteous-
« ness. For certain of ours, who were in atten-
« dance on their masters as they were sacrificing,
« by making the sign upon their foreheads put to
« flight their gods, so that they could not des-
« cribe in the bowels of their victims what was to
« happen ». He evidently alludes to what actually
happend in 302, when Diocletian was sacrificing at
Antioch; who upon it compelled the whole court to
come and sacrifice or be scourged, and all the soldiers to sacrifice or be disbanded. . The palace of
Nicomedia was twice set on fire, and, like the
burning of Rome under Nero, it was attributed to
Christian incendiaries. Eusebius says of the imperial edicts : « We have seen with our eyes the
« sacred temples levelled to the ground and over-

« turned from the foundations, the sacred books of
« divine scriptures burnt in the midst of the forum ».
But all the churches were not destroyed, for he says
that, under Licinius, many were levelled to the
ground, and others were closed by the provincial
Presidents; and he gives the decree of Licinius and
Constantine ordering the churches to be restored to
the Christian corporations. « And since the same
« Christians are known to have had not only the
« places in which they used to meet, but others
« too which did not belong to each of them pri-
« vately, but of corporate right, all these after
« the law commemorated by us you will, without
« any doubt, order to be restored to the same Chris-
« tians, that is to each body and assembly of them ».
It was, therefore, a necessity, at the peace of the
Church, to repair the old and build new ones.
« But now, » says the same Eusebius, « who can
« amply describe the numberless crowds of men dai-
« ly taking refuge in the faith of Christ ? Who
« the number of churches in each city ; who the
« illustrious concourse of people in the sacred *aedes?*
« whence it happens that now, not satisfied with
« the old buildings, they erect spacious churches
« from their foundations in every city ». And it
would have been strange if Constantine, who owed
his empire to the miraculous sign of the Cross,
and set it upon his statue in the imperial city, re—

mained indifferent to these buildings. Again Eusebius says: « He supplied God's churches with many « benefits out of his treasury, partly enlarging and « raising aloft the sacred buildings, partly adorn- « ing the august oratories of the churches with ve- « ry many votive offerings ». The preamble of the decree preserved by the same historian shews that it contemplated a general and public restoration. « Since up to this day impious presumption and ty- « rannical violence have persecuted the ministers of « our Saviour, I hold it certain and am evidently « persuaded, that the buildings of all the churches, » either through carelessness spoilt, or through fear « of the assailing iniquity of the times, are less « honourably cared for ». It is reasonable to suppose that the oratory of S. Clement was not forgotten in these Constantinian restorations. S. Jerome, in his catalogue of ecclesiastical writers, informs us that « of his name, the memory, the « church raised at Rome keeps up to this day » (1). We do not read of any other church ever having been dedicated to S. Clement in Rome except this one. Besides this, the word *memoria* has a technical meaning; it does not mean simply the remembrance of his name. S. Augustine writing against Faustus,

---

(1) Nominis ejus, memoriam, usque hodie Romae extructa ecclesia custodit. S. Hierom. cat. de script. ecclesiast.

the Manichean, says : « The Christian people fre-
« quents the *memories* of the martyrs, with reli-
« gious solemnity, both to excite imitation and that
« they may share in their merits, and by their
« prayers be helped : so however that we sacrifice
« to none of the martyrs but to the very God
« of the martyrs, although we set up altars in
« the *memories* of the martyrs » (1). Again he
says : « We build to our martyrs not temples as
« to gods, but memories as to dead men whose
« spirits are living with God; nor do we erect these
« altars on which to sacrifice to martyrs, but to the
« one God, both of the martyrs and our own, we
« immolate the sacrifice » (2). So the Pontifical
Book records that Felix Ist appointed Masses to be
celebrated over the tombs and memories of the martyrs ; and that « Anacletus built and put together
« the *memoria* of blessed Peter, whilst a priest or-
« dained by blessed Peter, or other places where
« the bishops might be laid in sepulture; but where
« he himself also was buried nigh the body of blessed
« Peter » (3). A Pagan inscription records that

---

(1) Lib. 20. cap. 21.
(2) De Civitate Dei, lib. 22. c. 10.
(3) Hic (Anacletus) memoriam Beati Petri construxit, et compo-
suit, dum presbyter factus fuisset a Beato Petro, seu alia loca, ubi
episcopi reconderentur sepulturae. Ubi autem et ipse sepultus est
juxta corpus Beati Petri.

« Servilius Troilus, whilst living, provided the *me-*
« *moria* for himself and his, and for his wife Ulpia
« Successa etc. » And in another to the Diis Manibus and eternal memory of Q. Vereius Laurentinus, an incomparable man of Lyons, their son records that he laid the said Laurentinus and his wife in the *memoria* which Laurentinus had made for his very dear wife, and dedicated in the mortar. In the case of the martyr Pope S. Clement there was a special reason why the *memoria* should be styled the memoria of his name. The religious inclination of the Christians naturally led them to build the *memoria* over the martyr's body. When the body of S. Boniface was brought from the East in Diocletian's time, « Aglae, straightway rising up, took
« with her clerics and religious men, and thus with
« hymns, and spiritual canticles, and all veneration
« went to meet the body and laid it five stadia
« from the city of Rome till she could build him a
« house worthy of his passion » (1). About the same time Primus and Felicianus were beheaded at Nomentanum (modern Mentana) and thrown into the fields, but the Christians carried them into an arenarium and buried them near it. Miraculous cures ensued ; and when the persecution of the Pagans had ceased many Christians built a basilica in their

---

(1) Ruinart, Acta Mart. p. 290.

honour at the fourteenth milestone from Rome. The martyrs Chrysanthus and Daria were buried on the Salarian way. Many years after, A. D. 284, a multitude of Christians was keeping their birth day, that is the anniversary of their martyrdom, when Numerian walled them in, and threw down a mass of gravel on them. « Among them were Diodorus « the priest, Marianus the deacon, and very many « clerics; but of the people neither the number nor « names were collected ». Ciampini says that small buildings were constructed over the cemeteries or their boundaries, called confessions, memorias, and martyria, (which has been illustrated by De Rossi's recent discovery of the entrance to the cemetery of S. Domitilla) and that the Acts of Chrysanthus and Daria, quoted by Arringhi, show it. There Hilaria, the relict of the martyr Claudius, is described as placing the bodies of her sons in separate sarcophagi; she is taken at prayer at the most holy confession, and in the hands of her captors utters this beautiful prayer. « Lord Jesus Christ, whom I « confess with my whole heart, join me with my « children, whom from my womb thou didst call « to martyrdom », and so expired. Her two maids buried her with the most loving diligence, and built a little church over her, for the place in which she died was her own garden, and, from the time the saints had suffered there, she made her dwelling at the spot. But in the case of S. Clement, his relics remained at the scene of his martyrdom until S. Cyril brought them to Rome in the ninth century. His *memoria*, then, was not of the body, but of some other title. The fifth council of Carthage (1) forbids *aedes* to be built for martyrs except there be on the spot either the body, or some sure relics, or the origin of some habitation, or profession, or of the passion of the martyr, handed down from a most faithful origin, « fidelissima origine ». The memory of Clement's name, preserved in the church mentioned by S. Jerome, was that of his traditional dwelling place. This saint and doctor (Jerome), to whom the Church owes the Latin version of the Scriptures, died in 420, only a hundred years after the Christian religion was made free throughout the empire, and we may well suppose that the basilica, which had been raised over S. Clement's paternal house at the base of the hill to which the Etruscan leader Coelius Viberna had given his name, would not have escaped that indefatigable restorer of shrines, S. Damasus, if it had need of repairs. De Rossi argues, from the collar (2) of a fugitive slave, that S. Clement's had its « pro-

---

(1) Can. 14.
(2) In the museum of Lelio Pasqualini, a contemporary of Baronius. De Rossi, in the Bollettino di Archeologia Cristiana N. 4, proves that the above mentioned collar is of the time of Constantine.

prio clero », that is its own clergy, or regularly constituted body of clergy, in the middle of the fourth century. The brand of slavery was abolished by Constantine, and such collars as that above mentioned substituted instead. Upon this thin bronze-plate, referred to by De Rossi, is engraved, on one side : « Hold me for I have fled, and recal « me to Victor acolyte of the *dominicum* of Cle- « ment », together with the Constantinian monogram of Christ. On the obverse side the inscription is « I have fled from Euplogius ex-prefect of the city ». This inscription is rudely scratched, as if with the point of a knife, and below it is the monogram of Christ encircled by a laurel crown having ᴾ_ᴱ on one side, and a palm branch on the other.

TENE ME Q	FVGI EVP
VIA FVG . ET REB	LOGIO EX .
OCA ME VICTOR	PRF . VRB .
I . ACOLIT	
O A DOMIN	
ICV CLEM	
ENTIS	

For our part, we will hope that if Victor of S. Clement's kept a serf at all he had him, as S. Paul says of Onesimus : « Not now as a slave,

« but instead of a slave, a most dear brother, espe-
« cially to me; but how much more to thee » (Phi-
lemon) « both in the flesh and in the Lord » (1).

CHAPTER II.

*Heresy of the Pelagian Celestius condemned in S. Cle-
ment's — S. Gregory the Great preaches in it —
Restored by Adrian 1st — Gifts by S. Leo III, and
S. Leo IV — Probable period of its destruction
and abandonment — When discovered — Visits, and
munificence, of Pius IX — Consists of a nave,
two aisles, and a narthex, see ground-plan —
Alexandria, its interest to the Church — S. Catharine V. M.*

We will not infer the primitive respectability of our clergy from the circumstance mentioned at the end of the preceding chapter, but rather from the fact that Renatus, the priest deputed by Leo the Great, and who fled from the Eutychian *latrocinale* of Ephesus, twenty years after S. Jerome's death, was titular of S. Clement's. Or from the fact that Pope Zozimus chose this church in 417 for his sentence of condemnation of the Pelagian Celestius: « We sat », says the Pope, « in the basilica of « S. Clement, who imbued with the discipline of

---

(1) S. Paul to Philem. v. 16.

« blessed Peter, with such a teacher amended an-
« cient errors, and had such sure confirmation as
« even to consecrate by martyrdom the faith he had
« learned and taught; to wit that for the salu-
« tary castigation the authority of so great a priest
« might be an example in present knowledge » (1).
Or because the beggar, S. Servulus, lived and died
in the porch of this church, and no less a man
than Gregory the Great found time amidst the incursions of the Lombards, the storms and earthquakes
everywhere, and his missionary engagements for the
conversion of the Angli, to come to this basilica
and preach his panegyric; we should conclude that
both Church and clergy were flourishing in 600. Two
hundred years after, whatever may have been the
cause, the basilica was falling into ruin. Anastasius the librarian tells us that Adrian Ist, who died
in 795, restored the roof. Stephen the third, who
died in 757, restored the basilica of blessed Laurence *super Sanctum Clementem*, which seems to
have been the chapel *Sancta Sanctorum*, at the Lateran palace, which Anastasius, in his lives of the
Pontiffs, frequently calls the basilica of S. Laurence

---

(1) « Resedimus *in Sancti Clementis basilica*, qui imbutus Beati
« Petri apostoli disciplinis tali magistro veteres emendasset errores,
« ratosque profecto habuisset, ut fidem, quam didicerat et docuerat,
« etiam martyrio consecraret, scilicet ut salutiferam castigationem
« tanti sacerdotis auctoritas praesenti cognitione' esset exemplo ».
Epist. S. Zosimi ad Africanos.

and S. Theodore. Of Adrian he says : « The title « of blessed Clement, which was even about to fall « and be laid in the ruins, of the third region, he « made anew ». One of the columns of the original basilica is broken, and perhaps the brick piers in which it and several other pillars of the old church are imbedded, are Adrian's work. Certainly that Pope, who sent his legates to that council against the Iconaclasts, which in its seventh session defined that not crosses only (which Iconoclasts admitted as do the Lutherans) should be set up in churches, and on the walls and ceilings of houses, but holy images and pictures be honoured with incense and candles, like the gospels and other holy things, would have been pleased to see depicted, on one of these piers, S. Clement saying mass and the miracle of Sisinius. His successor Leo III is said to have given several splendid vestments to S. Clement's. Perhaps they were antipendiums, or frontals, such as that which Anastasius says was given by Leo IV to another church, « and upon the altar itself he made a vest- « ment shining throughout with white pearls, and, « on the right and left, gemmed tablets having, with « disks of gold round about, the distinguished name « of the bishop written in full ». S. Leo IV deserved to have his portrait painted in the fresco of our Lady's Assumption in our basilica. He shewed that he knew how to use the sign of the Cross;

for by it he extinguished the great fire that broke out in the Vatican quarter of the Borgo. He might well have said, with David : « Blessed is the Lord « my God, who teacheth my hands for the battle « and my fingers for war » (1). He gave no countenance to the paradox that the Church is not to make use of the secular arm against Church robbers; for after the Saracens had carried off the silver with which Honorius Ist, in 626, had covered the confession of S. Peter and the doors of the basilica, he fortified that quarter of the city ; and hearing that they were on the march to plunder Porto, he went down himself to Ostia to meet the Neapolitan troops. He gave them his blessing and the holy communion, and they totally routed the infidels. He restored the doors of S. Peter's and enriched them with many silver bassreliefs. To our church of S. Clement he gave six silver salvers, cornucopia-lamps, a silver basin and the *regnum* of gold which used to hang over the high altar. When Leo died, in 855, the basilica, restored but six years before, must have been in good order. Then came that memorable event, in 867, when the apostle of the Sclavonians, S. Cyril, arrived in Rome with the relics of S. Clement, beside which his own body was one day laid. The miracles which followed on

---

(1) Ps. 143.

the translation of these saints, and the devotion they excited among the Romans, would naturally lead one to suppose that the pictures relating to them were painted soon after this event, rather than that the piety of individuals was rekindled at a later period. Whether they were painted upon the brick pier, which may be attributed to Adrian Ist, or on piers constructed at a later period, can only be conjecture. It is a matter of great regret that these paintings of an age from which modern European history may be said to date, the age of Charlemagne of France, and Alfred of England, should be now so damaged, and the history of some of them so obscure. The freshness of their colours when first discovered, shews that the basilica was, for some reason or other, abandoned and purposely filled up, and the modern church built upon it whilst its walls were yet in a highly decorated state. We can suggest but two reasons for this. The great earthquake of 896 which shook the old pillars of S. John Lateran's, and may have reached this church ; or the destruction of this quarter of the city from the Lateran to the Capitol by Robert Guiscard, who came to Rome, in 1084, to rescue the great monk of Cluni, Gregory VII, who died the following year at Salerno, saying : « I have « loved justice and hated iniquity ; therefore I die « in a strange land ». A thorough Italian, Tuscan by birth, educated at Rome in the monastery of

our Lady on the Aventine, consecrated Pope on S. Peter's day, wounded and imprisoned on Christmas night by a Roman baron, deposed by a mock council, confronted by an excommunicated antipope, besieged by foreigners in S. Angelo, driven into exile to end his days in that city where lies the body of the Evangelist whose Gospel ends with our Lord's words: « All power is given to me in heaven and
« on earth. Going therefore teach ye all nations,
« baptizing them in the name of the Father, and
« of the Son, and of the Holy Ghost, teaching them
« to observe all things whatsoever I have commanded
« you: and behold I am with you all days, even to
« the consummation of the world » (1). S. Gregory was a true type of the contest between Christ's Vicar and the ambition of temporal princes. Probably it was in his age that our venerable basilica disappeared, and as, though the stones of old Rome would speak again, it appears, once more, in the pontificate of Pius IX.

The basilica disappeared and was forgotten, so that, notwithstanding the industry of Roman archaeologists, every record and tradition relating to it was referred to the comparatively modern church built upon its ruins. However the basilican style was followed in all its details in the latter, which caused it to be regarded by all archaeologists as the most perfect example existing of the early Christian ba-

---

(1) Matt. c. XXVIII. v. 18. 19. 20.

silica. In fact any one who visits the subterranean basilica, will see that the upper church is simply a reproduction of it, though on a somewhat smaller scale. But a particular study of the topography of this part of the city, as well as a minute inspection of the marbles in the choir, induced the writer of these pages to suspect, so far back as 1848, that the church spoken of by S. Jerome, Pope Leo the Great, Symmachus, and Gregory the Great, could not be that described by Ugoni, Panciroli, Rondinini, Nibby and others; and, therefore, that the former must be either beneath, or somewhere near the latter. Just as these conjectures were about to be tested, Rome became the theatre of an unprovoked and sacrilegious revolution, which caused unheard of abominations within, and the most shocking desolation without, its walls. The contemplated researches were, therefore, deferred, but not abandoned. In progress of time, what had been but conjectures ripened into convictions, and, in 1857, the researches were commenced by opening a passage through a chamber containing some remains of ancient walls, and thence through another, quadrangular and vaulted. Here, having made an aperture in the wall, and removed a quantity of rubbish to the depth of fourteen feet, were discovered three columns standing erect, *in situ,* and some fragments of frescoes representing the martyrdom of S. Catharine of Alexandria, and a group of nineteen heads with an equally poised balance and the inscription, written vertically: « Stateram auget modium justum ». These discoveries removed all doubt, as to the site and existence of the primitive basilica.

It would be tedious to give a detailed account of the progress of the excavations year by year, and the difficulty of removing the immense mass of compacted rubbish with which the abandoned basilica had been purposely filled up to make a foundation for the church above, without damaging the walls and whole structure of that church. In fact some parts of the upper church had no foundation but that rubbish, more than one hundred and thirty thousand cartloads of which had to be carried up the same way in which Maximin made the martyrs Thraso and Saturninus carry gravel from the arenaria to build Diocletian's baths, that is in baskets on the shoulders. Suffice it to say that the architect Cavaliere Fontana succeeded admirably, and without a single accident, in supporting the upper church on brick vaults and arches; and that the lower basilica is made easy of access in its whole extent. From what was hitherto the sacristy of the modern church, a wide and admirably constructed staircase, of twenty three steps of Alban peperino, made in 1866, descends at once to the floor of the subterranean basilica. Here the first object that attracts the attention of the visitor is the following inscription engraved on a marble slab.

PATERNAS . AEDES
A . D . CLEMENTE . APOSTOLORVM . PRINCIPIS . DISCIPVLO . ET . SVCCESSORE
SACRO . RELIGIONIS . CVLTVI . DEVOTAS
PETRI . PAVLI . BARNABAE . APOSTOLORVM . PRECIBVS
BINIS . GREGORII . MAGNI . CONCIONIBVS
ET . DEBELLANDAE . PELAGIANAE . HAERESI
S . ZOSIMI . PONT . . CONCILIO . CELEBRES
VENERANDIS . LYPSANIS . SANCTORVM
CLEMENTIS . PONT . FLAVII . CLEMENTIS . VIRI . CONS . IGNATII . ANTIOCHENI . MM .
SERVVLI . C . NECNON . CYRILLI . ET . METHODII . SLAVORVM . APOST . DITATAS
TEMPORVM . INCVRIA . LONGO . SAECVLORVM . TRACTV . IGNOTAS
FR . JOSEPH . MVLLOOLY . ORD . PRAED . PROVINCIAE . HIBERNIAE
HVJVS . COENOBII . PRAESES
FELICITER . DETEXIT . MENSE . SEPT . MDCCCLVII
AGGESTAS . MACERIES . REMOVERE . INSTITVIT
SACRAE . ARCHAEOLOGIAE . COETVS . REM . ALIQVAMDIV . CONTINVAVIT
RELICTAM . PRAESES . RESVMPSIT . PERFECIT
SCALAS . AD . HYPOGEVM . CONDIDIT
ARCVS . ET . FORNICES . SVSTINENDAE . SVPERIORI . BASILICAE . EREXIT
PECVNIA . AD . TANTVM . OPVS . CONLATA
A . PIO . IX . PONT . OPT . MAX .
ET . MVNIFICIS . VNIVERSI . ORBIS . LARGITORIBVS

PIVS . IX . PONTIFEX . OPTIMVS . MAXIMVS
HANC . DIVI . CLEMENTIS . MEMORIAM
NON . SINE . DEI . NVMINE . INVENTAM
QVATER . INVISIT

AN. DOM. MDCCCLXVIII

The basilica consists of a nave, two aisles, and a narthex. Its entire length is 146 feet. The nave is 52 feet 3 ½ inches wide ; the width of the northern aisle is 18 feet 7 inches, and that of the southern 19 feet 10 inches; the narthex, which runs the whole width of the church is 91 feet 8 inches. From the narthex we enter the north aisle which is divided from the nave by a line of seven columns of various marbles imbedded in a wall, built, for the most part, of the *debris* of ruined temples and broken statues. These columns are twelve feet high, and eighteen inches in diameter, and all stand in their original positions. The first, *verde antique*, is of marvellous beauty and very remarkable for its vermillion spots varying its surface of vivid green and pure white: it is considered an unique specimen of its kind in Italy. The second is Parian ; the third and fourth (fluted) are of Numidian marble; two others of Oriental granite, and the seventh of *settebasi* of the rarest quality. Some of these pillars have been stript of their capitals, others retain them, and, although all are valuable and beautiful, they lack uniformity both in height and diameter, which shows that they must have been taken from still older edifices, perhaps porticoes or Pagan temples. Springing from these columns are arches of early construction supporting the northen wall of the upper church. The columns seem to stand on a uniform plinth, running along the aisle, but, in fact, it is a brick wall of the imperial period. The wall opposite this line of pillars was once entirely covered with paintings of which only some fragments remain. In describing them as they stand, we do not possess the necessary technical skill, nor have we much confidence in assigning the age or date of such pictures by mere comparison of hands and styles, seeing the very scanty materials even the learned in art possess for that purpose, and the egregious mistakes which have been made in classifying pictures so modern as those of the Italian schools. We will rather suggest thoughts naturally arising from the subjects themselves, and where we fail, those more skilful than we can easily correct us.

These fragments have more of what is called the Byzantine style than the other pictures of the church. The subjects also are more ancient than the rest, with the exception of the group of scriptural subjects at the west end of the south aisle and the heads in the narthex. Hence if we knew that the wall was repaired by Adrian, we might suppose that they were painted by pupils of artists who had fled, some seventy years before, from the image-breaking persecution of Leo the Isaurian at Constantinople. But the niche of the Madonna, the most Byzantine of all, was evidently broken through these pictures after they were painted. S. Gregory the Great had been at Constantinople before 590 , and it is not probable that the religious pictures which he sent to various missionary countries were all imported from the East, or that the city of the Popes was devoid of native artists. Whenever they were painted the modern plan of dividing the episodes of one subject into divers panels by gilt rectangular frames was not adopted. One large decorated border incloses a group separated only by the discrimination of the spectator's eye. In that of S. Catharine there were six. The eye soon becomes accustomed to this arrangement; and the perpendicular lettered inscriptions introduced in some places interfere much less with the general effect than the horizontal scrolls or tablets held by angels, in productions of a later age. The anxiety of these church artists was to tell the story well, because it had a religious interest, and they chose rather to write the saint's name beside him than that the beholder should make a mistake, or be forced to get by heart some conventional system of emblems that he might make out, among the well draped muscular figures before him, which was which.

Alexandria was as dear to Pagans as Mecca is to Mahommedans ; for there was the great temple and monstrous idol, of Serapis. In the reign of Julian the Apostate the Pagans again used Pagan ensigns in the army, and boasted that they would exterminate the Christians. Thirty years after , in

May 392, the emperor of the West, Valentinian II, was strangled, in his palace-gardens on the banks of the Rhone, by his Pagan general, Arbogastes, who set up Eugenius as emperor. That same year the Patriarch of Alexandria clearing out a deserted temple of Bacchus, by a rescript from Theodosius, to convert it into a Christian church, found infamous figures in the *adyta*, which he caused to be exposed for public reprobation. The Pagans rose and martyred many Christians. In 394, Theodosius, with difficulty, defeated Eugenius. He ordered the idol of Serapis at Alexandria to be burnt, and two churches were built on the site of his temple. All over Egypt the temples were demolished. In those of Alexandria the cruel mysteries of Mithras were discovered, and, in the secret *adyta*, the heads of many children cut off, mangled, and superstitiously painted. For the Church Alexandria had another interest. It was a great school of Christian philosophy. The method of the blind reading by touch was taught there; for Dydimus, born in 308, and deprived of sight in childhood, got his letters cut in wood, and became so great a scholar, especially of the scriptures, that he was set over the school, and S. Jerome profited by his teaching. The cemeteries that contained the memories of the martyrs to which, on the abatement of Diocletian's persecution, the faithful of Alexandria crowded, are now known. The most frequented was that of S. Peter their archbishop, situated in a suburb, where, on account of the martyrs' cemeteries, he had built a church to the Mother of God, Mary ever Virgin. One of these cemeteries contains a painting, perhaps a restoration of the seventh century, of the miraculous feeding with loaves and fishes, in which S. Andrew has his square nimbus and our Lady is indicated by name. The words « eating of the eulogia of Christ », found in this painting, refer to the well known passage of S. Paul: « The chalice of the *eulogia,* which we bless is it « not the communion of the blood of Christ? And « the bread, which we break, is it not the partaking « of the body of the Lord? » (1) S. Peter excommunicated Arius whom he had ordained deacon; and the patriarch S. Cyril, who died in 412, the great opponent of Nestorius, who denied the Incarnation, constantly uses the word eulogia for the sacramental species. S. Peter, whom Eusebius styles « a doctor « of religion, and a divine ornament of bishops », was beheaded with three of his priests, when Maximin Daza, who had been named Caesar by his uncle Maximin Galerius, came to Alexandria and renewed the persecution, in 311. The visitor who has admired in the chapel of S. Catharine of Alexandria, in the upper church, of S. Clement, Masac-

---

(1) 1. Cor. 10. 16.

cio's paintings of her life and sufferings, has there a proof of the tenacity of Catholic traditional devotion. The rude picture, in the subterranean church, of her martyrdom, is perhaps the oldest in existence that treats of the subject. The great emperor Basil says she was of royal blood, so true a scholar that she confuted and converted the philosophers sent by Maximin to argue with her ; they were cast into a fire and then beheaded. Some think that she was the Christian lady mentioned by Eusebius, illustrious for birth, wealth and singular learning, who resisted the brutal debauchery of the Caesar. But that lady, Eusebius says, Maximin saw ready to die and would not behead her, but seized her estates and banished her. Tradition says that our Saint was placed bound, between four wheels set with sharp spikes, to be torn asunder, but was freed by an angel loosening the cords; that while in prison she converted the persecutor's wife and his general Porphirius, both of whom were martyred. She was always honoured by the Greek Church. When the Saracens oppressed the Christians of Egypt, in the eighth century, her body was translated to the monastery on mount Sinai in Arabia, first built by the empress S. Helen and beautified afterwards by the emperor Justinian, as several old inscriptions and mosaics testify. There is an admirable composition, by Masaccio, in the upper church of S. Clement, of her entombment by angels. S. Paul the hermit of mount Latra in Bythinia, who died in 956, had great devotion to her. In the eleventh century a monk of Sinai, coming for the yearly alms of Robert duke of Normandy, left some of her relics at Rouen.

CHAPTER III.

Pictures discovered in S. Clement's.

NORTH AISLE.

MARTYRDOM OF S. CATHARINE OF ALEXANDRIA.

FIRST PICTURE FOUND.

On the wall to the right, a little beyond the second arch, as we enter this aisle, is a painting representing the martyrdom of the illustrious virgin S. Catharine of Alexandria, the colours of which are nearly obliterated. In the wide border, on the left, at the top, is an angel. The first subject is a private audience before Maximin, who is seated between two guards; a philosopher occupies a lower seat. Maximin and the philosopher are gesticulating with much animation; the Saint, richly robed, stands intrepidly addressing them. The middle compartment is destroyed; the stoles of one or two figures remaining on the left of it indicate ecclestastics. On the right the letters $_\Lambda^K$ identify the Saint, who is tied, almost naked, to the wheel, which a man is turning, while two others seem to hold her against it. The judge is seated in advance of the crowd, and a person, perhaps one of the discomfited philosophers, turns away. Three angels, over the judge's head, are flying towards her. Perhaps their number, besides the picturesque effect, is intended to refer to the blessed Trinity, as her cotemporary Arius denied the divinity of Christ, whose angel delivered her. The three lower subjects are scarcely visible. On the left she seems haranguing, perhaps, while in prison. In the centre is her beheading, before the judge. On the right a crowd of persons appears advancing, past two columns of a temple in the back ground, towards an elevated figure, but the subject cannot be made out. Nothing can be more dramatic than the closing scene of the Pagan Caesars. Diocletian was forced by Galerius to abdicate, and he died in 314, hearing that Constantine had thrown down his statues with those of Maximin and Maxentius. His own slaves could not bear the stench from the corpulent Galerius swarming with vermin, and he died wretchedly, after publishing an edict in favour of the Christians, whom, during his reign, he so barbarously persecuted. We have seen the boy Constantine present at Diocletian's sacrifices, and Galerius kept him a hostage for his father Constantius, ruling in Gaul, Spain and Britain. The young prince ran away, avoided pursuit by starting at night, and, taking all the post horses, he reached his dying father at York in 306. Licinius, whom Galerius had made his imperial colleague, extirpated the whole of Diocletian's family, beheading his mother and widow, and casting their bodies into the sea. Then came that famous march of Constantine on Rome : the Cross in the sky : « In this shalt thou « conquer » ; Maxentius in his flight perishing in the Tiber, and Maximin Daza, compelled by Licinius to repeal his edicts against the Christians, flying to Tarsus in 313, and dying a withered and dried up skeleton in acute torment, deprived of sight, his eyes starting from their sockets.

II.

COUNCIL-PICTURE.

Passing the niche of the Madonna for a moment, we find the Greek cross in the medallion at the top of the border of the next picture ; and at the foot a hart springing. « Flee away, o my beloved ; and « be like to the roc, and to the young hart upon « the mountain of aromatical spices » (1). The sub-

---

(1) Canticles, chap. VIII. v. 14.

ject in the centre of the picture below the window is well nigh totally destroyed. It represented some public spectacle or assembly, from the crowd arranged in rows. On the left are many female heads : some seem religious, and others have their hair gathered in decorated nets. There are also tonsured men of the Latin rite. On the right the figures appear to be Eastern, and one more prominent than the rest, is not unlike a Greek emperor in one of the diptychs. Over what seems the entrance there is the balance with the words « stateram auget » ; and over the large chalice or font below it « modium justum ». A female figure is next to the font or chalice, and a lighted taper appears behind it. The words so often quoted by S. Clement recur to the mind: « The city « set upon the mount cannot be hid ; nor do they « light a candle and put it under the modium, but « upon a candelabrum that it may shine to all who « are in the house, that those who are entering in « may see the light ». Or those assigned to him in his first epistle to S. James, where he directs the priests to hear the business of the bretheren instead of secular judges, and adds : « Weights, measures, « steelyards, keep most accurate for every place : de- « posits faithfully restore ». Possibly the subject may have been the condemnation of the Pelagians by S. Zosimus. Perhaps the very circumstance that the niche containing the Immaculate Mother of God full of grace, and Abraham's sacrifice, the type of the necessity of atonement for original sin, was broken into the border of the picture, may favour this idea. Such errors usually came from the East. The Pelagians held Unitarian errors, denying original sin, and the necessity of divine grace against which they extolled the philosophical virtues of the Pagans; hence the most direct answer was the divine provision by which the Virgin was filled with grace that she might never be subject in birth or life to the least sin. After the destruction of Jerusalem, Ebion and Cerinthus taught that Christ was only a greater angel, born of Joseph and Mary like other men, but surpassing them in virtue and wisdom. What the apostle who received our Lord's Mother from the Cross thought of this doctrine is apparent from the anecdote which Irenaeus heard from the lips of S. John's disciple Polycarp. That S. John going to bathe at Ephesus hurried forth from the bath without bathing, exclaiming: « Let us fly for fear the bath fall, as « Cerinthus the enemy of truth is within ». And that Polycarp when Marcion once met him and said: « Dost thou know us? » replied: « I know thee as « the firstborn son of Satan ». To Judaizing Christians the errors spoken of above were readily suggested by isolated texts. For instance « the Jews « murmured at him, because he said: ' I am the « living bread which came down from heaven '; and

« they said : ' Is not this Jesus the son of Joseph, « whose father and mother we know? How then « said he : ' I came down from heaven ? ' » (1) ; which evidently raises a difficulty, continuing to this day, in the consecration of the blessed Eucharist, for all who deny the teaching authority of the Church. The African Pope, S. Victor, A. D. 192, 202, excommunicated the Ebionites, Theodosius the banker, who pretended that Melchisedec was greater than Christ, and another Theodosius, the apostate' tanner of Byzantium, who asserted that he was nothing more than a mere man who called himself the Son of God. About the year 400 the Syrian Rufinus at Rome taught his errors to Pelagius. They were of the same bitter root; for evidently if Adam's sin did not prejudice posterity, and children are now born in the same state in which they would have been if Adam had never sinned, and if they, dying without baptism, inherit eternal life, there was no occasion for the atonement of a divine mediator. The African S. Augustine, who had experienced the call of divine grace, and personally felt that without it he could not rise from the degradation of carnal sin, wrote vigorously against Pelagius. S. Germanus of Auxerre, whose life was a perpetual miracle of grace, who on his way to Britain, as Legate of Pope Celestine, blessed S. Genevieve then a

---

(1) S. John, VI. 41. 42.

child of seven years, and foretold the sanctity which made her patron saint of Paris, silenced the British Pelagians at Verulam by word and miracle in 429. When Celestine's successor Zosimus sent his excommunication of Pelagius and Celestius to Africa and the East, the emperors Honorius and Theodosius published an edict throughout the empire banishing those heresiarchs, and condemning all, to perpetual banishment and confiscation of their properties, who maintained their doctrines.

III.

NICHE OF THE MADONNA.

We approach the little niche, between the two pictures we are after noticing, with feelings of reverence, for that little recess (six feet by three, sunk eighteen inches into the wall) contains the representatives of the Christian world : Christ in his incarnate nature and in his glory, his Immaculate Mother, angels, virgins, martyrs, saints, men instruments of his providence and heirs of his promise. These paintings were at first concealed by others, much ruder, painted upon a coat of plaster which fell away. The Byzantine school is here strongly marked, particularly in the overloaded jewelled headdress of our Lady, and the decorations of her throne. The artist knew very well that this exuberance of ornament, and the elon-

gated arm supporting the divine child on her lap were not natural. Let us try to see the spirit of his composition in that mystic art of which Angelico of Fiesole was the best exponent. In the crown of the niche a medallion shows our Lord ever youthful and radiant with glory. On the sides are heads of the virgin-martyrs S. Catharine of Alexandria and S. Euphemia of Chalcedon; and beneath them respectively Abraham brandishing a sword to strike and an angel shielding Isaac. The very difference between the heads of S. Catharine and S. Euphemia with hair flowing down from their jewelled crowns, human nature decked with the jewels of virginity and martyrdom, and the countenance of our Lady enshrined in the mass of ornaments without a single lock appearing, human nature totally transformed by grace, indicates the limner's scope. Our Lady is the chief figure, immediately opposite the eye, and occupying the whole front of the niche. Abraham's sacrifice is painted on the side of the niche. The painter does not give a naked Isaac tied up like a bundle and cast upon a heap of sticks. There seems a mystic meaning in the figure of Abraham, which when first discovered had a chalice of blood, in its left hand, since fallen away, and a shower of blood seems falling from a circle above his head. Whether it were an allusion to the passion, or a type of the avenging and destroying angel, whilst the opposite angel of healing taking

Isaac by the hands points to the true child of sacrifice upon his Mother's lap, we do not say. We are so accustomed to the mere natural outward form, from the days of Raphael downwards, that we are apt to miss the interior life. Not so the Fathers of the Church. They speak of the Mother of God with a tenderness which could not, and ought not, be found in earthly love. They regard her in a triple sense, as the human creature prepared by the perfect union of her will with God's to receive His gifts: as the divine seat richly prepared by grace: and as the Mother sustaining the human nature she had ministered to her Son. It would also be true to say that they look upon her, after her Assumption into heaven, as crowned with glory to be our advocate; because the interests of the Son are dear to the Mother, dearer as she is placed above the obscurity of earth in the full fruition of divine love, and nothing is so dear to the Son as the salvation of our souls. We see her in the cemetery of S. Agnes veiled, with a single necklace on her neck, and her hands outstretched in prayer, an unusual attitude when the child is seated on her knees. That face, as compared with others of hers in the catacombs, partakes of that peculiar set expression which is characteristic here of the calm, almost stern face, encircled with the halo of glory. « The queen hath stood at thy right hand, girt a- « bout with variety: all the glory of her, the daughter

« of the king, in golden fringes girt about with va-
« rieties, is from within: virgins after her shall be
« brought to the king, her neighbours shall be brought
« to thee » (1). We see them next to her. The head
of our incarnate Lord with its parted hair is marked
but by the glory of the Cross; but theirs are decorated with the triple row of gems, viz grace, virginity and martyrdom, which he bestowed upon them,
surmounted by the cross wherein they found their
great reward. But all the gifts of grace are signi-
fied by the necklace, breastplate, and the immense
jewelled headdress with its triple crown borne by our
Lady. It has no cross; for that is beaming about the
Saviour's head, sitting on her lap and sustained by her
hand beneath his foot. On earth his sufferings were her
cross; but now in the peace of glory, totally resplen-
dent from his beauty, as he is blessing, the Gospel
in his hand, so she who gave the Author of the Gos-
spel to the world has her hand also raised to bless.
From that hand nothing but blessing could flow; and
in their own private need or in public distress the
saints have held but one language, that she, his Mother, continually intercedes with her divine Son, imploring his compassion for that human nature which
through her he was pleased to take. S. Ephrem calls
Mary « My Lady » and he spoke the familiar lan-

---

(1) Ps. 44.

guage of the Church; just as says S. Peter of Alexandria sixty years before him : « Our Lord and God « Jesus Christ having been born according to the « flesh of the holy, glorious, Mother of God, Mary « our Lady ». Many prayers to the martyrs, and for the dead, are scratched in the catacombs; and it is supposed that, at some spots, where the names of priests are very numerous, they had descended to say mass. On the painting we are now speaking of, the names of two priests are scratched beside the throne, John and Salbius; and between them « Rosa, Bituli ». Who they were we don't know. S. Euphemia suffered in the same persecution as S. Catharine. She was a chief martyr amongst the Greeks, and her festival is kept generally in the East. The Council of Chalcedon often mentions her *martyrium* in that city, and sat in her church under S. Leo the Great, in 451, to condemn the Eutychian heresy which denied two distinct natures in our incarnate Lord. There was a church of hers in Rome in the days of S. Gregory the Great. We should almost suspect from the eastern figures in the Council picture here, and the heads of S. Catharine and S. Euphemia on either side of our Lady, that that picture represented the Council of Chalcedon rather than the condemnation of Celestius. S. Cyril, indeed, at Ephesus in our Lady's great church, had condemned, in the name of Pope Celestine, the successor of Pope

Zosimus, the opposite error of Nestorius who maintained a divine and a human person in Christ, and eastern figures would appear also in a picture of the Council of Ephesus. But seeing the inscription lately found among the relics under the high altar which refers to Leo Ist, the Council is more likely that of Chalcedon. That Council was, as it were, the summing up and anathema of three heresies: the Pelagian which left human nature as it was by itself without grace; the Nestorian which, indeed, admitted original sin, but denied the necessity of grace and that God was made man; and the Eutychian which out of horror to the Nestorians admitted only one nature in Christ, and the author of which wrote to Pope Leo Ist to complain of being condemned and anathematized in the Council held by S. Flavian.

IV.

MUTILATED FIGURE OF OUR SAVIOUR.

We pass on to the end of this aisle, and mount three steps leading to the ancient tribune. There, on the right, is a colossal figure of our Lord, the head and shoulders of which were destroyed in building the upper church. He stands with sandalled feet upon a jewelled footstool. Two books are in his left hand, one resting upon the other. They probably represent the Old and New Testament.

A little more to the left is a fragment of an inscription of which only the following can be deciphered : « Quisquis has mei nominis literas legeris lector dic indigno Joanni miserere Deus ». « Whoever reads these letters of my name, let him say ' have mercy on me, o God ', unworthy John ». Who this John was who is begging the prayers of the passing reader, we do not know. Under this, as well as under the southern aisle, several chambers have been discovered, and are supposed to be some of the original chambers of Clement's house. Only three of them have been, as yet, partially explored.

When the excavations reached the west end of the north aisle, it was found that this ancient basilica stands on the ruins of much earlier structures. Observing that the lower part of the west wall was built of a quality of brick far superior to that above it, the ground was dug to the depth of fourteen feet, and three walls of three different constructions, as well as of three different periods, were discovered. One is of the finest brickwork of the imperial times, probably belonging to the palace of Clement; a second of colossal blocks of travertine varying in length from eight to ten feet, of the republican period; and a third of *tufo lithoide*, which if it be not anterior to what is called, in our opinion, with but little truth, the foundation of Rome by Romulus, is certainly part of the walls of Servius Tullius the sixth king of Rome. The travertine and *tufo* walls run parallel to the brick one, and are only twenty five inches distant from it. In one direction, from north to south, all these walls have been traced ninety eight feet. The travertine and *tufo* walls have been traced from west to east two hundred and ten feet without finding either the beginning or end of them. The *tufo lithoide* wall lies still buried in the earth between twenty two and twenty three feet, which shows how low the level of Rome of the kings must have been. A thorough exploration of the length and depth of these walls could not fail to throw great light on the topography of this quarter of Rome. While passing between these walls let us turn to the right. Here three chambers have been found, one of which is supposed, with great probability, to be the ancient oratory or *memoria*, of S. Clement, for it is precisely under the tribune of the basilica, and consequently in the most sacred part of it. The vault is decorated with stucco ornaments and bas-reliefs of the very best style of art. Here also was disinterred a broken altar of Mithras sacrificing the bull, holding the horns whilst he stabs him, as he is usually represented. The oldest Roman mention of Mithras is an inscription in the third consulate of Trajan, about 101; the dedication of an altar « *Deo soli Mithrae* ». Is it possible that after S. Clement's martyrdom such an altar was purposely brought in to desecrate his oratory? It is said that the worship of this Persian deity was not known in Syria or Egypt in Origen's time, A. D. 263; this seems problematical, as it was known in Rome a hundred and fifty years before. The worship of Mithras was proscribed in Rome, in 378, by Gracchus the Praefect of the praetorium. According to M. Freret, the rites of Mithras were derived from Chaldaea, where they had been instituted to celebrate the entrance of the sun into Taurus. There are still remaining on the edges of this altar the sun and the fish; on the back a large serpent, and on either side two men assisting at the sacrifice with torches, in their hands, and wearing the Phrygian cap.

SOUTH AISLE.

V. VI.

CRUCIFIXION OF S. PETER, BAPTISM BY S. CYRIL, AND OTHER FRAGMENTS.

Returning from these rooms and continuing our route between the walls just spoken of, through the entire width of the basilica we ascend to the west end of the south aisle. Greatly do we deplore the ruin of the pictures which once covered the whole wall here, for the fragments that remain display a beauty and purity of style much beyond the other paintings in this basilica. The subjects appear to have been arranged in two horizontal lines, one above the other; and the figures in panels, singly, or in pairs. The ornamental border, a little above the floor, is a pattern divided into compartments, and in the centre of each compartment is a large globe and four small ones, and birds, like storks, on either side, pecking at what seems to be a stream of light descending from the large globe.

On the top line, at the right, two feet tied to a cross indicate S. Peter's crucifixion with his head downwards; beside it is the head of an aged saint tonsured and with the nimbus. On the extreme left are two very beautiful heads of angels. The centre of the lower line shows, in a circle, the feet of an animal, which, no doubt, was the mystic lamb; for a figure next it, on the right, of which the lower half only remains, extends the hands towards it in the manner of supplication, or adoration, so usual in Christian monuments. There seems to have been a kneeling figure behind this one: then two beautiful angels, and then two saints, standing in order, and what remains of the countenances exhibits great devotion. The subject on the left is clean gone. It had been replaced by a panel of very inferior execution. We say replaced, because it seems scarcely possible that the present painting, almost grotesque in character, could be the original design just placed side by side with the other well executed figures. The subject is a crowned emperor seated on a throne under a canopy. S. Cyril with a nimbus, his name painted vertically behind him, kneels before him. The monarch seems, by the action of his left hand, to be enjoining something upon two persons behind the saint. Most probably it represents S. Cyril's parting audience of Michael III to whom, in 848, the Chazari of the Danube had sent an embassy for priests, and he is directing the ambassadors to take care of the chosen missionary. Were this picture part of the original series, we should suppose that the figure on the right of the lamb with the one on its knees represented a subject we shall find on a larger scale in the narthex; for the spiral columns and their capitals behind the emperor are precisely the same as those on either side of the narthex picture. The subject at right angles to this, on the southern wall, represents an archbishop, with the Greek pallium, baptizing by immersion a young man of Barbaric type. From its position, next to the beginning of S. Cyril's first mission, it probably represents the baptism of the Cham of the Chazari: if not that of Rastices duke of Moravia, or Boigoris Michael duke of

Bohemia: for all these were converted by S. Cyril and his brother Methodius. A few steps further on along this wall is a projecting enclosure of brick, which may have been an altar, and which De Rossi supposes to have been the original monument prepared to receive the marble chest in which S. Cyril's body was removed from the Vatican where it had been buried at first.

VII.

LIBERTINUS.

No pictures remain along the rest of this wall. At the east end of the aisle, immediately under S. Catharine's chapel, there are rude remains of a group of Benedictine subjects. S. Gregory the Great, who out of his own estates built six monasteries in Sicily, and took the habit himself in that of S. Andrew which he founded on his father's house at Rome, had true Catholic love for the supernatural manifestations of God's providence, and has preserved many anecdotes in his Book of dialogues. He particularly mentions S. Benedict's prophecy of the plunder of Monte Cassino, and its accomplishment, by the Lombards a hundred years after, before his own eyes; and from his marked love for that saint and familiarity with his order, Mabillon maintains against Baronius that he chose S. Benedict's rule for his own monastery. The subjects here were taken from his dialogues, and were therefore probably painted shortly after his death in 604. Honoratus, an emancipated serf of the Patrician Venantius, built a Benedictine monastery at Fondi, in Campania, for two hundred monks, of which he was the superior. He was a holy man, and among the miracles wrought by him was his stopping, by invoking the name of Jesus, a descending mass of rock which threatened destruction to the house. At the upper monastery in Subiaco, even to this day, there is a rock in a similar threatening position, apparently detatched and ready to fall and crush the monastery. S. Benedict appears to have had skill in detecting shams, whether they were dressed to imitate his own monks, or in the more gorgeous habits of secular ambition. As, the Arian king of the Goths, Totila marched through Campania in 542, he sent word to the saint that he would visit him, but played a trick to test his powers. « Put off, my son, those robes you « wear, and which do not belong to you », said Benedict to Riggo who presented himself in the royal purple, attended by three noblemen and a train of pages. He afterwards saw Totila, rebuked him, and foretold his death. Libertinus, whose story is the subject of two of the paintings just referred to, appears to have lived in the time of Totila. We have in the one with the inscription « ubi Abbas Liber-

« tino véniam petit » « where the Abbot begs par-
« don of Libertinus », an example of how human
passions may break out in the peace of the cloister,
and how meekness and humility may overcome them.
The Abbot who succeeded Honoratus was not favourable to Libertinus. One day, in a rage, the
Abbot, for want of a stick, took up his footstool and
beat Libertinus severely with it about the head. He
went quietly to bed, and early the next morning
presented himself at the bedside of the Abbot, who
thought that he was leaving the monastery, and
that the abrupt departure of so holy a man would
not serve his own reputation. Stung with remorse
when he saw that Libertinus had come, as usual, to
ask for his blessing, before setting out on the business
of the monastery, he rose, and we see him prostrate
on the floor of his cell while Libertinus gives him
the benediction of forgiveness he had asked for.

Libertinus had such veneration for the deceased
Honoratus that he used to carry one of his clogs
or sandals in his bosom. On his journey to Ravenna, a woman with her dead child in her arms
seized his mule by the bridle, and insisted that he
should restore the child to life. The traveller could
not escape, and so strange a demand alarmed his
humility. Moved with compassion, he said: « Do not
« weep ». At length he alighted, placed the clog upon
the child's breast, and whilst in prayer life returned.

Laurence, who survived him, told these two anecdotes to S. Gregory, as well as the following. The monk, who was the gardener, was annoyed by some one stealing the vegetables. He found out the place where the thief used to get in, and seeing a snake by it told him to keep guard. While the monks were at their *siesta*, the thief stepping over, as usual, took fright at the sight of the snake, and fell so that he hung in the hedge by the leg. The monk on returning released him, and quietly conducting him to the door of the monastery, gave him some vegetables, saying : « My son, why will « you steal ? If you want any more, come to me « and I will give them to you ». If any of our readers are scandalized at this simple conventual gossip with which so great a Pope relieved his leisure, and others did not disdain to paint, we recommend to them the more serious remarks of Leibnitz. « It is not one of the least prerogatives of that « Church, which alone has retained the name and « character of Catholic, that she alone offers and « propagates eminent examples of all the excellent « virtues of the ascetic life. In truth, I own that « I have always singularly approved the Religious « Orders; the pious associations, and all the praise- « worthy institutions of their kind, which are a « sort of heavenly militia upon earth, provided that, « apart from abuse and corruption, they are directed

« according to the rules of their founder, and that
« the Sovereign Pontiff applies them to the wants
« of the universal Church. What can there be in
« fact more excellent than to carry the light of
« truth to distant nations across the seas, and fire
« and sword ? To be occupied with nothing but
« the salvation of souls; to interdict oneself every
« pleasure, and even the sweetness of conversation
« and society, in order to be at leasure for the
« contemplation of supernatural truths and divine me-
« ditations; to be devoted to the education of youth,
« to give it a taste for knowledge and virtue ; to
« go and carry help to the unhappy, to men lost
« in despair, to prisoners, to those who are con-
« demned, to all those who are stript of every thing,
« or in fetters, or in distant regions, and in those
« services of the most expansive charity not even
« to be frightened by the terror of the plague.
« Whoever does not know, or despises, these things,
« has only a cramped and vulgar idea of virtue ;
« and foolishly thinks to have fulfilled his obliga-
« tions to God when he has discharged outwardly
« some worn-out practices with that cold custom
« which is generally accompanied by no zeal or sen-
« timent ». Evidently the learned German philosopher who dwells upon these works of the active and
retired religious life would not have stript Commu-
nities of their houses, churches, and lands, and would

have subscribed to the condemnation contained in these words of Pope Pius IX : « With consummate im-
« pudence they do not hesitate to assert that di-
« vine revelation not only is of no use, but even
« injurious to human perfection ; and that divine
« revelation itself is imperfect, and therefore subject
« to a continual and indefinite progress correspond-
« ing to the progression of human reason. Nor
« thence are they ashamed to boast that the pro-
« phecies and miracles set forth and told in Holy
« Writ are the fancies of poets; and the most holy
« mysteries of our divine faith the sum of philo-
« sophic investigations; and that, in the divine books
« of either Testament, mythic inventions are con-
« tained , and that our very Lord Jesus Christ ,
« horrible to tell ! is himself a mythic fiction » (1).

NAVE.

The nave is separated from the south aisle by a line of eight columns , of which only five remain. One is broken and imbedded in a brick pier for support. The front and sides of these piers are covered with admirably well preserved frescoes. For preservation , beauty of execution, and their ecclesiastical subjects, they are the most interesting Christian compositions ever discovered in Rome, or perhaps

---

(1) Encyclical of June 1862.

elsewhere. The pictures in the catacombs give us indeed a class of parabolic and scriptural subjects familiar throughout the early Christian world, and some few figures of saints and Popes. But these, besides such figures, give us also well contrived compositions of Roman devotion, and spirited records of historical events in the Church, after the catacombs were disused, and long before modern pictorial art was developed. They appear to have been part of a series painted about the same time, and, when the colours were fresh, the basilica must have presented a brilliant appearance very different from that puritanical baldness, which some suppose, but very falsely, as we have proved in the Introduction to these pages, to have been the undefiled condition of church walls in the early ages.

VIII.

INSTALLATION OF CLEMENT BY S. PETER. S. CLEMENT SAYING MASS. MIRACLE OF SISINIUS.

Near the high altar, on a pier which is fourteen feet high, nine feet six inches in width, and three feet in thickness, we have a large, and admirably well preserved, series of paintings divided into three horizontal compartments. On the highest are nine figures the heads of which were destroyed during the building of the upper church, but the names inscribed beneath the feet of four of them — Linvs, S. Petrvs, S. Clemens Papa, Cletvs — enable us to understand that the subject represents the installation of Clement by S. Peter. S. Clement is standing on a highly ornamented throne. S. Peter, having one foot on the step of the throne, is leaning over Clement in the attitude of investing him with the *pallium*, symbol of universal jurisdiction. Linus is standing behind Peter; on the other side Cletus is next Clement; and both are in their sacerdotal vestments, but without the *pallium*: moreover they occupy lower positions than those occupied by Peter and Clement who are on the same level, so that it would appear that the painter embraced the opinion of Tertullian and others, and intended to represent S. Clement as the immediate successor of S. Peter. But, as we have already observed, that opinion is contradicted by several Fathers of the early Church, as well as by the Canon of the Mass. Ciacconius, Oldoinus and others say that Peter nominated Clement for his immediate successor, but that, either through humility, or divine inspiration, he did not accept of that dignity until after the martyrdom of Cletus. Behind Linus and Cletus are two other priests in the vestments of their order, and behind them again two soldiers in Roman military costume.

The central compartment represents the interior of a church, from the arches of which are suspended seven lamps, symbolizing the seven gifts of the Holy Ghost. That over the altar is circular in form, much larger than the other six, and contains seven lights, probably typical of the seven gifts of the same Holy Spirit. Anastasius, the librarian, who lived in the ninth century, makes mention of this form of lamp, and calls it a « *Pharum cum corona* », « a lighthouse with a crown »: a crown from its form, and a lighthouse from the brilliancy of the light it emitted. He also says that it was in common use in all the Christian Churches. S. Clement in his pontifical robes is officiating at the altar, over which his name – *S. Clemens Papa* –, Pope S. Clement, is written in the form of a cross. He has the maniple between the thumb and forefinger of the left hand. The altar is covered with a plain white cloth, and on it are the missal, the chalice, and paten. The missal is open, and on one page of it are the words « *Dominus vobiscum* », which the saint is pronouncing, his arms extended, as Catholic priests do, even to this day, when celebrating mass. On the other page « *Pax Domini sit semper vobiscum* », « the peace of the Lord be ever with you ». These two phrases were introduced into the liturgy of the Church by Clement himself and are still retained. On the right of the saint are his ministers, namely two bishops with crosiers in their left hands, a deacon, and subdeacon. They all have the circular tonsure, and the Pope in addition to the tonsure has the *nimbus*, or glory, the symbol of sanctity. On the left of the saint, but separated from him by the altar, is a group of fourteen persons probably representing the congregation. They are all admirably designed and carefully executed. Two of them have their names – Theodora, Sisinius – written beneath their feet. Theodora wears a rich and gracefully folded dress, and behind her stands a female of noble mien with jewelled headdress. Mombritius, James of Voragine, Panvinius and other early writers inform us that Theodora was the wife of Sisinius, that both were attached to the court of the emperor Nerva, that they were converted to the faith by S. Clement, and afterwards suffered martyrdom (1). Sisinius having intruded upon the mysteries, is struck blind, and his helplessness is admirably expressed. He grasps the shoulder of a youth who leads him towards the open door, and turns to gaze upon his eyes, whilst another assisting him behind seems to be telling, what had occurred, to Theodora who is looking at him with amazement and commiseration. It appears that Theo-

---

(1) « Hos inter Sisinius, necnon uxor ejus Theodora, atque alii « Nervae imperatoris familiares Christo nomen dederunt ». See Rondinini, page. 8. §. 9.

dora, who was converted to the faith before Sisinius, had been in the habit of frequenting, without her husband's knowledge, the oratory in which S. Clement used to give instructions to the faithful and celebrate the eucharistic rites. Sisinius, on a certain day, followed her to the chapel to discover what she was doing there. On entering it, he began, as Pagans in those days were wont to do, as well as many nominal Christians in our own, to ridicule the sacred mysteries, and was struck blind by the Almighty in punishment of his sin. But afterwards, repenting of what he had done, through the prayers of S. Clement, and of his pious wife Theodora, he recovered his sight, embraced the Christian faith, and sealed it with his blood. The following fourth stanza, or verse, of the very ancient hymn formerly sung at the first Vespers of S. Clement refers to this fact.

« Tunc convertuntur Christo sacrae virgines,
« Magnatum sponsae Deo peramabiles;
« Sed Theodorae sponsus zelotypio
« Caecus et surdus factus est continuo;
« Sed per Clementem credens sanus redditur ».

In the foreground, on the right of S. Clement, and in front of his attendants, are the figures of a man and woman holding in their hands lighted twisted tapers, called by Anastasius *kerostota*. They are of diminutive size, to indicate their humility, as may be seen in many more modern pictures painted three or four hundred years ago. The man has his name – Beno – written near him, and the woman's name is Mary, as we learn from the following inscription which separates this compartment from a beautiful border below it: « Ego Beno Derapiza cum Maria uxore mea « pro amore Domini et beati Clementis P. C. R. F. C. » « I Beno Derapiza with Mary my wife for the love « of God and blessed Clement had it painted ».

It is evidently mere pedantry to look for accurate representations of ecclesiastical costumes in these pictures. The artist has taken the liberty, as all artists do, to suit his compositions: thus the two assistants wear the maniple on the right wrist, which is always worn on the left, and S. Clement holds his maniple across the two fore fingers of the left hand.

In the lowest compartment there are four figures, one of which is in the attitude of giving instructions to the others who are engaged in dragging a column, and each has his name written near him: Carvoncelle, Albertel, Cosmaris, and Sisinius. The three first are clad in the short tunic, which is a badge of servitude. Sisinius wears the toga and paludamentum of a Roman tribune, and is addressing the men in the following terms: « Falite de reto colo palo Carvon– « celle », « get behind the column, Carvoncelle, « with a lever ». « Albertel, Cosmaris trai », « Al– « bertel, Cosmaris draw it up ». « Fili dele pute

« traite ». Interpolated under the arches « saxa traere « meruistis : duritiam cordis vestris (sic) ». « For « the hardness of your hearts you have deserved to « draw stones ». This compartment, perhaps, represents the building of the church of S. Clement.

The above phrases may also be referred to the following fact which is recorded by several early writers in their lives of our Saint. On a certain day Sisinius, a noble Roman citizen, went to a church which his wife Theodora was in the habit of frequenting, in order that he might discover her motives for going there. He found S. Clement celebrating mass, and the saint, knowing why he intruded on the sacred mysteries, like another Eliseus, prayed the Lord to strike him with blindness. Sisinius finding himself deprived of his sight as well as of his speech, intimated to his servants to conduct him out of the church, but they could not find the door until Theodora begged of S. Clement to allow them to go away, which he accordingly did. Some time afterwards S. Clement visited Sisinius and restored his sight; but the ungrateful man took the saint for a magician, and ascribing the loss and recovery of his sight and speech to his black art, ordered his servants to arrest him and cast him into prison. But a dense veil coming over their eyes concealed S. Clement from them, and seizing a column that was lying hard-by, they began to drag it along thinking they were dragging their prisoner. The holy man advised Theodora not to cease praying until the Lord should enlighten her husband with his heavenly light; and while she was praying, S. Peter appeared to her and said : « Your « husband shall be saved in order that the words « of Paul may be fulfilled : ' The unbelieving hus- « band is sanctified by the believing wife ' » (1). Sisinius struck with remorse of conscience for his treatment of Clement, desired Theodora to send for him. He came and instructed him, together with 424 members of his family and slaves, in the mysteries of the faith, and received them into the religion of Christ. The words « *falite de reto colo palo Car-* « *voncelle* » may be a corruption of the Latin « *fac* « *ibi te retro cum palo Carvoncelle* » , « get behind « the column with the lever (or stake) Carvoncelle ». « *Albertel, Cosmaris, trai* » , « Albertel, Cosmaris, « draw ». « *Fili |dele pute traite* » , « sons of « puts draw it up » , to which a voice replies : « *Saxa traere meruistis : duritiam cordis vestris* » , « You have deserved to draw stones on account of « the hardness of your hearts ». Other interpretations might be given of these antiquated sentences , but we shall leave them to those who are more profoundly versed in philology than we can have any claim to be.

---

(1) Corinth. VII. 14.

The date of this painting has afforded a theme for discussion to some of the most eminent living archeologists, philologists, and painters: some referring it to the twelfth century, others to the ninth, and others to the seventh. Without pretending to decide so difficult a question, we may observe that even the most modern pictures found here must be anterior to Robert Guiscard's devastation of the city in 1084, when very probably the basilica was abandoned, and it was found necessary to fill it with earth on account of the immense piles of ruins with which it was surrounded. But it may be objected that we cannot prove that the prefix (if it be a prefix) to Beno's cognomen, or even the cognomen itself, or any family of that name flourished in Rome before the twelfth century. We reply that this is a negative argument, and consequently proves nothing. Moreover there is a manuscript in the Lateran archives in which mention is made of a family of that name living in Rome in the eleventh century, and that same family may have flourished for centuries before. Finally it has been objected that some of the inscriptions are in vulgar Italian, which was not spoken before the twelfth century. To this we oppose the authorities of the learned cardinal Bembo and Cesare Cantu. The former, in his work « on the origin of the Italian language », says: « It is asserted by some writers that « the vulgar Italian language is coeval with the La-

« tin, on the supposition that the common people
« always had a language of their own; but it is
« certain that the vulgar Italian language was spoken
« shortly after the incursions of the barbarians, and
« as early as the sixth century ». The latter, in his
complete analysis of the formation of the Italian language (1), furnishes us with phrases similar to those
in our fresco, which were in use in the eighth and
ninth centuries « *Da ipsa casa − ire ad marito − a scrivere tolli − crotta, fenile − granario, orto, orticelle, corte* ». Therefore taking such examples
into consideration perhaps the ninth century may not
be too early a period to assign to these paintings.
The style of the figures, their execution and drapery might induce us to refer them to the early
Roman school of painting, but Beno's cognomen, or
surname, prevents us from doing so.

IX. X.

S. ANTONINUS. DANIEL IN THE LIONS' DEN.

On the side of this pier, at the top, is the
lowest half of a figure of a bishop in a richly ornamented dress, and jewelled buskins. His name,
Antoninus, is painted under his feet. It may be
Domitian's martyr of that name; or S. Antoninus,

---

(1) Storia universale, schiarimenti del libro XI.

or Antonius Caulcas, patriarch of Constantinople in 893, who laboured to extinguish the Greek schism begun by Photius, and held a Council for that purpose, the Acts of which were purposely destroyed by the schismatics. In 846, S. Cyril told Photius: « Your « passion against Ignatius deprived you of your « sight »; and in a series of pictures with which S. Cyril is intimately connected, the patriarch who proceeded against that schismatic intruder (Photius) might be here appropriately introduced. Below, in the centre, is the prophet Daniel. He is dressed in Roman costume, and has the ephod on his breast; his hands are outstretched, and his eyes raised to heaven, while two lions gambol at his feet beneath which his name – S. Danihel – is written. The incorrect drawing of these animals, and of five others in the panel below, show that the painter never saw a lion in his life. In the earliest known painting of this subject, which is in Domitilla's cemetery, the prophet stands on a mount with his hands extended in prayer, but without the nimbus, and the two lions are very natural as well as lively. They seem to have been painted by one who heard the cry: « The Chris- « tians to the lions ». On Christian sarcophagi the saint appears in a state of gladiatorial nudity, and the beasts, on either side, squatted on their haunches, have not quite lost the ferocious character of their nature, though approaching the stiff quaint heraldic character we see here. An ornamental border separates the middle from the lower panel, and shows a good deal of fancy and taste.

XI.

LIFE, DEATH, AND RECOGNITION, OF S. ALEXIUS.

Called from a palace to a pilgrimage, from Roman espousals to a hermit's life, in a hut near our Lady's church at Edessa; in youth's bloom to the austerity of solitary old age; from wealth to privations; in privations to return home, not as the prodigal son, but, that hardest trial of merely human nature, to his birth-place, self-stript of its ties and associations, to parents no longer known as a child, forgotten by all, a mendicant asking for charity, and with no place to lay his head; this young nobleman of the fifth century, Alexius, has bequeathed to the city of the Pontiffs an imperishable name. The artist, who painted the subject we are about to treat of, seems to have felt that the sweet odour of grace was wafted from that story of inspired devotion, and to have sought for appropriate ornament. The honey-suckle supplies the border below the picture of his death; the lower panel, of flowers, fruits, and gay birds of paradise, is res-

plendent in colour and in excellent taste. Above, the angels of our Lady and of the strength of the Church, Gabriel and Michael, censor in hand, stand beside the magnificent throne on which our Lord sits holding in his hands a scroll with the words « Fortis ut vincula mortis », « strong as the bonds « of death ». Thus He presides over the life and death of the saint. Saints Clement and Nicholas are there also. Upon the Aventine Hill, the beautiful campanile of S. Alexius on his father's house, looks down on one side upon the Tiber and the great hospice of San Michele; upon the Ripa Grande, the port of ancient Rome, and upon S. Francesco a Ripa, built on the ancient church of S. Blaze where the saint of holy poverty, S. Francis, used to live. On the other side upon the ruins of the forum and Coliseum, and the hills of Latium. The remains of the palace of Pope Honorius III, and of an antique Roman house are on the steep of the hill below towards the river. Honorius confirmed the rule of the order of S. Dominic in 1216, in which year the relics of S. Alexius were found in his church next the Dominican convent of S. Sabina. S. Adelbert of Prague, S. Boniface, the apostle of Germany, martyred at the age of seventy five, in 755, and S. Thomas of Canterbury martyred in 1170, lived in the convent of S. Alexius. There, once overlooking the busy grandeur of the world, the palace of the rich, and noble Roman Senator, Euphimianus, held a hidden treasure – the heart of his only child. Dear lover of the poor he gave incessant alms, and God rewarded him, calling him to a higher state, the greater sacrifice of voluntary poverty. « Yet one « thing is wanting to thee : sell all that thou hast, « and give to the poor, and thou shalt have trea- « sure in heaven; and come, and follow me » (1). His chaste soul was vowed to God alone. His parents urged him to marriage. His heart had already forsaken the world. If men have freedom, they should have freedom to live for religion. « Amen, I say to « you there is no man that hath left house, or pa- « rents, or brethren, or wife, or children, for the « kingdom of God's sake, who, shall not receive much « more in this present time, and, in the world to « come, life everlasting » (2). He fled. In the eyes of the world he was eccentric or insane; a son who rebelled against his parents, a husband who abandoned his bride. The Church, in him, vindicates the right, to make choice of a more perfect state, before the consummation of marriage; the pilgrim who hated father, and mother, and wife to come to Christ ; the ascetic who hated his own soul that he might thereby save it, and shouldered his cross to be Christ's disciple ; the saint obedient to grace and faithful to

---

(1) Luke 18. 22.
(2) Ibid. 18. 29.

death. And the eye, which gazes, from the cloister of S. Sabina, by the orange tree S. Dominic planted there, upon the palm tree waving its branches against the tower of S. Alexius, may turn itself within, and the soul ponder how sin is purged by suffering, and by what mysterious similitude young innocence seems to be called upon, in the hardship of religious life, to do penance for hardened vice. At Edessa, Alexius was recognized as a person of distinction. He returned to Rome and as a pilgrim received hospitality in his father's house, where he spent many years bearing with joy the taunts of the servants. The staircase under which he was allowed to stay is still preserved over one of the altars in his church on the Aventine.

In the central compartment of the painting we see him on his return to Rome, in the garb of a pilgrim, with his wallet and staff, accosting Euphimianus who is on horseback followed by two attendants, and evidently asking hospitality of him. Euphimianus is pointing with his right hand to his palace (from the balcony of which a lady is looking), and saying to Alexius: « That is my residence, in it you shall find « an asylum ». During his stay in his father's house he wrote an account of his life, but would not consign the manuscript to any one. At length, sickness came upon him, and he died holding the manuscript in his right hand with so stiff a grasp, that it could not be removed. At that moment the bells of the adjacent church began to ring a joyful peal, of their own accord. The inhabitants of the neighbourhood were seized with astonishment: the phenomenon could not be explained. After a little the news reached S. Boniface who then governed the Church. Euphimianus requested him to come and explain the marvel. The Pope consented, and he went up to the Aventine accompanied by his clergy and cross-bearer. On his arrival at Euphimianus' palace, he was conducted to the staircase where the dead pilgrim lay. He recited a short prayer, and leaning towards the pilgrim he took, without any difficulty, the manuscript from his hand, and blessed him. Euphimianus is standing by with an expression of compassion, not knowing, of course, who the dead man was. A little more to the right of the spectator is depicted his recognition. He is laid on a bier covered with a rich and highly decorated pall. His aged parents tear their hair through grief for not having known him, and the bride covers his face with kisses. The inscription below says: « The father does not recognize « who asks his pity: the Pope holds the scroll which « tells his austere life ». His interment was celebrated with great pomp by the whole city of Rome. How many parents have wept when the spirit whispers to the young heart: « Hear, my daughter, and see, « and incline thine ear; and forget thy people, and the

« house of thy father, and the king will desire thy
« beauty, for he is the Lord thy God and they shall
« adore him » (1). The final close of the devoted
soul is well indicated by the words upon the scroll
in the Pontiff's hands : « Come to me, all you that
« labour » (2).

XII. XIII.

S. AEGIDIUS, OR GILES. S. BLAZE.

On the side of this pier, at the top, is part of a figure with the name Egidius, that is Giles. The celebrated Athenian hermit of this name lived at the end of the seventh century near Nismes, and was greatly honoured in France where he built a monastery which became a great Benedictine Abbey, and gave his name to the town of S. Giles. But from the position of S. Giles here in connection with S. Alexius who lived in the fifth century, he may be the Abbot who was sent in 514 by S. Caesarius of Arles to seek confirmation of the privileges of his metropolitan church, from Pope Symmachus. The election of Symmachus, at the end of that century, was contested by an Eutychian antipope, and S. Caesarius condemned the Semipelagians in the second Council of Orange in 529.

---

(1) Psalm. 44.
(2) Mathew XI. v. 28.

S. Alexius lived in the same century with Zosimus and Celestine, whom we have seen condemning the Pelagians, Eutychians, and Semipelagians, and Leo the Great who by his presidency over the Council of Chalcedon may be said to have cut up this class of heresies by the root. In fact, S. Prosper, whose portrait we shall find near this, and whom S. Leo sent for from the South of France to become his secretary, wrote vigourously against the Semipelagians. Their error consisted in admitting grace, but stickling for man's own free will as moving to virtuous actions before the call of grace. One might suppose that the life of S. Alexius, so opposed to natural free will, and so inexplicable without the most powerful call of grace, was a practical refutation at the time; that that miracle of grace, the life of a young saint choosing privations and abstinence of every kind, in the very lap of fortune, and wooing of the world, might consume the error in the flames of divine love.

It is difficult to account for the choice of the martyr bishop S. Blaze placed below S. Giles, except by a reference again to S. Leo the Great, and the relics under the high altar, among which are those of the Forty martyrs of Sebaste in Armenia, of which city Blaze was bishop. A year after S. Sylvester had gazed from the walls of Rome in the direction of that battle which gave her a Christian emperor, he was chosen Pope, and sent his Legates to the Council of

Arles against the Donatists, a sect then seven years old, which pretended that the Catholic Church had failed elsewhere, and was to be found in its purity only in their own local metropolis. But if S. Sylvester was condemning heresy, and Constantine supporting his decisions, Licinius was persecuting Christians, and, in 316, S. Blaze was put to death. Four years afterwards, the twelfth legion, quartered in Armenia, was ordered to sacrifice. Forty stepped out before the governor Agricola who had tortured the bishop, declaring themselves Christians; and, like S. Blaze, their sides were torn with iron hooks. Were we to take this image of their bishop, placed beside the sudden call of S. Alexius, as a sufficient reference to their history, no more instantaneous and effective call of grace could be found; for when they were stripped upon the ice to perish by lingering cold, one only apostatized, and his place was instantly occupied. « Lord, we are forty who are engaged in « this combat; grant that we may be forty crowned, « and that not one be wanting to this sacred num— « ber ». Such their prayer. A sentinel, moved by a vision of spirits descending and distributing gifts to all except the apostate, threw down his arms, stript himself and took the deserter's place. S. Blaze appears extracting a thorn from a boy's throat, who is supported by his mother. He was patron of the wool-combers at Norwich, who kept his festival in the last century. In Rome, upon his feast (February 3), which is celebrated in the church of S. Maria in Via Lata, where S. Paul was lodged, a relic of his throat is venerated; and also in a church dedicated to him in Via Giulia persons with diseased throats are touched with another of his relics. The wolf carrying off a pig which he is said to have saved by his prayers, refers to a story recorded in his life.

XIV.

S. PROSPER OF AQUITAINE.

Passing down the aisle by two beautiful columns of *bigio* marble, one spiral, the other plain, we must take the picture of S. Prosper of Aquitaine as the only memorial left here of the condemnation of Pelagianism. A Welshman and Scotchman together were its patrons; Morgan a monk of Bangor who took the name of Pelagius, « by the « sea », and his pupil a noble Scot, and quondam lawyer, known as the monk Celestius « from the « skies ». But neither was the original inventor of this heresy which denied the necessity of grace. Morgan picked it up at Rome, about 400, from Rufinus the Syrian, and then went off to Palestine to perfect it. The root of it was disbelief in the divinity of Christ, a heresy vigourously maintained by the Nazarenes and Ebionites at Pella whither the Christians had retired before Vespasian attacked Jerusalem. « Is not this the carpenter's son ; is not « his mother called Mary, and his brethren James, « and Joseph, and Simon, and Jude: and his sisters « are they not all with us: whence therefore hath he « all these things? » (1) Ebion and Cerinthus attributed other children to the ever Virgin Mary before the birth of Jesus, as their followers since have done after that event: the whole being nothing else than a denial of the supernatural power of God and the fall of Adam, for if Adam had no grace to fall from, and Jesus were simply such as he, mere man, His blessed Mother needed no fullness of grace, and there was nothing but natural talent to recommend the New Testament to the human race. To follow its precepts became mere matter of choice, and no authoritative worship of the Creator could exist. The crucifixion became only a natural consequence of opposition to the world, and its victim a virtuous enthusiast. The presence of God in the pillar and cloud had passed away, and was expunged from the tabernacle, by the destruction of the only authorized Temple. The renewal of it by the Catholic Church could only be an illusion, or a trick. Sacraments were superfluous where grace, if they

---

(1) Mathew 13. 55.

could confer it, was not needed. Preaching could only be, at best, of the natural law, Christ a capital philosopher, the best exponent of God the Creator, and, the moral duties of His creatures; heaven the birthright of man, if this world was not to last for ever; eternal hell an unnecessary invention repugnant alike to the affections of man, and his Maker who loved him. In short, as the rites, and ceremonies of the synagogue, were come to an end, and man ought not to go back to all that preceded it, the perfectibility of his reason, and natural appetite for good, would lead him on in an indefinite progress of intelligence, and moral virtues to be happy for ever. This desolating system was a renewal of Satan's old trick : « No ! you shall « not die the death ; for God doth know that in « what day soever you shall eat thereof your eyes « shall be opened, and you shall be as gods know- « ing good and evil ». A voice from heaven : « This is my beloved Son » died away in idle echoes when men said it thundered, or an angel had spoken. The only answer was the conduct of the Church, which, as each phase of heresy appeared, condemned it in its turn. It is not worth while to pursue the subterfuges of Pelagius and his disciples. At Carthage in 412, and at Diospolis in 415, accused by the exiled bishop of Arles and Aix, and at both condemned, he adopted that policy, which we have seen in our own day, of private conversations, and letters to friends; and such a system received its check, when the Bishop of Rome was written to for information with a will to abide by his answer. In 415 the bishops of Jerusalem took this course. In 416 again at Carthage and Milevis; and in 417 Innocent excommunicated the two, Pelagius and Celestius. Celestius came to Rome. Pope Zosimus, in March 417, without removing the excommunication, deferred sentence for two months. In 418 a great Council at Carthage renewed the excommunication; Zosimus confirmed it, and sent the sentence to Africa and all the chief churches of the East.

It often happens in the history of the Church, that error is answered not merely by the pen, but by a living saint. Augustine the Manichaean (1), who at twenty two tested everything by reason, and turned his wit against the Catholics, was yet to be the converted child of his mother's tears, S. Monica; yet to hear of S. Antony of the desert; yet to hear the child singing « take up and read »; to snatch up S. Paul's epistles from the garden bench, and read with smitten heart: « Not in rioting and drunkeness, not in cham-
« berings and impurities, not in contention and en-
« vy; but put ye on the Lord Jesus Christ, and

---

(1) The fallen Chaldaean priest Manes had got his notion of two necessarily existing principles, good and evil, creating their like, from, the lapsed Arab Christian merchant, Scythianus.

« make not provision for the flesh in its concupiscen-
« ces ». Yet was this African, immersed in the pride of life, and the lust of the eyes, to become a convert, priest, bishop, founder of a religious Order, doctor of the Church, saint. On the grace of Jesus Christ, on original sin, on marriage and concupiscence, on the soul and its origin, are some of the works which, then thirty years a priest, he wrote against Pelagianism. Pelagius was scotched, not killed. In 429, Pope Celestine had sent his two vicars against him to Britain. Both were French: S. Lupus bishop of Troyes, who abandoned the married state to become a priest, and at the head of his clergy boldly met Attila « the scourge of God », and saved his city. S. Germanus bishop of Auxerre, called by compulsion to the ecclesiastical state, for he was a military man, when the then bishop shut the church doors upon him and tonsured him. On his journey he received the virginal vow of S. Genevieve the future patroness of Paris, and foretold her sanctity. Confounded by their successful preaching, the heretics came to a conference at S. Alban's. It ended by Germanus taking his reliquary from his bosom, and laying it on the eyes of a blind girl who was restored to sight. He ordered the protomartyr's tomb to be opened, placed the reliquary within it, and took a little of the martyr's dust which he used in the consecration of a church at Auxerre. The devil,

finding himself checkmated at S. Alban's, carried his game to the South of France. Some priests thought that by grace Augustine destroyed free will; and they compromised by granting that supernatural grace was necessary for actions conducive to eternal life, but that free will must start the first desire. Like most compromises it was a bad one. Thus, Semipelagianism, ascribing to the creature alone the beginning of virtue, gave the whole to him and not to God. S. Prosper of Aquitaine applied to Augustine who replied, two or three years before his death, by Books on the predestination of the saints, and the gift of perseverance. Prosper went to Rome about it, and Celestine commended Augustine's doctrine to the bishop of Marseilles and others. When Leo the Great became Pope in 440, he called Prosper to Rome and made him his secretary. The final overthrow of the heresy was due to S. Prosper; or, as he himself describes it in his poem upon the Semipelagians ungrateful to divine grace (1).

« Pestem subeuntem prima recidit
« Sedes Roma Petri, quae pastoralis honoris
« Facta caput mundo quicquid non possidet armis
« Religione tenet ».

« The stealing pestilence, the first cut off
« Rome Peter's Seat of Pastor's honour made

---

(1) Carmen de ingratis.

« Head to the world; what'er not owned by arms
« By true religion held ».

XV.

CRUCIFIXION.

On the pilaster, forming a right angle at the end of the nave, is a group of subjects, if not arranged in connection with S. Prosper to vindicate the doctrine of original sin and sacramental grace, yet happily illustrating them. We turn with pleasure from the discomfited heresies to the Author of grace upon the cross. The painting is old and rude, but true human hearts stand beside it « You are they who have « continued with me in my temptations » (1). Our Lady is appealing to her Divine Son. S. John with his Gospel roll stretches a supplicating hand to Him. Could the painter better indicate the words: « Wo- « man, behold thy Son; after that he saith to the « disciple: ' Behold thy Mother '; and from that « hour the disciple took her to his own » (2)? Mistress of the little house of Nazareth; Mistress of every Christian home, in the house and in the temple wherever the Cross of Christ is venerated that Mother is found beside it. Our Lord is not repre-

---

(1) Luke 22. 28.
(2) John 19. 27.

sented as dead: there is suffering compassion in His face. This is probably the earliest church picture we have of the Crucifixion, and, if poor in art, there is Christian feeling in the simplicity which gives us the union of those three hearts in the hour of agony and death. Red streams of grace flowed down upon the guilty earth: the appointed Mother stood. That loud cry rent the veil of the useless temple, and so shook nature that the dead came forth from their graves; still she stood. For in that temple she had presented the Child, and for her a prophecy was yet to be fulfilled. His heart was pierced and her's; and as the blood and water flowed that marriage type of Cana lived again before her eyes. The mystery of the Cross was consummated.

XVI.

THE MARYS AT THE SEPULCHRE.
DESCENT INTO LIMBO.
MARRIAGE FEAST AT CANA.

High up on the pilaster, at right angles with the one we are after noticing, is depicted the open arch of our Lord's sepulchre with the lamp suspended from it. The angel seems saying to the two women bringing the spices they had prepared: « He « is risen, he is not here ». The roll in the hand of her with the alabaster box may refer to the prediction « Wheresoever this Gospel shall be preached « in the whole world, that also which she hath « done, shall be told for a memory of her » (1). The last unction of His feet for burial was no common act. It was done with a pound of ointment of rich spikenard of great value, and the house was filled with the odour of the ointment. « If », says Augustine, « you will be a faithful soul, anoint « the Lord's feet with the precious ointment. But « that ointment was that of faith. By faith the « just man lives; anoint the feet of Jesus by living « well. Hearken to the Apostle when he says: ' We « are the good odour of Christ in every place ' ».

The subject below the sepulchre is the descent into Limbo to release the souls which could not be admitted to the presence of God until the merits of Christ's passion had been applied to them. When the women returned from the sepulchre, their words seemed to the apostles as an idle dream. But to Adam it was no dream when our Lord entered and raised him by the hand. In his state of glory, indicated by the azure cloud in which He is enveloped, our Saviour, with a grave and affectionate action, is releasing the parents of the human race. Adam presses one hand upon his breast, whilst Eve behind extends both in energetic supplication. Adam

---

(1) Mathew 26. 13.

by his fall had not lost the inherent qualities of human nature, but forfeited the grace with which that nature had been endowed. To recover grace was the whole aim of a virtuous life, and purgatory the means to clear away the faults which marred the aim. So S. Gregory of Nyssa expresses it: « Some
« there are who throughout their life in the flesh
« regulate their lives in a spiritual manner, and free
« from passion : such we are told were the patriarchs
« and prophets, and they who lived with them and
« after them, men who hastened back to the per-
« fect by means of virtue and the pursuit of wisdom.
« While others, through their entry into the future
« state, have cast aside in the purgatorial fire their
« propensity to the material, and have returned gladly
« from an eager desire of good things to that grace
« which was at first the inheritance of our nature » (1).
The most efficacious means to obtain this grace is the sacramental action of the Eucharist ; and the Catholic painter ends his group of mysteries with its type in the miracle of Cana. The master of the feast who is addressing Christ, is indicated by ARCHITRICLINVS written vertically over his head. Our Lady with the nimbus stands next to him. In the grave look of our Lord, with his eyes cast down, there is an expression becoming the importance of

---

(1) De anim. et resurr. p. 636.

the Sacrament. All flows from the life-blood of Christ.
« A cluster of cyprus my love is to me in the vine-
« yards of Engaddi » (1). « We preach », says
S. Ephrem, « the cluster which when squeezed has
« filled the chalice of salvation with its own liquor ».
And he represents our Lady saying to the Magi :
« I do fear Herod the polluted wolf, lest he dis-
» turb me and grasp the sword to cut off the sweet
« cluster yet unripe ». For the Daughter of Sion
knew what David had sung : « Thou hast prepared
« a table before me, against them that afflict me.
« Thou hast anointed my head with oil, and my cha-
« lice which inebriateth *me,* how goodly is it ! » (2).
We easily connect, the vintage scenes of the catacombs
and the dove with the full cluster of grapes, with
the juice poured into the chalice. Christ described
in various figures pours himself through the Church :
Himself with His grace under the veils of the bread
and the wine, but His grace alone in the other
Sacraments. Grace is the sap of the Church, the life
blood of the mystic vine. Those who reject it, cry
with the Jews: « His blood be upon us and upon
« our children ». Reject any fact of the divine
testimonies, and the connexion of the fact is lost ;
but deny the necessity of grace, and the whole of

---

(1) Canticle 1. 13.
(2) Psalm. XXII. v. 5.

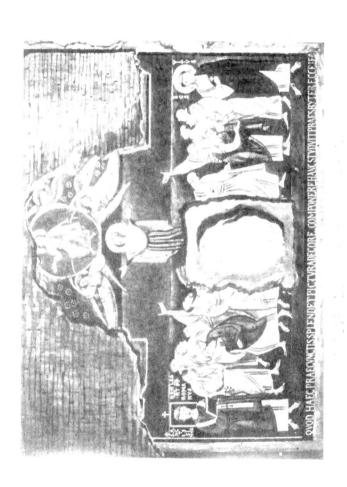

the testimonies are withered, for the Church exists only to distribute it. When treason was at the table upon the very issuing of the great Sacrament of Grace, the words of warning were added. « Abide
« in me, and I in you. As the branch cannot bear
« fruit of itself, unless it abide in the vine, so
« neither can you, unless you abide in me. I am
« the vine; you the branches: he that abideth in
« me, and I in him, the same beareth much fruit:
« for without me you can do nothing » (1).

XVII.

ASSUMPTION OF THE BLESSED VIRGIN.

As we approached with reverence that old niche where, in the northern aisle, we found the Mother in glory with the Son, here again we greet the sequel and consummation of the triumph of the Cross in her Assumption. Come, cried the Jews blaspheming in the ears of that faithful Mother, « let
« Christ the King of Israel now come down from
« the Cross that we may see and believe » (2). Come, « let us put the wood on his bread, and
« blot him out from the land of the living, and

---

(1) John XV. v. 4. 5.
(2) Mark c. XV. v. 32.

« his name shall be remembered no more » (1). The Church replies :

« Impleta sunt, quae concinit
« David fideli carmine,
« Dicendo nationibus :
« Regnavit a ligno Deus » (2).

« O Sacred Wood ! in thee fulfill'd
« Was holy David's truthful lay ;
« Which told the world, that from a tree,
« The Lord should all the nations sway ».

That triumph would not, in a certain sense, be complete if she who had borne the heat and burden of the day were not beside the throne to share it. S. Alphonsus Liguori, considering why Mary, altogether sinless in soul and body, was yet permitted to undergo the common penalty of death, says that God wished to give the just the model of a sweet and happy death. It is a sweet thought that the Son who gave himself to the human race in the form dearest to their affections, that of the first born Child, and had no dearer gift upon the Cross than her he loved so well, was showing S. John, in her, how to die. That

---

(1) Jerem. 11. v. 19.
(2) Hymn. « Vexilla regis ».

living death of her's — the constant anticipation of Simon's prophecy in the passion of her Son, all those toils and travels she had borne for Him, all those pangs and insults, that patient woman was meekly sharing at the foot of the Cross, so naturally prepared her to minister at the bed of death, and disposed her so well to die, that were there nothing supernatural in the invocation of her name, it would rise of itself on dying lips with that of Jesus. As Irenaeus says: « As the human race was « bound to death by a virgin Eve, it is saved « through a Virgin ; the scales being equally ba- « lanced, virginal disobedience by virginal obe- « dience ». If Henoch and Elias were translated, that perfect will of Mary was not to lose the merit of « obedient even unto death ». And if the Collyridian heretics strove to worship Mary, as Gentiles did Astarte queen of heaven, death proving her mortality gave her a triumph in the act. For that pure body (such is the tradition of the Church) was not to know the corruption of the grave, but, reunited with her soul, anticipated the general resurrection, and abides with God in glory for ever. Before this picture, of nigh a thousand years ago, the theologian must bow his head. It is the earliest known picture of the Assumption (1) ; and in the

---

(1) The feast of the Assumption of the Blessed Virgin is mentioned as having been celebrated with great pomp before the sixth

fact of her Assumption is contained the reprobation of that heresy which Pius IX has had occasion to condemn, that life is distinct from the soul. For if the most perfect and privileged creature of divine love, after the sacred humanity of Christ, thus lost life and recovered it by the reunion of the soul, the triumph which the Church celebrates in this circumstance is an evidence of the true faith on this point. « Arise, o Lord, into thy resting place; « Thou, and the ark which Thou hast sanctified » (1). The angels and saints, accustomed though they were to the wonders of heaven in which God displays the magnificence of His power, at the sight of the dazzling beauty with which Mary was adorned as she ascended on high full of grace, cried to their Lord : « Who is she that cometh up from the de- « sert flowing with delights, leaning upon her be- « loved » (2). And if human will would seek to persuade itself that this refers to the beauty of the soul of the just, to what soul so much as to hers ?

---

century, both in the Greek and Latin Churches, as appears from the most ancient sacramentaries extant, with complete calendars, before the time of Pope Sergius, as is clear from the Pontifical; and before the reign of the emperor Mauritius, as is gathered from Nicephorus, lib. 17. 28. See also Baronius Annot. in Martyr. Mabillon in liturg. Gallic. lib. 2. p. 118. Pagi in Brev. Gest. Rom. Pont. in Sergio n. 26. Martene de Eccl. discipl. in divin. Offic c. 33. n. 25. Thomassin etc.

(1) Psalm. 131.
(2) Canticles 8. 5.

If it were expedient that their Master should depart, and prepare a place for the apostles, His mother truly would not be left behind, and her place is at His right hand. « At thy right hand the queen hath « stood in a vesture all of gold, girt about with « variety » (1).

Our Saviour is above, seated on His starry throne, in a nimbus supported by four angels. In His left hand He holds a closed book, while the right is extended. The design is not unworthy of Beato Angelico. Below, the apostles, finding the tomb empty, are in various attitudes of emotion and surprise, and all have their eyes fixed on Her who is mounting aloft, and disappearing from their sight. They are in two groups, six on each side of the tomb, and two have their hands elevated, probably to indicate the desire they had to follow Her. The beloved disciple, who took his Mother to his own house, holds the Gospel roll with one hand, and places the other before his mouth in a manner reverential and full of astonishment. S. Vitus, holding a small cross in his right hand, stands at the extreme end to the right. He has his name – Sanctvs Vitvs – written vertically near his head, which is tonsured and surrounded with the halo. We cannot positively affirm which of the saints of that name he represents; but very proba-

---

(1) Psalm. 44.

bly he was a member of the Order of the *Crociferi* – Crossbearers –, founded by Pope S. Cletus. Or it may be that he was the celebrated archbishop of Vienne in France, who died in 525, and that he is placed near S. John on account of his opposition to the Arians who by denying our Lord's divinity deprived the incarnation of its supernatural value as a remedy for sin, and by thus degrading the Son to their own level reduced the Mother whom all generations shall call « Blessed », and the Angel saluted « full of grace », to the condition of any ordinary woman. S. Vitus was held in great esteem by Clovis, king of France, while yet a Pagan, and by Gundebald the Arian, king of Burgundy, whose son, and successor, Sigismund, he converted to the Catholic faith. Ennodius, in his life of S. Epiphanius, says of him « that he was a treasure of learn-« ing and piety ». Perhaps if we may conjecture why a prelate of Vienne is found in the same composition with Pope Leo IV, A. D. 847, 855, the reason is that S. Ado, who was consecrated bishop of that See in September 860, and next year received the pallium from Nicholas I[st], with the decrees of a Roman Council to check disorders which had crept into several churches in France, had lived five years previously in Rome, and from his distinguished character, and connexions with that See, may have had an influence in the selection of the saint. On the corresponding extremity to the left is Pope S. Leo with the square green nimbus, or glory, to indicate that he was living at the time this picture was painted, either by himself while yet a simple priest, (for the halo and pallium might have been added after he had been made Pope), or by a priest of the same name, for the inscription underneath records « Quod haec « prae cunctis splendet pictura decore, componere « hanc studuit presbyter ecce Leo ». « That this « picture may outshine the rest in beauty, behold « the priest Leo studied to compose it ». From the inscription « Sanctissimus Dom. Leo . . . rt. PP. Ro- « manus », « Most holy Lord Leo... Pope of Rome », it is not easy to determine whether he is Leo III, or Leo IV, for the letters preceding ri are almost effaced, and cannot be read. If it be Leo III, it must have been painted before 795 ; if Leo IV, before 847. The latter had been priest of the church of the Four crowned martyrs opposite S. Clement's. His feast is on the same day as that of S. Alexius, July 17. The following names are scratched on two narrow fillets running parallel to the inscription under the feet of the apostles: « Hier. Ego Mercurius. Mercurius Presb. « Petrus Larissa. Ursus Presb. XXX Novembris « obiit Kalaleo. ✝ Salbius Presb. Flori. Florus Presb. « S. Theodori. Joannes Presb. de Titu. Ego Rufi- « nus Presb. Ven. Dom. Clemens Presb. Georgius. « Ego Mercurius Presb. ». Probably they are the names of the priests who were attached to this basilica, except that of Florus of S. Theodore's, but at what period they lived we have not been able to discover. The priests John and Salbius may be the same who scratched their names in the niche of the Madonna in the north aisle.

NARTHEX.

Two of the paintings in the narthex, as well as the one we have noticed, at pages 161-2-3, of the miracle of Sisinius, refer to the history of S. Clement. It is not easy to describe them without repetition. They have this peculiar interest that they are the earliest votive pictures we possess; or at least that we are acquainted with. No doubt the Catholic custom of giving expression in this way to feelings of religious gratitude for the benefits of Providence, for hair-breath escapes, graces of healing, and answers to prayer, always existed; and just as Pius IX invoked the help of our Lady when the floor was giving way beneath his feet at S. Agnese, and that most remarkable escape was followed up by the restoration of the church, and by commemorative pictures; so the authors of these pictures in our church seem to record their great devotion to S. Clement. « Who then », says S. Basil of Seleucia, « will
« not be in admiration of the great power of the

« Mother of God, and how far she goes beyond
« whatever other saints we honour? For if Christ
« bestowed so much power upon his servants as
« not only to cure the afflicted by their touch, but
« to do this even by their shadow, what must we
« think of the power given to the Mother? » He describes many miracles in answer to prayers addressed to the virgin martyr S. Thecla (who suffered in the first, and he wrote in the middle of the fifth, century), so that her church was, in some way, a public hospital, and propitiatory for the whole earth from diseases, and sufferings and demons; and men went their way singing hymns, giving thanks and blessing. In the preceding century S. Basil of Cappadocia says of the Forty martyrs of Sebaste : « The
« afflicted flies to the Forty, the gladdened runs to
« the same, the former to find deliverance from his
« troubles, the latter that his more fortunate lot
« may be continued to him. There the pious mother
« is found praying for her children, supplicating for
« her husband on his journey, and begging health
« for him when afflicted with sickness ». S. Augustine says : « This question surpasses the power
« of my understanding, in what manner the mar-
« tyrs succour those who are certainly helped by
« them ». He says he was himself a witness of the great glory of the martyrs, SS. Protasius and Gervasius, discovered in Milan by S. Ambrose. Nor was

the belief in miraculous cures in the fourth century confined to Milan; for S. Asterius of Amacea says: « Thus does a father, or a mother taking her sick « child and folding it in her arms, hurry by hos- « pitals and physicians, and fly unto help that « knows nothing of their art; and having come to « any of the martyrs, through him she offers up a « prayer to the Lord ». And he adds, what travellers to Italy will recognize as an evidence of the continuity of Catholic habits in the West: « The « crowds of beggars and the swarms of poor re- « gard the resting place of the martyrs as their « common asylum ». And if any of them have shared in the sprinkling of the holy water at S. Antony's at Rome, they may witness an exemplification of what S. Paulinus says: « You may see not « only parents from the country bearing in their « arms the pledges of their affection, but even of- « tentimes bringing in with them their sick cattle ». Or they may have been scandalized by the practice mentioned by Theodoret, « that those, who faith- « fully petition, obtain their requests, the votive of- « ferings, significative of their cures, plainly testify. « For some bring representations of eyes, others of « feet, others of hands, some of which are of gold, « others of silver. For the God of these martyrs « receives the gifts though small, and of little cost, « computing the gift by the means of the giver ».

It is evident that the donors of these three pictures in our church were of the same way of thinking, and wished to record their great devotion to S. Clement. One is given by Beno Derapiza, another by Beno with Mary his wife, and another by Maria Macellaria. As they all pointedly refer to S. Clement, all are in the same style and give the same formula « P. G. R. F. C. pingere fecit », « had it painted »: and as the joint gift of the husband and wife shows the motive for their grateful devotion to the saint, we suppose them to be the same people. An eminent authority ungallantly suggests that Maria Macellaria was the wife or daughter of a butcher. We feel bound to shed every drop of our ink in her defence; and if we cannot trace her origin to the Sicilian town of Macella, and cannot prove that she was not Maria of the provision market, and no dealer in meat, fish, or vegetables, we appeal to our fair readers whether Lady Mary and Beno, on the other side of the medallion of S. Clement, have the least look of the slaughter house about them. S. Ambrose says of S. Helen, whom the Jews and Pagans nicknamed *Stabularia*, « a good Stabularia « who sought so diligently the will of the Lord, « and chose to be reputed as dung that she might « gain Christ ». A good Macellaria, we think, who did not scruple to paint the penitential spirit of her fear of God upon the walls of our basilica (1).

Maria Macellaria's votive picture is a funeral procession, and there is a difference of opinion whether it is intended for the translation of the relics of S. Cyril or S. Clement. Our own opinion is that it represents the latter. We have spoken of S. Cyril and his mis-

---

(1) Among the ancients *macellum* was a provision market, and got its name from Macellus, a thief whose house was pulled down by the censors and the ground used for the sale of victuals. Plautius says: « I come to the market *(macellum)* ask for fish, they « show them dear: lamb dear, beef, veal, dogfish, pork, all dear ». There was a very large *macellum* on the Coelian, probably near to where S. Stefano Rotondo now stands, and whoever knows how local names are kept up for centuries in Rome, and how nicknames are given, may see that Lady Maria lived thereabouts long after the *macellum* had disappeared. The Livia *macellum* was on the adjoining hill of the Esquiline. The Suburra, which the Roman antiquaries have shifted so often, seems to have been connected with those two hills. There, in the evening, stolen things were sold and ladies walked: the barber clipt and eatables were bought.

> Birds of the hoarse crowd, their mother's eggs,
> And yellow Chian figs the steam among,
> The plaintive goat's rough progeny,
> Olives as yet unequal to the cold,
> Hoary the greens with chilling rime.
> Think'st thou our country sent to thee?
> How diligently dost thou wander boy!
> Nought ours, myself except, the fields do bear.
> What'er the Umbrian bailiff sends to thee,
> Rustic of Tuscia or of Tusculum,
> Or country by third milestone pointed out.
> The whole for me is in Suburra born.
>   *Martial.*

sions befóre. Now we will step a few paces further on and consider first the upright picture referring to the place whence S. Cyril brought the relics of S. Clement. Those who in thought, or in printed articles, have accused Christ's Church of eight hundred years idolatry, have made a mistake in the date. Men are certainly prone to idolatry; and, long after Simon Magus and his Helena, one of the most pretentious capitals of Europe saw the goddess of reason, and the streets she presided over reeking with the blood of Christian priests. Eight hundred years after their Master had died for man, Cyril was striving to extirpate that Paganism among the Sclavonians against which in Holland and Germany, a century before, so many English and Irish missionaries were spending their toil and blood : for that Apostolic seed which Celestine and Gregory had sent to Ireland and England, was to bear rich fruit in the northern regions of Europe. The Vandals of Prussia, the people about the Baltic, the Hungarians and Poles, parts of Germany and Sweden, were to welcome the harbingers of the good tidings a century after S. Cyril. The Norwegians, the Swedes, and the Russians, of the eleventh century, have left us the names of many of their missionary saints, and in the twelfth century Pomerania, Finland and Sweden bore witness to the zeal of Rome for conversion. Pagan habits were more inveterate than faith, and

14

relapses frequent, though priests and kings watered the ungrateful soil with their own blood : and the thirteenth age , which saw the reconciliation of the Greeks at Lyons, also saw that Hyacinth who in March 1218 received his habit from S. Dominic at S. Sabina, and died at 72 on the feast of the Assumption of our Lady in 1257, a saint and apostle of the barbarous idolaters of the North. Scarce three hundred years after, was the charge of idolatry made against the Church; and it is evident, were we to accept it, that the unhappy infidels of Europe had been converted from one form of idolatry to another. If we get a little out of this chained cycle of years, we shall find the Jews of Smyrna suggesting that the mangled limbs of Polycarp might be worshipped instead of Christ, and the Centurian, to get rid of their contention, putting the body into the fire. We shall find the Pagan persecutors threatening others to have their remains utterly destroyed that silly women may not wrap them in linen cloths , and venerate, and anoint, and worship them. We are brought back to the first century ; to that priceless treasure of the church of Antioch , to what the lions had left of S. Ignatius in the amphitheatre at Rome , and to the relics of Trajan's other victim S. Clement. We see again the Christians weeping on the shore when their venerable benefactor was carried out three miles at sea , and his body an-

chored there, as his executioners thought, for ever. Incorrigible idolaters they weep that they cannot prostrate themselves before a dead man's bones. At least they did not need the warning given by S. John Chrysostom in the fourth century : « Do not fix thy
« contemplation on this, that the martyr's body lies
« there deprived of the energizing power of the soul,
« but reflect on this that there reposes in that body
« power greater than that of the soul itself, the
« grace, to wit, of the Holy Spirit, which, by the
« miracles that it performs, gives proof to all of the
« resurrection ». Eusebius is not ashamed to say of another martyr : « The body of the divine mar-
« tyr was cast up at the gate of the city by the
« waves of the sea, as though unable to hold it ». In the case of S. Clement, the sea simply receded, and repeated the miracle every year.

XVIII.

MIRACLE AT THE TOMB OF S. CLEMENT.

In this beautiful composition we have lost the first finding of the relics of our Saint. High up on the wall, the inscription, now nearly obliterated, only remains – « in mare submerso tumulum parat « angelus istud » « the angel is preparing that « tomb » (to S. Clement) « submerged in the sea », refers to the tradition that when Trajan had S. Clement thrown into the deep with an anchor about his neck, and the Christians on the shore wept that they could not recover his body, the sea retired three miles, and it was found with the anchor in a little marble temple prepared by angelic hands. The miracle of the receding waters was repeated for several centuries on the anniversary of his martyrdom, and during the octave of his festival, thus leaving a dry path for the Christians to go and venerate his relics. The temple surrounded by the sea full of fishes is seen in the central compartment, and within it a marble urn containing the sacred treasure. The urn serves for an altar which is covered with a white cloth, and upon it are two candlesticks with lighted candles. Three lamps are suspended from the vaults, and from the canopy over the altar hang two looped curtains very gracefully arranged. On the left is a city, from one of the gates of which a procession issues headed by the bishop going to say mass, and carrying a crosier in his left hand, while his right is raised towards his breast. His assistants clothed in the vestments of their order accompany him, and an immense crowd of people follow behind. The name of the city is designated by the word *Cersona,* or Cherson, which is written under the arch of the gate. This ancient city has been, long since, destroyed, and modern Inkerman built on its ruins. Between the bi-

shop and the temple is a woman of comely aspect, and in a graceful dress, carrying in her arms her child who is lovingly embracing her. Again at the altar we see the same woman and child: she is stooping to raise him up, while he extends his little arms towards her. The words, *mulier vidua*, widow woman, are written in the form of a cross over her head, and *puer*, or little boy, over the head of the child. Underneath, in one line, is the inscription « *integer ecce jacet, repetit quem praevia mater* » « behold unhurt he lies whom his returning mother « seeks again ». The scene here represented and expressed by this epigraph is recorded by S. Ephrem martyr bishop of Cherson, by S. Gregory of Tours, the blessed James of Voragine, S. Antoninus, and many other early writers. They tell us that when S. Clement was thrown into the sea, about three miles from the shore, the Christians who were spectators of his martyrdom were grieved that they could not recover his body, and begged of God to let them know how it could be found. The Lord hearkened to their prayers, and consoled them by causing the sea to retire to the very spot where the holy Pontiff was drowned. Following the receding waters they found his body enshrined in a marble temple, with the anchor that was attached to his neck. For several centuries, on the anniversary of S. Clement's martyrdom, a similar reflux of the sea took place, and continued throughout the octave of his festival, during which the martyr's shrine was visited not alone by the pious inhabitants of Cherson, but by pilgrims from remote regions. On one occasion, a woman brought her little boy with her to visit the tomb of our Saint, and after having satisfied her devotion she went away thinking that he was following her. Having missed him, she determined to go back to the temple, but after travelling a short distance, she saw the sea flowing in and could not proceed any farther. She then retired slowly before the advancing waters, bewailing her only child whom she thought she had lost for ever. On the following anniversary she returned hoping to find even the bones of her dear little one, but, to her great consolation and joy, she found him alive at the tomb of the Martyr, and opening his eyes, as if awaking from sleep, he stretches out his little arms to his mother who takes him up and embraces him. This touching fact should teach us that we should never despair of God's protecting providence, and that we should not measure His ways by those of man. Lower down is a medallion of S. Clement, of the finest style of art. He is tonsured and has the nimbus. In his left hand he holds a closed book, and is blessing with his right. On a beautiful border, which is intersected by the medallion, are four doves turned towards the Saint. Beno, the donor of the picture, holds a candle on one side of the medallion;

the Lady Mary is on the other side with her little boy Clement, both hold candles in their hands. Little Attilia, the sister of little Clement, has also her candle, and stands with her governess behind her father. Under the medallion-head of S. Clement is painted the very expressive and suggestive motto « *me prece querentes estote nociva caventes* » « seeking me in prayer beware of hurtful things ». At the extreme left is an inscription showing that this picture was a votive offering made by Beno to S. Clement, the patron of his boy:

| † IN NOMI NE DN̄I EGO BENO DERAPIZA P̄ AMORE BEATI CLE MENTIS ET REDEMP TIONE ANI MEE PIN GERE FE CIT (sic) | - | « In the name of the Lord,
« I Beno Derapiza,
« for the love of blessed Clement
« and the salvation of my soul,
« had it painted ». |

XIX.

TRANSLATION OF THE RELICS OF S. CLEMENT FROM THE VATICAN TO HIS OWN CHURCH.

The devotion of the Derapiza family being accounted for, we have had at their hands the miracle of Sisinius' conversion; and that of the original locality of S. Clement's relics, of a miracle wrought there, and of their own connection with his name. But is there none of an event so important to his church, and so consonant with their devotion, as the deposition of his relics here? The funeral procession may perhaps be the answer. S. Nicholas Ist invited S. Cyril to Rome. S. Cyril from the time he had stirred up the bishop of Cherson to recover the relics, took boat and found them, bore them back himself and ultimately begged them, always carried them about with him. He brought them to Rome, died and was buried in the Vatican, and was translated to S. Clement's. Certainly there was nothing to warrant the licence which the painter took in representing him carried bodily on the bier wearing the pallium borne by four youths, and two others swinging their censers in the air; because they were only the bones of S. Clement, which were in a marble ark; and even if S. Cyril's body were embalmed, it was similarly shut up in another sealed by the Pope. The

painter fór pictorial effect has not chosen to paint a mere ark. The body is followed by a youth with uplifted hands, incongruous if a mourner, but appropriate if hymning the glory of his relics. Nicholas was dead or dying when Cyril arrived, and Adrian did the rest. The anachronism of the painter is deliberate, in representing Nicholas with his nimbus behind them. The cross is borne behind the Pope who is between two eastern ecclesiastics, and two crosiers near them seem to denote two bishops. The one on his right has the nimbus. This might well be Cyril, and the other Methodius; for, like Nicholas, Cyril was reputed a saint at his death, which followed soon after the deposition of S. Clement's relics; but Methodius survived him many years, and could not be considered a saint at the time of either translation. The painter has also lowered the pall which covers the body to show the crosses of the pallium on the shoulder, precisely as he gives them on that of the Pope. If the venerable head with the nimbus on the bier is that of Cyril, we have no picture of the recovery of S. Clement's relics; and the saint on the Pope's right, thus supposed to be Methodius, occasions a double anachronism by being sainted with Nicholas, though he certainly was not till probably fifty years after him: and the eastern bishop on the Pope's left is altogether unaccounted for. The three spangled banners surmounted by Greek crosses, at the back of the crowd, were most probably intended to carry the imagination to the first mission from Constantinople, and the triple conversion of the Cham of the Chazari, the king of the Bulgarians, and the duke of Bohemia. The artist has shown ingenuity in breaking the line of the procession so as to bring the Pope prominently forward. As the head of the procession arrives, the Pope is celebrating at the altar, upon which is the missal, the paten, and the host. The deacon has the chalice upon a cloth, as we see it in the picture opposite to the temple in the sea. Upon the missal, which is open, are the words « *per omnia secula seculorum - pax Domini sit semper* » « for all ages: « may the peace of the Lord be ever with you ». Over the altar is a large circular lamp, and two smaller ones. The inscription underneath repeats the anachronism « † *Huc a Vaticano fertur pp. Nicolao hymnis divinis quod aromatibus sepelivit* » « Hither « from the Vatican is borne (Nicholas being Pope) with « divine hymns what with aromatics he buried ». The notices we have of the circumstances attending the arrival of S. Clement's relics and the burial of S. Cyril are too brief and obscure to supply any accurate details. That S. Cyril was first buried at the Vatican, and afterwards removed to S. Clement's, they do say. It is most probable that S. Clement's relics were also presented to the Pope at the Vatican ; but there is no mention if it. The artist clearly chose to

represent the subject in his own way, and without strict historical accuracy either in the event or the accessories. The time at which these pictures were painted might be supposed rather soon after Rome was moved by the arrival of the relics than a couple of hundred years after. Besides the devotion of the Derapizas to S. Clement, and not necessarily to S. Cyril, there is in the picture opposite the temple in the sea a sufficient exhibition of the devotion of the Romans to the stranger saint.

XX.

OUR SAVIOUR BLESSING ACCORDING TO THE GREEK RITE.

This large votive picture opposite the temple of S. Clement in the sea presents some difficulties; and unfortunately the funeral or liturgical inscription beneath it is illegible. Whether this was the very ancient chapel mentioned by Baronius, in which S. Cyril's relics were said to be discovered in his time, or why this composition should be found here and the miserably painted actions of his life (the audience of Michael and the baptism) be in the sanctuary, who can say? The style is bolder and somewhat more Byzantine than the other two pictures in the narthex, but looking to the larger scale and votive nature of the subject it is not of a different age. It was evidently meant for a grand commemorative picture of S. Cyril; and was probably an altar-piece, framed as it is between two pillars, and immediately opposite the temple from the ruins of which he removed S. Clement's relics to Rome. And, whether to a person entering by the great door of the basilica, or passing from the church into the narthex and turning to look at the patron saint of the basilica, it is on the right hand, as the place of Cyril's deposition is described by Baronius, Panvinius, and Panciroli, and where the devotion of the Romans would naturally place his honourable memorial. In the centre our Lord, represented as a young man with parted hair and very little beard, stands upon a footstool. In one hand he holds the book of the Gospels, and with the other gives his blessing according to the Greek rite, a peculiarity appropriate to the saint from the Bosphorus. Two ecclesiastics kneel one on each side: the elder tonsured and bearded, not unlike one of the bishops beside Nicholas in the procession, does not aspire to the honours of a saint, for he has no nimbus. His dress is rather that of a philosopher, or monk, and in his left hand he holds the Gospel whilst his right seems to appeal modestly to the Saviour. The younger, close-shaved after the manner of the Latins, and wearing a rich chasuble, kneels reverently holding a jewelled chalice upon the cloth which covers both his hands. It is natural to suppose that the elder represents S. Cyril. S. Clement, whose name is written vertically behind him, wearing the pallium, precisely as S. Nicholas, and the body on the funeral bier before described, is very conspicuously presenting him ; a natural action for one to whom he was indebted for the finding of his relics and bringing them to Rome. The angel Gabriel stands behind the aged ecclesiastic , whom we suppose to be Cyril , with one hand in the action of prayer , and with the other affectionately shielding the bosom of his client, his hand reaching down almost to touch the Gospel which that client holds in his left hand. This appears a natural action in the angel interceding for a missionary of the Gospel in the circumstance of his death, pleading for that blessing which our Lord , if he is blessing either of the persons in this picture, is directing to the elder. Were we to suppose that the younger is meant to represent Methodius, notwithstanding the incongruity of his Latin appearance, he is not so presented nor so shielded, and might be simply offering the chalice of his affliction. Behind him is the angel Michael appealing, to the Saviour, with his left hand in behalf of his client, and holding his rod in his right. « And he that spoke « with me had a measure, a golden reed to measure

« the city, and the gates thereof, and the wall » (1). In the mosaics of S. Agatha in Ravenna, supposed by Ciampini to have been executed about 400, our Lord is seated giving his blessing, and on either side of him an angel with a rod. If this client is Methodius, we remember his conversion of Boigoris-Michael. If we had any doubt that this picture referred to the missionary enterprize of S. Cyril, the figure of S. Andrew on this side, which corresponds to that of S. Clement on the other, would remove it. The apostle takes no part apparently in the subject of the picture, but with his right hand refers to the Gospel roll in his left. He was the earlier apostle of the countries traversed by Cyril and Methodius, and the Russians have long gloried that he carried the Gospel as far as the mouth of the Borysthenes, to the mountains where Kiow stands, and the frontiers of Poland. Immediately under this picture a tomb of brick was discovered, on 10th of February 1868, containing the skeletons of two men of more than ordinary size, probably those of the brother missionary saints.

XXI.

On the wall under the *luminaire,* or skylight, at the south end of north aisle is the head of a

---

(1) Apoc. 21. 15.

female with the halo. It is of a high style of art, and is supposed to have been painted about the beginning of the fifth century.

XXII.

Nearly opposite the fresco of our Saviour blessing according to the Greek rite, is the head of some unknown personage. It belongs to the early Roman school of painting, and is supposed to have been executed about the year 300. Beneath it is an inscription scratched on the plaster – *graffito* – which has puzzled the ingenuity of paleographers to decipher.

XXIII.

OUR SAVIOUR DELIVERING ADAM FROM LIMBO.

LAST PICTURE FOUND.

The Saviour of the world having expired on the Cross, and by His death paid the ransom due to the Divine Justice for the sins of men, descended into the infernal prisons to deliver thence the souls of the just, who were so long debarred from Paradise, their heavenly home. The fresco before us, which is on the right of the hight altar, represents that scene. Our Divine Lord wears a flowing mantle, and is surrounded with a cerulean halo.

He takes Adam by the right hand and tramples on the demon who is vomiting balls of fire at Him. The enemy of the human race, unwilling to let Adam go, holds him by the foot and knee. Hovering in the dark back-ground, are heads and hands, symbolizing, according to archaeologists, the *shades*, or souls of the disconsolate prisoners. Our Redeemer holds the Cross in His left hand, and behind Him is the monogram $\overline{C-S}$. Behind Adam, only three fingers remain of a figure probably representing Eve. He is in a standing posture, and there is an expression in his face which says, he has been long enough here. A small spiral pillar separates this from another compartment to the left. It contains a half figure of a venerable ecclesiastic of oriental type, holding in his left hand a gemmed closed book, while the right is raised in the attitude of supplication. He wears a gemmed chasuble, and an embroidered amice, or cowl, decorated with five Greek crosses.

It is somewhat singular that Limbo should be found twice in this church, and if the picture raises fresh antiquarian guesses at dates and styles, the middle state of souls is too old and Catholic a doctrine to be disturbed by its incredulous opponents. S. Cyril of Jerusalem says: « Then we also com-
« memorate those who have fallen asleep before us,
« first patriarchs, prophets, apostles, that God, by

« their prayers and intercessions, would receive our
« petition : then also on behalf of the holy Fathers,
« and bishops, who have fallen asleep before us, and
« of all, in short, who have already fallen asleep
« from amongst us, believing that it will be a very
« great assistance to the souls, for which the sup-
« plication is put up, while the holy and most awful
« Sacrifice lies to open view. And I wish to per-
« suade you by an illustration : for I know many
« that say this : ' What is a soul profited, which de-
« parts from this world, either with sins, or without
« sins, if it be commemorated in prayer?...' Now sure-
« ly, if a king had banished certain persons who had
« offended him, and their connexions, having woven
« a crown, should offer it to him on behalf of those
« under his vengeance, would not he grant a respite
« to their punishments? In the same way, we also,
« offering up to him supplications on behalf of those
« who have fallen asleep before us, even though they
« be sinners, weave no crown, but offer up, for our
« sins, Christ crucified, propitiating, both on their
« behalf and our own, the God that loves man » (1).

---

(1) Catech. Mystag. V. (Alit. Catech. 23.) n. 9-10. p. 328.

SARCOPHAGI

AND

MONUMENTAL AND LAPIDARY INSCRIPTIONS.

The sarcophagi arranged along the walls of the narthex were found during the progress of the excavations. That on the right near the bell-tower contains the remains of a man and woman, probably Beno and Maria already noticed; and the one opposite it those of a man. The small one *vis-à-vis* the miracle at the tomb of S. Clement contains the bones of a little boy, or little girl, each in its natural place. The inscription on it is Pagan, but we know that the Christians sometimes appropriated, for the purpose of interment, pagan sarcophagi. It is:

D. M.
JVLIAE C. FIL.
FELICITATI
SPIRITO DVLCISSIMO
DEFVNCTO ACERVO
QVAE VIXIT ANNO VNO
MENSIBVS XI, DIEB. TRIBVS
FECERVNT JVLII VERNA
ET FELICITAS PARENTES
SIMILITER ACERVI ET
INFELICISSIMI

Near the stairs is a large *terra-cotta* coffin which contained the body of a bishop, or mitred abbot, but the moment it was exposed to the air, the human form disappeared; for it was not thicker than a cobweb. There are three other sarcophagi containing human bones, but they have no inscriptions.

Opposite the door leading to the nave is a large marble slab with the following inscription:

MIRE INNOCENTIAE IENNARIO V. P. QVI
VIXIT AN: LI. MENS V. D. XXV. NAM MECVM
VIXIT AN: XXV. MEN. V. D. XXV. SINE ALIQVA
DISCORDIA AVT CONTROVERSIA . FLO-
RENTIA VXOR BENEMERENTI IN PACE
FECIT ET SIBI DEPOSITVS PRID:
IDVS IVNII VRSO ET POLEMIO
DP. FLORENTIES N ONIS AVG. VIXIT ANNIS V
M. X. VIXIT SVPER MARITVM SVVM ANNVS III. M. II. IN PACE

De Rossi in his « Inscriptiones Christianae » (1) gives a part of the above; for the slab was broken, and only about one half of it was found at the time this eminent archaeologist published that work. Ursus and Polemius were consuls in 338.

Over a grave, a little to the right, is the following:

SVBTVS HAC TERRA NRA . SEPVLTA SVNT MEMBRA
NEPTIS CVM AVA , DVLCISSA NEPE . VOCATA

---

(1) Vol. I.

PETRVS ET DARIA . BIOLA SIMVLQ. MARIVLA
CVM HIS QVIB: ADJVNCTIS ALIIS TRIBVS
CAL . MAD . OB . DVLCISSA . TEP . GREG . VI .
PP . IND: IIIIX .
ANN . I . NICL . PP . OB . MARIA IND:
M . SEPT . D . XVIII .   IIIX .

Gregory VI governed the Church in 1045.

Another slab has an inscription on both sides,
one pagan, the other christian.

D.   M.
M. AVR. SABINVS CVI FVIT ET SIGNVM VAGVLVS
INTER INCREMENTA COAEQVALIVM SVI TEMPORIS
VITAE INCOMPARABILIS DVLCISSIMVS FILIVS

SVRO IN PACE QVESQENTI
EVTICIANVS FRATER FECIT

IOVINIAN
NEOFITO

On the floor opposite the picture of S. Alexius

DEPOSITVS LEONAS VI . KAL . FEB .
IN PACE

¡ PRAESBYTER

and various other fragments of inscriptions in Damascene characters.

INNOCENQVAE VIXIT ANN V
M V

This epitaph is of the second century

CLEMES VIXIT
ANNIS XXV

DIS . MAN
CLAVDIAE VITALI . FI
CLAVDIANVS
SABINIANVS
NVTRICI PIEN
TISSIMAE

M . LVCCIVS . CRESCES
VIXIT . ANNIS XXVIII

SCIATHIS . MAGIAE . LIBRAR
VIXIT . ANNOS . XVIII
PROS . POCTAVI . CVBICVL . FECIT
FECIT . CONIVGI . SVAE . ET . SIBI

Inserted in the wall of the narthex are several other inscriptions and fragments of inscriptions, partly pagan, and partly christian; some exquisitely sculptured capitals, divers pieces of broken columns, fragments of marble candlesticks, ornamental sculpture, pieces of mosaic pavement, and several tiles with the marks of their makers. Close by the bell-tower is a fragment of an altar of Mithras.

MODERN BASILICA OF S. CLEMENT.

PRELIMINARY REMARKS.

The Church of God is a society existing everywhere throughout the world, bound by its own laws, acknowledging its own head, comprised, as to some portion or other of its members, within the limits of temporal kingdoms, but bound by the secular laws of those kingdoms only so far as they agree with her laws, and are accepted by her. It is evident, therefore, that in every case of conflict between the liberties of the Church and the law or practice of any temporal kingdom, the subjects of the Church must appeal to the decision of their own tribunal; that is for the direction of their consciences on the point, to the judgment of the Pope who is their supreme judge in morals. In point of practice, whatever intermediate judgments may be given by theologians, doctors, or bishops, the last resort is the conscience of the Vicar of Christ. The Church does not judge those who are without; and whether the Sultan is right or wrong in practising polygamy, whether the government of England is right or wrong in setting up divorce-courts, the Church merely prescribes to her own subjects, that is to the faithful of Christ, that they cannot avail themselves of such relaxations or inducements' held out by sovereigns and governments to those who obey them. Hence, without going into theories or details, it is easy to understand the principle of sentences of deposition which the Pope has pronounced, from time to time, against Catholic sovereigns. He releases their subjects from an oath of allegiance, because he is the sole judge of all oaths. He is the final judge of the morals of Catholics, and a sovereign is no more exempt from his excommunication than a slave; and were the subjects of the sovereign truly Catholic, he would find himself, as isolated and helpless as the merest beggar in his dominions, when once named as a person excommunicated, and to be avoided. Under what circumstances, or for what crime, a thief or a king is to be so sentenced, rests entirely with the conscience of the Pope. This, indeed, is a tremendous power; but it is tremendous only because the Church has a real existence, and not one of mere opinion. The atheist is free from it: the infidel is free from it : all who despise it, in a certain sense, are free from it ; for to enforce the sentence the Pope has only the word of Him who said : « Ven-« geance is mine; I will repay, saith the Lord ». When the society of Europe was more Catholic, and more free, the sentence of the judicial power of the Pope reached sovereigns in spite of their array of physical force ; because men of good will did not choose for their sake to encounter the vengeance of God. Rebellion, hateful to the Church, was equally denounced with the crimes of the sovereign, which might seem to justify it. The extreme sentence of deposition from the throne was a proof that Christian men were not chattels to be squandered by the caprice of a man mad, or wicked enough, to set at defiance, with impunity, the laws of man and God.

We have often heard it asked : « What right « have Popes to dethrone kings ? » but few take the trouble to enquire what right have emperors, or kings, to rob, and dethrone Popes. We have heard the cry of « vox populi, vox Dei », and have generally seen the omnipotent voice ending in mock elections under loaded cannon. We have heard the wail of suffering populations, and it has risen louder when they found themselves stript the more, the more they were supposed to be enjoying the sunshine of new liberty : a precious possession of which Brutus seems to have bequeathed nothing to his admirers

but the dagger. We have seen nations all professing peace, all anxious for unity, inimitably national, marching hither and thither, strewing the earth with the thousands of their dead, boasting of their virtues in the list of which they left out self-denial. It is an old story. Let us look at the Germans playing their part under Henry IV. In 1054 Hildebrand had been sent legate to France against simony in the collation of ecclesiastical benefices. In 1073, upon the point of being elected Pope, he begged Henry to use his influence against it, telling him that he could never tolerate his scandalous crimes. We will take the new Pope's character from his adversary Du Pin. « It must be
« acknowledged that Gregory VII was an extraor-
« dinary genius capable of great things, constant
« and undaunted in their execution, well versed in
« the Constitutions of his predecessors, zealous for
« the interests of the Holy See ; an enemy of si-
« mony and libertinism (vices he vigorously op-
« posed), full of Christian thoughts, and of zeal
« for the reformation of the manners of the clergy ;
« and there is not the least colour to think that
« he was not unblemished in his own morals. This
« is the judgment which we suppose every one will
« pass on him who shall read over his letters with
« a disinterested and unprejudiced mind. They are
« penned with a great deal of eloquence, full of

« good matter, and embellished with noble and pious
« thoughts; and we say boldly that no Pope since
« Gregory Ist wrote such strong and fine letters as
« this Gregory did ». To what emperor shall we
compare Henry IV ? The bastard of Normandy who
swept away the village churches of England to make
room for his deer, was a bold soldier; bold in his
vices, and not a mere plotting debauchee. To
what king ? Henry was more like the passionate
church-robbing murderer of Thomas a Becket. He
caused the seals and crosses of every deceased bishop and great abbot to be delivered to him, and
sold them to whom he pleased ; but we do not know
that he stooped so low as the cabbage gardens, and
poor convents of Capuchin Friars, and Franciscan
Nuns. Brutish in his life, affecting penitence for
his usurpations of the temporalities of the Church,
as if he were urged on to draw the sword by his
unhappy fate, receiving the letters of the Pope with
tears, not ashamed in his insatiable lust even to
offer violence to women who had the misfortune to
be his subjects ; ever bold to do wrong and, like
the drunken sot, never able to do right, personally
endowed with the animal courage of the chamois-
hunter, or the *condottiere:* to what king shall we
liken Henry IV ? In an age when Romans wore
swords and knew how to use them, when, under the
sanction of religion, there was some show of justice in

Italy to punish the violation of morality, and a condemnation by the Pope, even though frustrated by violence, was not yet become mirth for the printers of pamphlets at Paris, or the street preachers of London or Turin, we may imagine a scene that followed in the capital of the Christian world. The Sovereign Pontiff upon his throne was presiding over a Council in the Vatican when a priest from Parma, Roland by name, entered and presented his credential letters. His errand was to deliver two letters from the emperor of Germany and the sentence of a mock Council held by him at Worms. In the name of his sovereign, Roland commanded the Pope to resign the Chair of Peter; and turning to the bishops and clergy bade them present themselves on the festival of Pentecost to Henry IV, who would appoint for them a lawful Pope in the place of the ravening wolf and tyrant Hildebrand. The soldiers and nobles on duty at the Council rushed towards the debased priest, who was scarcely saved by taking refuge at the feet of his Holiness. When this imperial messenger had been removed, and order restored, Gregory opened Henry's letter and read it in a loud voice to the bishops. « Henry, not by
« usurpation but by the will of God, king of Ger-
« many, to Hildebrand not a Pope but a hypo-
« critical monk ». The reading of these words

caused such indignation that the Council had to be prorogued to the following day.

The question in dispute was simple. In 1075, the Pope directed his legates to summon Henry king of Germany and emperor elect, to Rome, under pain of excommunication for having simoniacally usurped the investiture of bishoprics, and promoted unworthy persons to ecclesiastical dignities. The enraged king ordered the legates out of the country, and he himself presided over a number of excommunicated simoniacal bishops at Worms, where cardinal Hugo distinguished himself by his invectives against the head of the Church. Ambassadors were at once dispatched to Italy to persuade the Italian bishops to accept their mock sentence of deposition; those of Lombardy, and the Marches of Ancona, were easily gained over, and in their assembly at Parma ratified the work of Worms. Henry sent the Romans a copy of the sentence : « I Henry, king « of Germany, finding that you have forfeited all « your rights, and usurped the Papacy, command « you to descend from the Chair of that city of « which I have been elected patrician and sovereign « by the free suffrages of the people ». And in another letter he urged them to rebel, and condemn and dethrone Hildebrand the tyrant, the usurper of the Holy See, the betrayer of the Roman empire, and the enemy of the common weal. These were the two letters Roland undertook to present to the Pope. History repeats itself. The only difference appears to be that, the blustering violence of the *lansquenet* is replaced by the impudence of the « pe- « tit-maître » of the salon, the cajoling of the multitude, and the actual use of military oppression, remaining constant quantities in diplomatic permutations. In countries that boast of more conspicuous plain-dealing, the statesman writes the pamphlet of the prison-spy; the conspirator is supplied with the passport, the fleet protects the landing of the brigand. In others more jealous of military empire than of liberty or peace, the pamphlet, the plot, and the purse, the advice of the envoy, and the judicious presence of a few troops to preserve order, and countenance fair play, pave the road to the modern ovation, and the ballot-box brings to perfection what some discharges of artillery, rendered necessary by the inconceivable stupidity of the human race, had begun.

The Council which had been so rashly interrupted, met again the next day, and Gregory addressed the one hundred and ten bishops and prelates present at it, palliating as far as he could the conduct of the German king and exhorting him to liberate the bishops and abbots he had cast into prison. The fathers all rose and besought the Pope to unsheathe the sword of Peter, and cut the rebellious,

blasphemous, and tyrannical monarch off from the Church. Standing on his throne, his Holiness pronounced this sentence amidst the acclamations of the Council : « Strong in the faith that the Vicar of
« Christ can loose and bind on this earth whatever
« should be loosed or bound in heaven, not through
« any worldly intention but for the safety and ho-
« nour of the Church, I, the legitimate Pope and
« Vicar of Christ, excommunicate, in the name of
« the Father and of the Son and of the Holy Ghost,
« Henry king of Germany, son of Henry emperor
« of the Romans, who with unexampled pride per-
« secutes and oppresses the Church : I interdict him
« the government of the kingdoms of Germany and
« Italy : I absolve all Christians from their oath of
« allegiance to him, and prohibit obedience to be
« rendered to him as king, because whosoever re-
« nounced the authority of the Church forfeits the
« authority he has received from her ». It was not the fashion of that age for imperial librarians to vilify the life of Jesus Christ : nor could an emperor outrage the moral sense of his countrymen, with impunity. When the Frenchman Berengarius broached errors against marriage and infant baptism, and his impiety denied transubstantiation and the real presence, a Council at Paris unanimously condemned him ; and the Catholic king deprived him of the revenue of his benefice, and an

archbishop of Canterbury, Lanfranc, wrote an excellent confutation of the heresy. In his letters to the Germans the Pope stated « that Henry was guilty
« of crimes so heinous and enormous as to deserve
« not only to be excommunicated, but, according
« to all divine and human laws, to be deprived
« of royal dignity ». The imperial appetite was not satisfied to pick up vile mistresses in public places. The head of the state was charged with dishonouring the wives and daughters of the princes, with cruel oppression of his subjects, with disregard of public interests, and the butchery of many innocent persons. The German princes declared in the national Council they held in 1076, that he had wantonly shed the blood of his subjects and laid an intolerable yoke on the necks of a free people. In modern days, it would be that he had broken his promise to protect the Church. But then the Germans had not adopted that heresy which lines the royal mantles of the nineteenth century. « For many there are who,
« set over the handling of public affairs, call them-
« selves patrons and champions of religion, extol it
« with their praises, cry it up as most especially
« suited and useful to human society; neverthless
« wish to moderate its discipline, to rule the sacred
« ministers, to put hands upon holy things : in a
« word, strive to encompass the Church within the
« limits of the civil state, and lord it over her, who,

« however is *sui juris*, and by divine counsel ought
« to be pent up within the boundaries of no empire,
« but to be propagated to the utmost bounds of the
« earth, and embrace every race and nation, to
« point out to them, and set free, the way of eternal
« blessedness ».

In the language of the modern historian « Free-
» men put over themselves Henry as king, on condi-
« tion that he should judge his constituents with
« justice, and govern them with royal care, which
« compact he had constantly broken and disregarded.
« Therefore, even without the judgment of the Apos-
« tolic See, the princes could justly refuse to acknow-
« ledge him any longer as king, since he had not
« fulfilled the pledge which he gave at his election,
« the violation of which brought with it the viola-
« tion of kingly power » (1). But the sagacious
Germans holding yet to the unity of faith did not
think the common Father of the faithful an alien to
their welfare; nor did they need to exclude the judgment of the Apostolic See from what affected its own
supremacy. They had not learned that Cisalpine hypocrisy with which the satellites of rebellion rejoice
in the liberty of the Church, whilst they trample its
laws and rights under foot, drive religious women
from their homes, strip them of all that could be

---

(1) Muratori, An. d'Italia, tom. 4. pag. 245. 246.

sold, and thrust the clergy and prelates into prison. When such things were done in the eleventh century they were not supposed to savour of liberty, but to be acts of violence against the common conscience; acts of shame which no pretext or excuse could palliate; nor were kings held to be religious who violated, more conspicuously than other men, the common obligations of humanity. If great crimes too often disgraced the throne, men who had not laid aside the traditional respect of the German tribes for chastity, and reverenced the Church which taught and practised it, were not easily to be persuaded that the sceptre in the loathsome grasp of the vulgar debauchee gave him a right to proclaim himself to the civilized world as the man of destiny, the saviour of the nations, the Caesar harbinger of universal peace. The tradition was not lost, that when the Pope of Rome confronted Attila, the Hun had seen S. Peter and S. Paul standing by him. And if common sense could not teach men that royal power was a great responsibility before God, the words of S. Leo to another prince were not yet expunged from Europe, that the royal power had been conferred upon him not alone to rule the world, but chiefly to protect the Church. It was the law of the empire that a king or emperor who remained a whole year under excommunication was virtually dethroned; yet if the Germans had acted on their own opinion, as Muratori suggests, they would simply have been violating fundamental law and rejecting the ultimate court of appeal. They sought the sanction of the Pope. Whether the ideas of the men of that age were logical or not, whether the pretensions of the Holy See were rightful or not, there was at least this advantage that there was somebody to appeal to, and that somebody must of necessity have some fixed principles, or he would not be appealed to. It was not a common hodge-podge of interests pitched into a congress to be got out of it in what condition they might be, and with no power but the fortuitous concurrence of interests to enforce a decision, if it were worth while to enforce it. The Pope had interests to maintain which he believed to be sacred: which Popes have maintained at Fontainebleau, at Gaeta, or when reduced by a robber king almost to the gates of Rome. It is an advantage to have something tangible to defend, and that something is the Cross of Christ which Judas and the Caesars have made more glorious by their treason and their hate.

Anxious to get absolution before the year's end, Henry crossed the Alps in the depth of winter, and prostrated himself, in the garb of a pilgrim, at the gates of the fortress of Canosa, where Gregory was stopping on his road to Augsburg to preside over the Council in which the question about the throne was to be decided. For three days he was not admitted;

judging, by his former duplicity, that the sincerity of his professions was not to be relied on. He received absolution on condition that, if his trial before the German nobles at Augsburg were against him, he should renounce all pretensions to the crown. Promising this, the Pope embraced him, and gave him the kiss of peace, after which he prepared to celebrate mass. At the time of communion, holding the Blessed Sacrament in his hand, Gregory appealed to his Lord as witness of his innocence, and invited the king to do the like. Conscious of his guilt he dared not, but promised to do it at Augsburg. Six days after he made a league, with the excommunicated bishops of Lombardy and Tuscany, to make the Pope a prisoner; and not succeeding declared war against him. The archishop of Magonza with the bishops of Wurtzburg and Metz, and other prelates, dukes Rodolph, Guelph, Berthold, with the Margraves, counts and barons, assembled at Forcheim, were informed by the papal legates of Henry's perfidy. Rodolph proposed to elect a new king, but the legates suggested that the Pope ought to preside at the election. The nobles maintained that procrastination was detrimental to the vital interests of their country. The legates persisted that the Pope as head of the Christian world should first be consulted. At last the right of election was ceded to the prelates, and Rodolph duke of Swabia was chosen. Otho of Nordheim, Guelph and

Berthold approved of the election, the legates sanctioned it, the people acclaimed it; and messengers were despatched to beg the Pope to anathematize the dethroned king. Still Gregory hesitated, hoping for Henry's amendment. At length, in 1080, seeing that he went on adding crime to crime, he excommunicated him anew in a Council at Rome, and acknowledged Rodolph. War ensued between the competitors, and Rodolph was slain. In 1081 Henry descended into Italy with a powerful army and besieged Rome, but was repulsed by the people who adhered unflinchingly to the Sovereign Pontiff. In 1082 and 1083 he renewed the siege, but without success. In 1084 he returned a fourth time, bribed the nobles, whose castles and estates had been ruined in the three preceding sieges, and the gates of the city and fifty hostages were delivered into his hands. The antipope Clement III, Guibert archbishop of Ravenna, titular of S. Clement's, who had been chosen, by Henry's party at Brixen, upon the election of Rodolph, was consecrated at the Lateran, and in the Vatican crowned his protector who took up his residence on the Capitol as the lawful successor of Augustus and Charlemagne. Gregory took refuge in the Castel S. Angelo; whilst Rusticus, his nephew, defended the Septizonium, an insulated mausoleum built by the Antonines where the church of S. Lucia in Selce now stands, near the basilica of S. Maria Maggiore. Twenty five years before, at the end of Easter, Rome had seen the bishop of Toul, in the habit of a pilgrim, alighting from his horse some miles from the city and walking barefoot to be crowned as Leo IX. To repress the Normans who, after having expelled the Saracens and Greeks out of the kingdom of Naples, became very troublesome neighbours to the Holy See, he made over his German lands of Fuld and Bamberg to Henry III, receiving in exchange Benevento and its territory. By means of this exchange he hoped to check the Normans, but his army was defeated by them and himself made prisoner. After about a year he was honourably sent back to Rome. In his last illness, he had himself carried before the altar of S. Peter's where he remained prostrate for an hour, then heard mass, received the viaticum and expired. Now, the Norman duke of Calabria, Robert Guiscard, Henry's implacable enemy, advanced from Salerno with an army of six thousand horse and thirty thousand foot. Three days before he reached the gates of Rome, Henry retreated into Lombardy, exhorting the Romans to drive back the Normans and persevere in their rebellion on his behalf. In Lombardy the Tuscans gave his army a great overthrow. Within twelve years his eldest son Conrad and his second son Henry rebelled against him. The latter, crowned emperor of Germany, stript him of the imperial insignia and forced him to renounce the throne. He took refuge at Cologne, and then at Liege, where he mustered an army against his son Henry V who defeated him. Reduced to extreme misery, he supplicated the bishop of Spire to nominate him to the prebend of a lector or precenter in his cathedral church, but was refused. At length abandoned by every one, he implored the bishop of Liege to afford him an asylum, and there he died in 1106. The antipope Guibert, after wandering through various parts of Italy and Germany, died suddenly at Ravenna in 1100 or 1101. Meantime schism and rebellion had wrought their usual calamities. Guiscard fought his way into Rome by the Porta Asinaria on the Naples road, and took up his quarters at the fortified monastery of the four crowned Martyrs opposite S. Clement's. The imperial faction, still strong in the city, rose against the Normans, and a hasty word from the conqueror was the signal for fire and pillage. As Italy has seen the Arab infidels of Algiers imported by the occupant of the throne of Catholic France against the Christian forces of Austria, so the Saracens of Sicily formed a large contingent of Guiscard's army, and seized the opportunity of plunder. From the Lateran to Castel S. Angelo, and from the Flaminian gate to the church of S. Lorenzo in Lucina, was a scene of wreck and ruin. Great part of the buildings of ancient Rome were then destroyed, and the fragments that remained supplied materials for ordinary buildings. Whatever was habitable from the Lateran to the Capitol was swept away. We might surmise that the basilica of S. Clement perished in the general wreck at that time; and that the clear waters which fill the subterranean chambers of Clement's palace had filtered through the soil after the destruction of the baths of Titus on the hill hard by. But in the absence of information lost, or possibly existing still in manuscripts of the Vatican and other libraries, though we have searched for it in vain, we have no proof that the churches were then destroyed. The succeding century was one of church restorations. Paschal II, in 1118, re-dedicated S. Adrian's in the Forum, and it is said that he rebuilt that of the four crowned Martyrs. In 1145 Lucius II placed the Lateran basilica of the Salvatore under the invocation of the Baptist and Evangelist S. John, and repaired and consolidated the foundations of S. Croce in Gerusalemme. In 1191 Celestine III made the ceiling of S. Maria Maggiore. But these are all negative indications. On the 13th of August 1199, a conclave was held in S. Clement's, and its titular cardinal Raynerius elected Pope. This was only fifteen years after the devastation by Guiscard's troopers, and it is difficult to understand how in so short a period of time the subterranean basilica could be filled up, and a new one built upon its site. But this difficulty disappears when we view the carelessness and evident haste with which the walls of the modern basilica were constructed; and moreover S. Clement's being obnoxius as the title of the antipope, and standing in the valley at the foot of Guiscard's position, it is probable that it was not spared in the fight. But in that case how can we account for the preservation of the pictures whose colours were so wonderfully bright when first cleared of the soil? By assuming that the church was only partially destroyed and immediately filled up after the devastation. Those who refer these paintings to the years intervening between 1085 and 1099, do so without a shade of probability; for, as we have already stated, they must have been executed when the circumstances they represent, and the devotion of those saints were fresh and fervent in the minds of the Romans. We confess, however, that in the midst of this obscurity of data, and dearth of positive proof, we can find only two facts of which we are certain — 1st that the original basilica existed in 1058, as we learn from a monumental inscription lately found in the pavement of the narthex with the names of Gregory VI and Nicholas II; 2^{d} that the modern church was built before 1299, because the tabernacle of the holy oils bears that date, and is an insertion later in style than the rest of the church.

MODERN CHURCH.

The modern church of S. Clement was entirely restored by Clement XI in 1715, as is recorded by this inscription over the door:

ANTIQVISSIMAM HANC ECCLESIAM
QVAE PENE SOLA AEVI DAMNIS INVICTA
PRISCARVM VRBIS BASILICARVM
FORMAM ADHVC SERVAT
EO IPSO IN LOCO AEDIFICATAM
AC IN TITVLVM S. R. E. PRESBYTERI CARDINALIS ERECTAM
VBI S. CLEMENTIS PAPAE ET MARTYRIS PATERNA DOMVS
FVISSE CREDITVM
A SANCTO GREGORIO MAGNO
GEMINIS HIC HABITIS HOMILIIS
ET SACRA QVADRAGESIMALI STATIONE
CONDECORATAM
CLEMENS XI. PONT. MAX.
IPSO ANNIVERSARIAE CELEBRITATIS EJVSDEM S. CLEMENTIS DIE
AD CATHEDRAM ECCLESIAE REGIMEN ASSVMPTVS
IN ARGVMENTVM PRAECIPVI IN EVM CVLTVS
INSTAVRAVIT ORNAVITQVE
ANNO SALVTIS MDCCXV. PONTIF. XV.

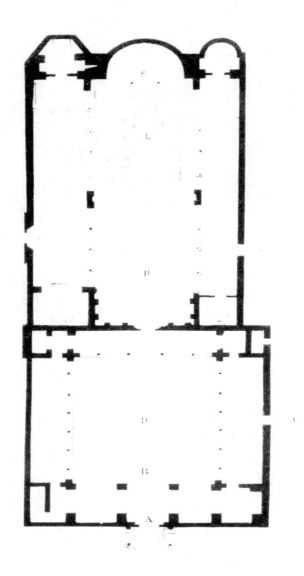

GROUND-PLAN OF EXTERNAL PORTICO, QUADRIPORTICO, AND MODERN BASILICA.

A. Entrance to. B. Atrium. bbb. Quadriporticus. C. Entrance to convent. D. Fountain in which the Faithful used to wash their hands before entering the church. D. Nave. E. Choir. 1, 2. Ambones. 3. Ancient marble screen. 4. High altar. F. Presbytery and tribune. 5. Episcopal chair. 6, 7, 8, 9. Chapels of S. John, of the Rosary, of the Crucifixion, and of S. Dominick. a. Side entrance to the church from the street. b. Entrance to the sacristy and subterranean basilica.

« This very ancient church which almost alone
« unconquered by the damages of time, yet pre-
« serves the form of the old basilicas of the city,
« built upon the very spot, and erected to a Title
« of cardinal priest of the Holy Roman Church,
« where the paternal house of S. Clement Pope and
« Martyr is believed to have been : graced by
« S. Gregory the Great with two homilies delivered
« here and the holy station of Lent. The Supreme
« Pontiff Clement XI elected to the government of
« the Catholic Church on the very day of the an-
« niversary celebration of the same Clement, in
« token of his particular devotion to him restored
« and ornamented it, in the year of salvation 1715,
« of his Pontificate the fifteenth ».

We must regret that the restorations are not in keeping with the style of the church; and particularly that the heavy carved and gilt flat ceiling substituted for the open timber roof, existing in 1690, presses upon and conceals some parts of the mosaic apse. The stucco ornaments and pictures above the arches of the nave are also of the last century. A series of frescoes is painted over the colonades that divide the nave and aisles. We give them in the following order.

I.

Death of S. Servulus. — On the right next the door, is depicted the death of S. Servulus by Chiari, a Roman artist, 1654, 1727, and pupil of Carlo Maratta. He is sitting on a pallet listening to a man who is reading the scriptures: a pilgrim kneels before him, and two other men are earnestly looking at him: his aged mother leans on her staff behind, and an angel is distributing bread to the poor. S. Gregory the Great, in his first Book of morals (1), thus speaks of Servulus: « In the porch of S. Cle-
« ment's church, Servulus, whom many of you knew
« as well as I, spent his days. He was poor in
« this world's wealth, but rich in heavenly trea-
« sures. He was paralyzed from his infancy. His
« mother and brother attended him, and the alms
« he received he caused them to distribute among
« the poor. He was utterly ignorant of letters, but
« he bought the books of the sacred scriptures, and
« had them continually read for him by the pil-
« grims and other pious persons to whom he gave
« hospitality, so that he committed them all to me-
« mory. In his sufferings he never ceased, either
« day or night, to give thanks to God, and sing
« His praises. But when the time arrived for him

---

(1) Homily 15. n. 4.

« to receive the reward of his sufferings, the pain
« attacked the vital parts, and knowing that he
« was near death, he asked the pilgrims, and those
« persons whom he had lodged with him, to arise
« and sing with him the psalms for his death. And
« while they were singing, he suddenly interrupted
« them, saying with a loud voice: ' Be silent;
« don't ye hear the melodies of the celestial choir? '
« And while listening to the angelic chant, he
« expired ».

II.

S. Ignatius condemned to death by Trajan. — This fresco, by Piastrini, represents the emperor Trajan sentencing S. Ignatius to be sent to Rome to be devoured by wild beasts for the entertainment of the people. Two soldiers are shackling his left hand, whilst he points with his right to heaven, joyfully exclaiming: « I thank thee, o Lord, for vouchsafing « to honour me with this token of perfect love for « thee, and to be bound with iron chains in imi- « tation of the apostle Paul for thy sake ». Shipped at Seleucia, sixteen miles from Antioch, bound to ten leopards, (so he calls the soldiers who guarded him night and day), at Smyrna he met the bishop S. Polycarp his fellow-disciple under the Evangelist S. John. To reach Rome before the shows were over, they hurried him again aboard. From

Troas he wrote to the church at Smyrna, styling the heretics who denied that Christ had taken true flesh, and that the Eucharist is that flesh, wild beasts in human shape, and prohibiting all communion with them.

III.

S. Ignatius parting from S. Polycarp. — The two martyr bishops are embracing each other, and the soldiers hurry S. Ignatius, who is in chains, to the ship in the back-ground. In front of a building behind the saints, is a group of men and women; some of them earnestly conversing with each other. The composition is very good, and tastefully executed. It is by Triga.

IV.

S. Ignatius devoured by lions in the Flavian amphitheatre. — Ghezzi of Ascoli, 1634, 1721, an imitator of Pietro da Cortona, gives the last scene of the holy martyr's life. Ignatius longed to land on the track of S. Paul at Pozzuoli, but a strong gale drove the ship to Ostia. He reached Rome on the last day of the shows, December 20, was presented with the emperor's letter to the prefect, and immediately taken to the amphitheatre. He had begged Polycarp and others, and wrote the same to the Romans, to pray that he might be devoured at once, lest, as happened

to some Christians, the beasts refusing to touch them, he should lose the crown of martyrdom. A letter of the church of Antioch reveals that the prayer was heard. « Thus was he delivered to the wild beasts
« near the temple, that so the desire of the holy mar-
« tyr might be accomplished, as it is written ' to
« the just their desire shall be given ' (1), that he
« might not be burdensome to any of his brethren
« by the gathering of his relics according as in his
« epistle he had before wished that so his end might
« be. For only the more solid parts of his holy re-
« lics were left, which were carried to Antioch and
« wrapt in linen, a priceless treasure bequeathed to
« the holy church through the grace which was in
« the martyr ». Four fierce lions were let loose and instantly devoured him, leaving only the larger bones. We see him kneeling with his arms extended, his eyes raised to heaven : two lions upon him, a third rushing forward, and another looking gently at him. Angels are in the air, one of whom flies towards him with the palm. « After being present at this sad
« spectacle », say the authors of the letter, « which
« made us shed many tears, we spent the following
« night in our house in watching and prayer, beg-
« ging God to afford us some comfort by certifying
« us of his glory ». They add that several saw him in great bliss.

---

(1) Prov. X. 24.

V.

S. Clement giving the veil to Flavia Domitilla. — The pictures on the left of the nave are all of the life of S. Clement. Sebastian Conca of Gaeta, 1676, 1764, a pupil of Solimene of Naples, and an imitator of Pietro da Cortona, painted, near the door, S. Clement giving the veil to Flavia Domitilla, who is kneeling before him.

VI.

S. Clement causing water to gush from a rock. — This is by Grechino. It represents the miracle at the marble quarries in the Crimea, recorded in the first responsory of S. Clement's festival. « At the « prayer of S. Clement there appeared to him the « Lamb of God : from under whose foot a living « fountain flows : the gushing of the stream makes « glad the city of God. I saw upon the mountain « the Lamb standing ». The Christians parched with thirst from their toil in quarrying and cutting the marbles, are gladly drinking.

VII.

S. Clement cast into the sea with an anchor tied to his neck. — Odasi of Rome, one of the chief fresco-painters of the day, 1663, 1734, under the patronage of Benedict XIII, depicted the martyrdom of S. Clement. The Pope is seen on a precipice over the sea, with the anchor fastened to his neck. Two men are holding it, and an officer commands the soldiers to hurl him into the waves. An angel bears the palm above. « When he had taken his way to « the sea, the people cried aloud: ' Lord Jesus Christ, « save him. ' Clement was saying with tears: ' Fa- « ther, receive my spirit ' » (1).

VIII. IX.

Translation of the relics of S. Clement. His entrance into glory. — We might expect the last subject to be that of the third responsory. « Thou « hast given, o Lord, a dwelling to Thy martyr Cle- « ment in the sea, in the form of a marble temple « prepared by angelic hands: affording a way to the « people of the earth to tell forth Thy wonders ». But Chiari has chosen the more ordinary translation of the relics. At the head of the saint, laid on the bier in his pontifical robes, there are two torch-bearers, and the Pope and his attendants stand at his feet: angels hover in the air. The same painter has represented the glory of the saint in the large painting on the ceiling over the centre of the nave.

---

(1) Benedictus Antiphon at Lauds.

X. XI.

SS. Cyril and Methodius. — On the wall over the door opposite the apse are the figures of SS. Cyril and Methodius, clothed in their episcopal robes. They wear the Greek pallium, and hold in their hands the Greek crosier. All those frescoes are very fair specimens of that feeble, mechanical, conventional, school of which Carlo Maratta was the chief.

CHAPEL OF THE CRUCIFIXION.

Injured as they have been, it is a relief to turn to the frescoes in the chapel of the Crucifixion, at the east end of the south aisle. There is, at least, a unity in its Gothic conception; and if the costumes are quaint medieval, poetry and good drawing, and sweet expression, yet remain. They are the very opposite of the Academic style; and their Tuscan author, 1402, 1443, Masaccio, as Tommaso Guidi was nicknamed, was a man who gave a great impulse to the art by studying individual forms. Masolino and Fra Filippo Lippi were of his age and school. Unfortunately for himself, the young Carmelite Lippi left his convent, and, after having been captured by a pirate and sold to slavery in Africa, became a painter of great repute, and carried off a young Florentine from the convent of S. Margaret, in which she was being educated. Their son Filippino became a great artist, and finished the frescoes of the Brancacci chapel, in the Carmine at Florence, interrupted by Masaccio's death. Vasari mentions twenty four eminent artists who studied Masaccio's style. His forms were similar to those of his contemporaries, the sculptors Donatello and Ghiberti. This is the only chapel he painted in Rome. On the isolated pier to the left, is S. Christopher who suffered martyrdom in Lycia under the emperor Decius. He seems to have taken the name of Christopher, that is, carrier of Christ, from the same motive as Ignatius did Theophorus, that is, carrier of God, to express his ardent love and intimate union with Christ whom he always carried in his breast. Vida, the poetical bishop of Alba, 1470, 1566, quaintly says of him :

« Christophore, infixum quod eum usque in corde gerebas,
« Pictores Christum dant tibi ferre humeris » (1).

« O Christopher, whom thou in inmost heart didst bear
« Thy Christ, the painters on thy brawny shoulders bare ».

And it is said that his great stature and wading through the stream represent his courage in his tribulations. But, seeing how very often our Lord appeared to saints in the form of a little child, it is very possible that a lost tradition of some such vi-

---

(1) Hymn. 26. t. 2. p. 150.

sion applies to S. Christopher. The entrance to the chapel is an introduction to the consideration of the humanity of Christ. Our Lady at prayer, in an arcade, receives the Angelic Salutation : « Hail full of « grace ». We pass under an arch on which are painted the twelve apostles, and stand before the Crucifixion of our Divine Lord. The eyes raised to heaven are met, upon the vault, by the only sources whence the Christian can learn of the God made man, to wit, the four evangelists with their emblems, and the four doctors of the Church. The still landscape behind the cross represents the repose of that world which its Creator meant for peace. Human passions, and the dereliction of the chosen people, fill the foreground. « What more ought I to have done for thee, and did « it not? I planted thee my vineyard most goodly « to behold; and thou art made to me very bitter, for « with vinegar hast thou given my thirst to drink, « and with the lance pierced through thy Saviour's « side » (1). Nor is the author of evil absent, nor the quick help given to repentance. The demon violently drags the soul of the reviling thief; whilst an angel receives the soul of the forgiven penitent. The centurion on horseback, clasping his hands, gazes up at the world's victim. She to whom much had been forgiven, because she had loved much, embraces

---

(1) Adoration of the Cross on Good-Friday.

the Cross, at the foot of which the beloved disciple stands weeping; and the will of the Virgin Mother fails not, but her human nature, worn out by suffering, faints in the arms of the women supporting her. The individuality of the painter's conception is strongly marked in the boy with a basket, and in the group of four men, one of whom is pointing to the Cross, while the others seem to listen to him.

On the wall to the left is depicted the martyrdom of S. Catharine. The first act of the saint shows her discoursing of the Trinity to the pagan Philosophers of Alexandria. She converted them, and the consequence of their conversion is seen in the fiery death they are doomed to suffer, under which the virgin encourages them to perseverance. Higher up, the idol she despised stands upon the pillar before which she is reproving the idolaters. Then from the window of her prison-cell she converses with the empress and converts her. The convert is decapitated, and an angel receives her soul. Ordinary tortures were not sufficient to punish, what seemed to the Pagans, crimes so enormous. The wheel, which bears her name, is contrived to tear her in pieces, but an angel descends and the broken engine wounds the executioners. In the presence of the soldiers leaning on their shields, the martyr kneels to receive the last stroke of the executioner, and an angel carries her soul to its reward. A small, but very delicate and graceful design shows three angels laying her body in the tomb on the summit of Sinai. When we praised Masaccio for turning to nature, it was not as if he were a mere copyist of living forms : the difficulties he had to contend against in painting eastern costumes certainly not familiar to him, and of using medieval soldiers for Roman legionaries, or spectators in the dress of Florentines, would have overcome the mannered artist who had not his talent for giving expression to the face. The subjects on the opposite side, next the street, have recently been detached from the wall, put on canvas, and replaced, in order to prevent their perishing altogether from damp. The one near the altar represents a flood which inundated the city of Alexandria as a punishment for the death of the martyrs. Several persons are seen drowning in the waters, while S. Catharine is praying at the window of a palace. We do not know what the others represent, and therefore must leave them unnoticed.

We are enabled to fix the date of an inscription on the outer wall of this chapel, near the great door of the church, by the introduction into it, of the name of Pope S. Zachary. He succeeded Gregory III in 741, and died in 752. The inscription records a gift, by Gregory the titular of our church, of the deutero-canonical and other books of Old and New Testament. It is as follows :

« Hisraheliticus dona offerebat populus ruri
« Alius quidem aurum, alius namque argentum,
« Quidem quoque aes, quidem vero pilos caprarum,
« Infelix autem ego, Gregorius primus presbyter almae
« Sedis Apostolicae, hujusque tituli gerens,
« Curam beati, supremus cliens Clementis,
« Offero de tuis, haec tibi Christe thesauris
« Temporibus SSmi Zacchariae Praesulis summi
« Per martyrem et sanctum, parva munuscula tuum,
« Clementum cujus meritis merear delictis carere,
« Atque ad beatam aeternam ingredi vitam.
« Aisti quantum habes, regnum valet coelorum.
« Suscipe hos Domine, velut minuta viduae quaeso,
« Veteris novique Testamentorum denique libros
« Octateuchum, Regum, Psalterium, ac Prophetarum
« Solomonem, Esdram, historiarum illico plenos.
« Require syllabarum, lector, sequentiam harum ».

The last line is engraved on a different quality of marble which shows that the inscription is incomplete.

CHAPEL OF S. DOMINIC.

The little chapel of S. Dominic, on the other side of the great door, is incrusted with rich and various marbles. The altar-piece which represents the saint dying in the arms of angels is said to be by Roncalli, a follower of Barocci of Urbino; and the two on the side walls are attributed to Sebastiano Conca. But, judging from their style, it is much more probable that all three are by Ignatius Hugford who was born in Florence of Scotch parents in 1695, and afterwards became president of the Academy of the « Fine Arts » in that city. The two last subjects have been repeated by the late Father Besson O. P. on the walls of the chapter-room in S. Sisto, where they actually occurred. The painting on the right represents S. Dominic restoring to life a mason who had been crushed to death by the fall of a vault, during the building of the convent of S. Sisto. That on the opposite wall represents the same saint restoring to life the young prince Napoleon Orsini, the only surviving stock of the Orsini family. Theodoric Apolda (1), Fr. Humbert (2), a third historian quoted by Echard (3), Fleury (4), John Longinus (5), and many others record this miraculous fact to have occurred in the following way. Honorius III committed to S. Dominic the reformation of the nuns in Rome, many of whom then lived without keeping enclosure, some dispersed in small convents, and others in the houses of their

---

(1) C. 7. n. 89.
(2) C. 33.
(3) T. 1. p. 30.
(4) 1. 78. n. 32.
(5) C. 6. Hist. Poloniae, ad an. 1218.

parents and friends. In order to facilitate the success of this commission, the saint requested that three cardinals should be appointed to assist him, to which the Pope assented, and named for that purpose Hugolini, dean of the Sacred College, Nicholas bishop of Tusculum, and Stephen, of Fossa Nuova, cardinal priest of the twelve Apostles. S. Dominic, having obtained the consent of the Pope, offered to give his own convent of S. Sisto to the nuns, and to build a new one for his friars on the Aventine. The nuns who lived in the small convents were easily induced to embrace the reform, but those of the great convent of S. Mary's beyond the Tiber obstinately refused. The saint repaired thither with the three cardinals already mentioned and addressed the nuns with such force of reasoning, and so much charity, that they all, except one, promised to obey. But the devil was not to be discomfited so easily. Immediately after the cardinals and S. Dominic had gone away, the parents and friends of the nuns went to S. Mary's to implore them not to take a step which could never be recalled; that, if they did, they would repent it; and that they ought never abandon their convent which was enriched by so many privileges. Such discourses were too flattering not to please women, who, although vowed to religion, held a certain amount of uncontrolled freedom too dear; so they all changed their minds and resolved to remain where they were. On hearing this, S. Dominic returned to S. Mary's to say mass, and after he had offered the holy sacrifice he addressed them with tears in his eyes, saying : « Can you then repent of a pro-« mise you have made to God ? Can you refuse « to give yourselves up to Him without reserve, « and to serve Him with your whole hearts ? » He went on in a strain of such affecting exhortation that after his discourse, the abbess and all the nuns confirmed by vow their readiness to comply with his directions. On Ash-Wednesday (1218) they took possession of their new convent, and while they were assembled in the chapter-room with the three cardinals treating of the rights and administration of the community, a messenger came to inform them that the young prince Napoleon, cardinal Stephen's nephew, had fallen from his horse, near the Porta S. Sebastiano, and was killed. The news so stunned cardinal Stephen that he fell speechless on the breast of S. Dominic who was sitting by his side. The saint, after in vain endeavouring to alleviate his grief, ordered the lifeless body to be brought to the chapter-room, and told brother Tancred to prepare the altar that he might say mass. The holy sacrifice being ended, the man of God put the broken limbs in their proper places, and, after spending some time in prayer, made the sign of the Cross over the body, and lifting up his hands to heaven, cried out with a loud voice : « Napoleon, I say « to thee, in the name of our Lord Jesus Christ, « arise ». That instant the young man arose safe and sound, in the presence of the three cardinals, the friars, and nuns, and an immense concourse of people.

CHAPEL OF THE BLESSED SACRAMENT.

This chapel, at the end of the aisle opposite S. Dominic's chapel, is dedicated to S. John the Baptist, whose statue, by Simon the brother of Donatello, is over the altar. On one side is painted the Baptist reproving Herod for having married his brother's wife; and on the other his decapitation, and his head given to the dancing girl on a dish. The chapel is vaulted, in a manner rare in Rome, with white glazed terra-cotta sunk panels, in the centre of each of which is a rose in alto-rilievo.

The two monuments immediately outside the chapel are very good specimens of cinque-cento work, especially that of cardinal Roverella, which bears the date of 1476. The cardinal is in a recumbent posture with two angels keeping watch over him, one at his head and the other at his feet. In the arched top of the monument is the Almighty surrounded by angels, and below them the Blessed Virgin with the

Divine Infant sitting on her knees. Two angels stand by their side. On the right, S. Peter is presenting the cardinal to our Lord and His Blessed Mother. S. Paul is on the opposite side. Two exquisitely carved candelabra, in bas-relief, form a border for the sides of the monument; and the sarcophagus is highly decorated with very graceful arabesques, and the symbols of the fine arts of which it would appear the cardinal was a generous protector. At the base of the tomb there are angels, one on each side, admirably designed and executed. A little to the right, towards the sacristy, is the tomb of John Francis Brusati, nephew of cardinal Roverella, and archbishop of Nicosia in Cyprus.

CHAPEL OF THE ROSARY.

The altar-piece of the Rosary chapel, on the left of the apse, representing the Madonna and Child giving Rosaries to S. Dominic and S. Catharine, is by Conca. It is well designed and admirably executed. On the wall to the left, S. Francis of Assisi is depicted receiving the Stigmata on Mount Alverno, and on the right S. Charles Borromeo distributing alms to the poor. Outside the chapel to the left, is the monument of cardinal Venerio of Recanati who died in 1479. The columns sculptured with vine-tendrils, and birds pecking at the grapes, are very beautiful. The capitals are admirable specimens of fine pierced work. On the rim of one of them is engraved the name « Mercurius « Presb. S. Clementis » : very probably the same John Mercurius, titular of the basilica, who erected an altar in it under the Popedom of S. Hormisdas, 514, 523, and therefore they must have been removed from the underground basilica. On a pilaster, opposite this monument, is a pleasing picture, by an unknown artist, of the Virgin and Child, and S. John. The children are playing together, and our Lady, kneeling with her hands joined, earnestly looks at them. Angels are scattering roses on their heads. On the floor, to the right, is the tomb of cardinal Henry of S. Allosio who died in 1450.

PORCH, QUADRIPORTICO, AND VESTIBULE.

Having described the modern portions of the church, we will proceed to examine it as carrying out the primitive arrangements of a Christian basilica reproduced from the original beneath. First the porch, once painted, is roughly built with four antique columns sustaining a Gothic canopy, three of the columns being of granite and one of cipollino, differing in order and diameter, two having Corinthian and two Ionic capitals; the door-jambs are rudely sculptured with tracings of dissimilar designs ; there are also remains of other buildings, and the whole is carelessly constructed.

The hangings and tapestry at the door of Roman churches on feast-days keep up a custom Pagan as well as Christian. Pliny says Zeuxis was so rich that he displayed his name woven in gold in the curtains shown at Olympia. And Aristotle gives a minute description of one of purple bought from the Carthagenians, embroidered with animals and gods, which when it was exhibited by Alcisthanes at the great festival of Juno Lacinia, to which all Italy used to flock, drew all eyes from the others. The iron rod is still in its place for those curtains of which the poet of the fourth century Aurelius Prudentius Clemens says : « Quae festis « suspendam pallia fortis ? » The bishop of Uzales in Africa, who lived in the fifth century, mentions that before the oratory, in which were preserved the relics of the protomartyr S. Stephen, a veil was placed on which the saint was painted carrying a cross upon his shoulders. From this outer porch we enter the quadriportico which is oblong, being 62 feet by 50, and surrounded on three sides by 16 pillars, twelve of grey Bigio marble, three of Numidian marble, and one of Oriental granite. The pavement of the atrium contains many fragments of green and white serpentine, and in the centre of the court is the *impluvium* to receive the rain. So far we have the usual arrangement of the Roman palace. The fountain at which the Christians purified themselves before entering the house ˵of God, was restored in 1868. In the porticoes of the ancient palaces family busts and other ornaments were found. In those of the church were placed pictures. In the fourth century, S. Asterius, after having prayed at leisure in the church, was passing hurriedly through one of the porticoes when he was arrested by a painting representing the martyrdom of S. Euphemia. It was in the fifth century, when the holy Cross was exposed for public veneration at Jerusalem, that Mary of Egypt was withheld from entering a church by an invisible hand thrice and four times. Smitten by her bad life she retired into a corner of the court. There she perceived a picture of the Mother of God; and, fixing her eyes upon it, begged her by her incomparable purity to help a lost woman to consecrate her life in penance, and allow her to venerate the sacred wood of her redemption. Then with ease she went up to the very middle of the church, kissed the pavement in tears; knelt again before the picture, and asked the witness of her promise to guide her. She seemed to hear a voice « if thou goest beyond « the Jordan, thou shalt there find rest and comfort ». Weeping and looking at the image, she begged the Blessed Virgin never to abandon her; and followed

up her conversion by that forty years' solitary penance in the desert, which has made her one of the most marvellous penitents in the history of the Church. We might accuse Jerome the austere, beating his emaciated breast in the wilderness, of harshness when he writes : « Gird yourselves and lament » (1).
« He that is a sinner, whom his own conscience
« reproves, let him gird himself with sackcloth, and
« lament both his own sins and those of the peo-
« ple; and enter into the church which he had left
« on account of his sins, and let him sleep in
« sackcloth, that by austerity of life he may com-
« pensate for his past delights ». The bishop of Barcelona, S. Pacian, writes about 374 : « What
« shall I do now, the priest that am required to
« effect a cure ? It is late for such a case : still
« if you can bear the knife and caustic, I can
« yet cure. Here is the prophetic knife: ' Be con-
« verted to the Lord your God in fasting, and in weep-
« ing, and in mourning, and rend your hearts ' (2).
« Be not afraid dearly beloved of the cutting. David
« bore it : he lay in filthy ashes, and was disfigured by a robe of a mean sackcloth. I beseech
« you therefore, brethren, by the faith of the Church,
« let not shame overcome you in this work: let it

---

(1) Joel 1. 13.
(2) Ibid. 2. 12.

« not be irksome to you to make, your own, the
« seasonable remedies of salvation: to humble your
« minds with sorrow, to strew yourselves with ashes,
« to wear yourselves with fasting and grief ; and
« to obtain the help of others' prayers ». Let us
now turn to a bishop, who when told that the emperor, who had already done eight months' penance after he had met and repelled him from the church-porch, was again approaching, answered : « If so,
« I tell you plainly I shall forbid him to enter the
« church-porch; and if he think good to turn his
« power into force and tyranny, I am most ready to
« undergo any death, and to present my throat to the
« sword ». S. Ambrose again says: « I have known
« some who in penitence have furrowed their cheeks
« with tears, have worn them away with continual
« weeping, have cast themselves down to be trodden
« on by all, and with a countenance pallid with fast-
« ing have had the appearance of the dead in a breath-
« ing body ». In another place he says : « I have
« more easily found those who have preserved their
« innocence, than those who have done penance in
« a befitting manner. The world is to be renounced,
« sleep less indulged in than nature demands : dis-
« turb it with groans, interrupt it with sighs, set
« it aside for prayers : a man must so live as to
« die to the uses of this life, he must deny himself

« and be entirely changed » (1). If we would turn to S. Augustine the convert of S. Ambrose, we are encouraged by the communion of saints: « As regards, « daily, momentary, light sins, without which this life « is not passed, the daily prayer of the faithful satis- « fies » (2). But he advises a man who is conscious of deadly sins to come to the prelate through whom the keys are ministered to him in the Church. « So « that if his sin is not merely to his own injury, « but also to the great scandal of others, and it « seems to the prelate a thing expedient for the « utility of the Church, let him not refuse to do « penance in the presence of many, or even of the « whole people : let him offer no resistance, nor, « through shame, add the tumour of pride to his « deadly mortal wound ». Two hundred years before, Tertullian enforced the same practice: « Con- « fession is a discipline for the abasement and hu- « miliation of man, enjoining such a manner of life « as invites mercy. It directs also even in the mat- « ter of dress and food, to lie in sackcloth and ashes, « to hide the body in filthy garments, to cast « down the spirit with mourning, to exchange the « sins which he has committed for severe treatment; « for the rest, to use simple things for meat and

---

(1) T. II. Lib. II. de Poenit. c. X. n. 96. 436-7.
(2) T. II. Enchirid. de Fide, n. 17.

« drink"; to wit, not for the belly's, but for the
« soul's, sake; for the most part also to cherish
« prayer by fasts, to groan, to weep, and to
« moan, day and night, unto the Lord his God, to
« throw himself upon the ground before the priests,
« and to fall on his knees before the Altar of God;
« to enjoin all the brethren to bear the message
« of his prayer for mercy » (1). Besides hearty repentance and private penance, the sinner had in some cases to humble himself, as S. Augustine notices, in the sight of all the people, and beg to be restored to their communion. For in the unity of the Church it never entered men's minds to haggle, and make terms as to the conditions on which they would condescend to be received, but they deplored their separation as an evil intolerable to their own consciences, worth any humiliation in exchange for that kiss of peace which they could only deserve by submission to authority. « Should any one, hav-
« ing secret sins, yet, for Christ's sake, hearti-
« ly do penance, how shall he receive the reward,
« if he be not restored to communion? I would
« have the guilty hope for pardon: let him beg
« it with tears, let him beg it with sighs, beg
« it with the tears of all the people: that he may
« be pardoned, let him implore. And, in case com-

---

(1) De Poenitentia, n. 8-12. p. 126.

« munion has been deferred a second and a third
« time, let him believe that he has been too remiss
« in his supplication : let him increase his tears,
« then let him return in deeper distress, embrace
« their feet, cover them with kisses, wash them
« with his tears, nor let them go that the Lord
« Jesus may say of him : ' Many sins are for-
« given him, because he hath loved much ' » (1).

When such was the spirit of the Church we know with what vigour the archbishop repulsed the guilty Theodosius ; yet S. Paulinus of Milan relates, in his life of S. Ambrose, that whenever any one confessed his sins to him, he wept so as to compel the penitent also to weep. Zozomen of the Greek Church, A. D. 450, who remarks that « it is a sacerdotal law « that the things done contrary to the sentiment of the « Bishop of the Romans be looked upon as null », has preserved for us a graphic picture of the public penitents. Of auricular confession he says : « As not to
« sin at all, seems to belong to a nature more divine
« than that of man's, and God has commanded pardon
« to be granted to the penitent even though he may
« often sin, and as in begging pardon, it is neces-
« sary to confess also the sin, it, from the beginning,
« deservedly seemed to the priests a burthensome thing
« to proclaim the sins, as in a theatre, in the cogni-

---

(1) S. Ambrose, T. II. L. I. de Poenit. c. XVI. p. 414.

« zance of the whole multitude of the church, they
« appointed to this office a priest from among those
« whose lives were best regulated, one both silent
« and prudent, to whom they who had sinned went
« and acknowledged their deeds ». And, in 460, S. Leo
the Great prohibited public Confession. « I ordain
« that, that presumptuous conduct, which, I have
« lately learned, is by an unlawful usurpation pursued
« by certain persons, in opposition to an apostolic
« regulation be by every means set aside. That is, as
« regards the penance which is applied for by the
« faithful, let not a written declaration of the nature of
« their individual sins be publicly recited; since it is
« sufficient that the guilt of their consciences be made
« known to priests alone by secret confession » (1).
The priest, in fact, gave his absolution upon condition
of the penitent performing his penance. « But »,
says Zozomen, « nothing of this was required by
« the Novatians, who make no account of repentance;
« though among the other sects (heresies), this
« custom prevails even unto this day. And in the
« church of the Romans, it is carefully preserved.
« For there the place of those who are in penitence,
« where they stand in sadness, and with signs of
« grief, is visible (to all). And when the liturgy

---

(1) Ep. CLXVIII. ad universos Episcopos per Campaniam, Samnium et Picenum constitutos, c. 2. p. 1430-1.

« of God is at length completed, without partaking
« of the things which are the privilege of the ini-
« tiated; with groans and lamentations they cast
« themselves prone upon the ground, and the bishop
« meeting them face to face, in tears, falls in like man-
« ner upon the pavement, and with loud lament, the
« whole assembly of the church is drowned in tears.
« And after this, the bishop raises the prostrate: and
« having offered up a suitable prayer for the sinners
« who are penitent, he dismisses them. But pri-
« vately each one being voluntarily afflicted, either by
« fasts, or abstinence from food, or in other ways
« appointed him, he awaits the time which the bishop
« has assigned to him. But, at the appointed time,
« having discharged the punishment, as it were a debt,
« he is freed from sin, and associates with the people
« in the church. The priests of the Romans observe
« these things, from the beginning, even unto our
« days » (1). And we have from an African Synod
of the fourth century the rationale of this conduct of
the bishop, and the place appointed for the penitent.
« Let the periods of penance be adjudged to penitents,
« by the determination of the bishop according to the
« difference of their sins: and a priest shall not recon-
« cile a penitent without consulting the bishop, except
« necessity, arising from the absence of the bishop, com-

---

(1) H. E. Lib. VII. c. 16. p. 299. 301.

« pel him : but as to the penitent whose crime is public
« and most notorious, disturbing the whole church, he
« shall impose bonds on him before the apsis » (1).
S. Basil mentions all the classes of these penitents
when he says in his 44th Canon that the adulterer
should be excluded from participation in the holy
mysteries for fifteen years : to spend the first four
among the mourners, then five among the listeners,
then four among the prostrate, and the remaining two
among the standers. The Council of Nicaea directs
that persons who fell away without compulsion, as happened under the tyranny of Licinius, if truly repentant, should pass three years among the hearers as
believers, and during seven years shall be among the
prostrate, and during two years shall communicate
without the oblation. The Council of Ancyra directs
that persons who fell before the idols, but had not
eaten the meats that had been offered to them, should
prostrate for two years, and communicate in the
third without the oblation in order that they might
receive full communion in the fourth year. « But
« the bishops have the power, having considered
« the manner of their conversion, to deal indulgently
« with them, or to add a longer period. But above
« all things, let their previous, as well as their
« subsequent life, be enquired into, and so let the

---

(1) Codex Can. Eccl. Afr. Can. XLII. Col. 1069. Labb. T. II.

« indulgence be measured out » (1). S. Gregory of Nyssa says: « The Canon law for fornicators is « that they shall be utterly cast forth from prayer « during three years, and be allowed to be *hear-* « *ers* only for three further years. But, in favour « of those who with special zeal avail themselves « of the time of conversion, and in their lives « exhibit a return to what is good, it is in his « power, who has the regulation of the dispensation « of the church for a beneficial end, to shorten the « period of *hearing*, and to introduce such men « earlier to the state of *conversion*, and, further « to lessen this period also, and to bestow *com-* « *munion* earlier, according as, from his own judg- « ment, he comes to a decision respecting the state of « the person under cure » (2). Evidently under such discipline persons could not travesty the religious dress and sneak into Catholic churches to commit sacrilege against the Eucharist by receiving it. S. Gregory notices that penitents were not to be deprived of the Viaticum, but, if they recovered, were to complete their period of penance. Of the practice of the West, S. Innocent I, A. D. 417, writes: « As regards penitents, who do penance, whether for « more grievous or for lesser offences, if sickness

---

(1) Can. V. Col. 1456-7. Labb. t. I.
(2) T. II. Ep. Can. ad Letoium, p. 119.

« do not intervene, the usage of the Roman Church
« demonstrates that they are to have remission grant-
« ed them on the Thursday before Easter. For the
« rest, as to estimating the grievousness of the trans-
« gressions, it is for the priest to judge, by attend-
« ing to the confession of the penitent, and to the
« grief and tears of the amending sinner, and then
« to order him to be set free when he sees his satis-
« faction such as is suitable : or, if any such fall
« ill, so as to be despaired of, he must be par-
« doned before Easter, lest he depart this world
« without communion » (1).

As we passed through the quadriportico to the great door of the church, persons excommunicated, and utterly cast forth from prayer for a time, weepers, and mourners in sackcloth and ashes, winterers as abiding the elements; would lament their exclusion, and beg for prayers. The vestibule of the modern church being precisely over the ancient one, the first steps into it would bring us among the catechumens and penitential hearers, both of whom were obliged to withdraw at the consecration. They were under the rod of the ostiarius, and hence this place probably got its name, narthex signifying a rod.

---

(1) Ep. XXV. Decentio, n. 10. Galland. T. VIII. p. 589.

INTERIOR OF THE CHURCH.

The interior of the church before us is 170 feet 6 inches long, by 70 feet 9 inches in width. On either hand the sixteen antique columns separating the nave from the aisles form a perspective to the apse : five of them are Parian marble, and of these four are fluted and one plain; five others of Numidian marble, three of granitello, two of Oriental granite, and one of *bigio*. The pavement is of beautiful « *Opus Alexandrinum* » in varied patterns. The greater part of the nave is occupied by the choir with its paschal candlestick and elevated ambones on either side. At its further end is the shrine of the Martyr to whom the church is dedicated, with the altar over it, raised in front of the bishops throne and the sedilia for the priests. The sight is arrested, at this most important point of a Christian basilica, by the ciborium over the altar and the rich mosaics of the apse. The floor of the church was given up to the laity. We will not attempt to assign the precise places occupied by the other penitents after passing the catechumens and *hearers* in the narthex. Butler says that the prostrate were at the bottom of the nave, and the *standers* above the ambones. S. Charles Borromeo revived the separation of men and women; and Ciam-

pini says, the men were in the south aisle, and the women in the north. The Pontifical book says, Pope Symmachus made the Oratory of the holy Cross on the men's side, Sergius I made a golden image of S. Peter on the women's side; Gregory III an oratory next the triumphal arch on the men's side. In the East the separation was made effectual by enclosures with doors. The empress S. Helen would be in her proper place in the women's department. Theodosius prayed in the chancel till S. Ambrose reproved him for it; and the emperor's throne was placed in the upper end of the men's apartment next the sanctuary. In the plan which Ciampini gives of S. Clement's he assigns the chapel of the Blessed Sacrament as the *Matronaeum*, or the place appointed for matrons; and the chapel of our Lady of the Rosary, as the Senatorium, or place for the Senator and other persons of distinction.

The object of the separation was not merely to prevent remarks upon bonnets and dress, and glances directed anywhere but to the altar. It was most important for the sacrifice and the communion. The Apostolical Constitutions of the third century direct some of the deacons to attend upon the oblation ministering the body of our Lord with fear, and others to watch the multitude, and keep them silent. During the sacrifice the people were to stand and pray in silence: then to communicate each rank

by itself, women with their heads veiled : the doors guarded lest an unbeliever, or one not initiated entered in. S. Hilary says: « We must not treat indis-
« criminately, nor unwisely, and without caution, of the
« Incarnation of the Word of God, and the mystery of
« the Passion, and the power of the Incarnation » (1).
In the nineteenth century when grace is made a jest for flippant lawyers, baptism an open question, ordination a ceremony signifying nothing, theology the staple of lay reviews, and the filth of the divorce court the entertainment of the people, the reticence of the fourth century will, doubtless, appear, to the scoffers of religion, antiquated and over nice. S. Ambrose remarks that he was on the Lord's day, after having dismissed the catechumens, expounding the creed in the baptisteries of the basilica. « These
« mysteries which the Church now makes known
« to thee who art transferred from among the ca-
« techumens, it is not the custom to make known
« to the Gentiles; for to a Gentile we do not make
« known the mysteries concerning the Father, Son,
« and Holy Ghost: neither do we speak plainly of the
« mysteries before catechumens ». And precisely because the doctrine of the Trinity was not communicated to them, the Lord's prayer was not to be published, nor the apostles' creed written. « A fortiori » the

---

(1) Comm. in Matth. c. VI. n. 1. p. 696. t. I.

real presence was not to be exposed, as S. Chrysostom says, before Gentiles who might scoff at it, or before catechumens whose curiosity might be roused and ignorance scandalized. In the present day the depths of ignorance cast a dark cloud, indeed, about the consecrated host, but do not prevent the scandal. The ancient practice was effectual. « When « the catechumen has joined his praise to that of « the initiated, he withdraws from the more se- « cret mysteries, and is excluded from Christ's sa- « crifice » (1). In the same fifth century, Theodoret says of the divine food, and the spiritual doctrine, and the mystic and immortal banquet which the initiated recognize: « These things are plain to « the initiated and do not need explanation : for « they are acquainted both with the spiritual oil « wherewith they had their heads anointed, and with « that inebration which weakens not, but strengthens, « and that mystic food which he, who has become « bridegroom, besides a shepherd, sets before us » (2). We are thus prepared to listen to the ancient discipline of the Church, to see the propriety of not tempting ignorant persons by their own ignorance, to accept the teaching of the Church without which ignorance is an inheritance; and even, in the rite,

---

(1) S. Cyril of Alexandria, de Ador. in Sp. et Ver. p. 445.
(2) T. I. in Ps. XXII. p. 746-50.

to see the utility of these eastern flabella which excite the derision of the uninstructed, when the chant rises in S. Peter's, and the tiared Pontiff is dimly seen in the distance borne onwards upon the shoulders of the faithful to the altar of sacrifice. « Let « other deacons walk about, and watch the men « and women that no noise be made, that no one « nod, or whisper, or slumber; and let the dea« cons stand at the doors of the men, and the « subdeacons at those of the women, that no one « go out, nor a door be opened, although it be « for one of the faithful, at the time of the obla« tion. Let one of the subdeacons bring water to « wash the hands of the priests, a symbol of the « purity of souls devoted to God. Then shall the « deacon immediately say : ' Let none of the ca« techumens, none of the hearers, none of the un« believers, none of the heterodox stay; you who « have prayed the foregoing prayer depart, let the « women take their children. Let no one have aught « against any one : let no one come in hypocrisy : « let us stand upright before the Lord with fear « and trembling to offer. ' When this is done, let « the deacons bring the gifts to the bishop at the « altar ; and let the priests stand at his right hand « and at his left, as disciples standing by their mas« ter. But let two of the deacons on each side of « the altar hold a fan made of thin membranes,

« or of peacock's feathers, or of linen, and let
« them silently drive away the flies, and the gnats,
« that they may not come near the chalices » (1).
Before we consider the part of the church especially devoted to the clergy, we will ask any of our readers who have been at the ceremonies by the tomb of the Apostle whether if religion is venerable by antiquity as well as by precept, the things they have seen there, and not understood, deserve to be laughed at?

The high altar is separated by marble panels from the laity, the penitents and catechumens. We have authority for this separation of the clergy from the lay congregation from so early a Pope as S. Clement, who says: « There are proper liturgies
« delivered to the chief priest, and a proper place
« assigned to the priests: and there are proper mi-
« nistrations incumbent on Levites, and the layman
« is adjudged to the appointments of laymen ». And we suppose S. Jerome speaks of what was the custom in his day, when the church of S. Clement kept his *memory* still. « It is not the same thing to shed
« tears for sin, and to handle the body of the Lord:
« it is not the same thing to lie prostrate at the feet
« of the brethren and to minister from an elevated
« spot the Eucharist to the people ». Before we ap-

---

(1) Apostolical Constitutions.

proach that elevated spot, which, in all the ancient basilicas, is nearly the same, a platform from wall to wall mounted by steps on either side of the altar, let us examine the choir on a lower level, but raised also, by one step, above the floor of the church. It is paved with Alexandrine work; the entrance gates are enriched with mosaics; the great marble panels are carved with wreaths, and crosses, and one conspicuous monogram frequently repeated: and on the jambs supporting them are engraved the fish, the dove, and branches of the vine.

The monogram is one of those puzzles of which Symmachus says to his friend : « I should like to « know whether you got all my letters sealed with « the ring in which my name is more readily un- « derstood than read ». S. Avitus of Vienne, like a sensible man, had his name in full round his monogram, that people might readily make it out. When Roman antiquaries confounded this choir with that of the basilica whence the panels had been brought up, they used to say it meant Nicholas. Ugonius, Alemannius, and Du Cange said so; but Ciampini thought it was *Johannes,* though what John he did not know. The distinguished author of Murray's Guide-Book said « John VIII ». If it means John, we have the name of John Mercurius in one of the carved capitals of cardinal Venerius' monument, which were probably the capitals of the ancient ciborium; and under the choir-panels are two marble beams, evidently the architraves of the same ciborium, on one of which is the inscription « *Salbo Hormisda Papa Mercurius presbyter cum sociis offert* », which shows that cardinal Mercurius, afterwards Pope John II, A. D. 532-535, put up the altar in the pontificate of Hormisdas, A. D. 514-523, and we naturally infer he put up the choir-panels also. And in addition to the guesses as to the period of the modern church, it is not improbable that the great earthquake of 896, twenty nine years after the death of Nicholas I, may have shaken the basilica, and perhaps thrown down the roof, when the frescoes of S. Clement, S. Alexius and S. Cyril, were fresh upon its walls. In which case the basilica, that was not filled up with casual ruin, but with soil and débris purposely compacted, may have given place to the new church two hundred years before Gregory VII and Paschal II, and the new church not have been destroyed by Guiscard at all. Paschal II may have repaired it, and executed the mosaics of the apse, in memory of his election in it, when he was repairing or rebuilding the four crowned Martyrs. And two hundred years after him, the nephew of Boniface VIII restored the mosaics in the concavity of the apse and inserted the tabernacle for the holy oils. The erudite author of Murray observes that the blocks of the choir are adjusted in a careless manner; and that the gospel-ambo being on the left

instead of the right hand, as in the basilica of S. Lorenzo, and in some other churches, is another reason for supposing that the choir, was carelessly set up, when removed from the church beneath. But the panels and pavement appear to have been carefully removed, and the different parts of the ancient choir accurately copied; and it is not likely that the builders did not know on which side the ambo ought to stand, although, without any haste or want of accuracy in placing the blocks, the settlement of the soil dislocated the joints and threw the panels out of the horizontal line. That very careful antiquary, Ciampini, engraves the gospel-ambo of S. Lorenzo without a hint that its position is more correct than that of S. Clement's. « We have thought », says he, « to
« note these things first, that as this kind of join-
« ings of dissimilar parts is everywhere occurring
« as well in S. Clement's as in the other very old
« basilicas, persons entering the vestibules of these
« churches may not stick in over nice animadver-
« sions, but rather go on with us to the more useful
« observation of the chief internal parts ». An ancient heretic used to ask: « What is the Easter that
« you celebrate ? You are again made to take up
« with Jewish fables. There is not to be any cele-
« bration of the Passover, for Christ our Passover is
« sacrificed ». To such a one the lofty spiral mosaic of our paschal candlestick is an eyesore, and,

instead of being lighted at the Gospel, the blest candle ought to be extinguished for ever. That striking of the flint on Holy Saturday and blessing the new light in the church; that prayer « Lord God, Father Omni-
« potent, light never failing, who art the Maker of
« all lights, bless this light which is blest and made
« holy by Thee who hast enlightened the whole world,
« that with that light we may be enkindled and il-
« luminated with the fire of Thy brightness; and as
« Thou wert a light to Moses going out of Egypt,
« so do Thou give light to our heart, and sense that
« we may deserve to come to light through Christ
« our Lord ». And the successive lighting of the church-lights when the sun is shining in the heavens, is surely superfluous and ridiculous excess. That chant of the deacon has no meaning when he goes up to the gospel-ambo and sings: « Now let the an-
« gelic host exult: the mysteries divine exult: and
« for the victory of so great a King the trumpet of
« salvation sound! Let the earth also rejoice illumi-
« nated with such splendour, and enlightened with
« the brightness of the eternal King, let it feel that
« the darkness of the whole world is dispersed. Let
« mother Church rejoice, adorned with the brightness
« of so great light; and may this temple resound
« with the loud voices of the people. Wherefore I be-
« seech you, most dear brethren, who are here pre-
« sent in the wonderful brightness of this holy light,

« to invoke with me the mercy of Almighty God.
« That He who has vouchsafed to number me among
« the Levites, without any merits of mine, would
« pour forth His brightness upon me, and enable
« me to perfect the praise of this light ».

And then follows « Oh surely necessary Adam's
« sin which by the death of Christ is blotted out!
« Oh happy fault which deserved to have such and
« so great a Redeemer! Oh truly blessed night,
« which alone deserved to know the time and the
« hour in which Christ rose again from worlds
« below. This is the night of which it is written:
« ' And the night shall be illumined as the day,
« and the night is my light in my delights ' ». And
when the ceremony goes on and the consecrated
hand waves the water to the four quarters of the
world, and the mystic candle thrice plunged in
the plenitude of the Holy Ghost within the baptismal font, we cannot think without pain of the
thousands of children who, in some countries where
Christianity is said to be part and parcel of the
law of the land, are never purified by that water, and whether baptism is a sacrament at all is a
question free to dispute. Ennodius of Pavia who
died in 521, and was styled a glorious Confessor by
Nicholas I, wrote two forms of blessing the paschal
candle in which the divine protection is implored
against storms and all danger from the malice of

invisible enemies. Some attribute the rite to Pope Zosimus A. D. 418: and the *Agnus Dei*, found with the relics under the altar of our church, may be of that date, for the archdeacon used to bless, on Holy Saturday, wax mingled with oil and impressed with the figure of a lamb, such as was found in the tomb of Mary Stilicho. S. Zeno, A. D. 362-383, says of the font « haste ye brethren who are about to be « washed. The living water tempered by the Holy « Spirit, and with the pleasantest fire, with soothing « murmur now invites you » (1). And S. Pacian, A. D. 371, says that the justice of Christ must need pass into the human race, Christ begetting in the Church by means of the priests : « These things « cannot be otherwise fulfilled than by the sacrament « of the laver, and of the chrism of the bishop » (2). And any one who considers that lights were borne before the emperors, and the fondness of the Christians for lights, incense, and balsams, in the catacombs, will hardly suppose that so obvious a figure as the descent of light into the illuminative waters was neglected.

On either side of the choir are the *ambones*. The word *ambo* is said to be derived from the Greek ἀναβαίνειν, to go up, which might apply to any other

---

(1) Lib. II. Tract. 35. Invit. 6. ad Font. Galland. T. I. p. 149.
(2) Sermo de Baptism. n. 3. Galland. T. VII. p. 308.

staircase, so that it is possible that *ambones* may be a colloquial corruption of *umbones*, that is convex projections, or elevated promontories. They are of remote antiquity. S. Augustine recounts (1) that Victorinus, the Rhetorician, read his profession of faith from the ambo. On the east side of the gospel ambo is a beautiful spiral candlestick, in mosaic, for the paschal candle. The connection between the light to lighten the Gentiles represented by the paschal candle, and the higher step in the *ambo* from which the deacon reads the gospel is evident. Ciampini says that S. Cyprian calls *ambo* the tribunal. The gospel *ambo* in our church has a double staircase, on one side towards the altar, on the other towards the narthex. According to an old Roman *ordo*, the two accolytes with their candles separated when they reached the *ambo*, two subdeacons with thuribles, and the deacon with the gospel passing between them; and going up into the *ambo* by one staircase, the subdeacons immediately descended by the other and there stood. A third subdeacon, preceding the deacon, held in his left hand the gospel to be opened at the mark, and the deacon read on that higher step in the *ambo* which a subdeacon was not to mount, it being especially reserved for the gospel. The deacon

---

(1) Confessions of S. Augustine, book VIII. c 11.

read the gospel with his face turned to the North. The gospel ambones in S. Lorenzo and S. Pancras are similar to that of S. Clement's. All three having that central projection from which the modern pulpit is taken: in S. Pancras, put up, in 1249, by Innocent IV, it is ornamented by twisted columns, and supported by a pillar below as some pulpits are. But Ciampini remarks that S. Clement's has a double *ambo*, and that it is an indication of the greater antiquity of the church to suit that very ancient rite of the Roman Ordo, by which the deacon stood turned to the south aisle in which the men were wont to be, but otherwise to the north, a rite not everywhere observed in the eighth and following centuries. The explanation he supposed to be that if the southern aisle was quite full of men and the middle of the nave also, the deacon turned to the women's side on the north, thus comprising the centre nave as well; but if the men were fewer and the southern aisle held all, then he turned to that side. On the women's side to the north we have another ambo, but lower, with its two marble desks, of which the highest, next the altar, was for the subdeacon who turned towards the altar to read the Epistle without regarding East or West. The altar in S. Clement's is at the west end, but the celebrant, standing in front of it, always faces the East. The lower desk turned to the East was for the cantor to sing the gradual, responsories, and allelujas ; and is only found where the subdeacon by turning to the altar had his back to the East , whereas if he faced the East a second desk for the cantor would be superfluous. Anastasius the librarian says it was Celestine I who, before the year 432 , had the gradual sung at Mass. We have thus considered the choir, raised and separated from the laity , and its uses; but it was a lower ecclesiastical place, and we must see whence the deacon had come down into it to read the gospel.

Speaking of that holy table in the cathedral church of Rome, once covered with plates of silver, a modern guide-book says : « It is shown as that « on which the last supper was laid ; and that, at « S. Pudentiana, the table on which S. Peter ate was « placed under the altar ». But these descriptions, materially true, hardly reach the truth. The French protestant critic, Le Clerc, observes that « certain « protestant writers, who fancy that the traditions « of the four or five first centuries ought to be « joined with the scripture , have denied that the « saints were prayed to in the fourth century; but « they should not have framed a material system « before they were well instructed in facts , since « they may be convinced of this by several places « out of Prudentius ». And he also says : « It « ought to be observed that, upon the grave, there

« is a table, or an altar, on which they cele-
« brated the Eucharist, so that the image was placed
« upon the altar, precisely where they are wont to
« place images now in the church of Rome ».

Leaving the *ambones* behind, and returning with the deacon up the choir, the following arrangement is before us; a porphyry slab with the inscription:

FLAVIVS CLEMENS
MARTYR
HIC
FELICITER
EST TVMVLATVS

« Flavius Clement martyr is here happily buried ».

Lower down, on the cornice over the *transenna*, behind which are preserved the relics of SS. Clement and Ignatius, is the following inscription:

HIC
REQVIESCVNT
CORPORA SANCTORVM
CLEMENTIS PAPAE
ET
IGNATII EPISCOPI
ET MARTYRVM

In the basilicas, with some rare exceptions, the body of the saint was placed beneath the altar protected by *transennae;* and at S. Alexander's, on the Nomentan way, were discovered, in 1854, the remains of such an altar, and the *transennae,* with the name of the saint and the bishop who dedicated it. As we stand below the altar before the slab of the martyr consul Clement, on either hand are two white marble *transennae* admirably worked, and they were once, probably, in their proper place in the lower basilica. These net-work panels sufficed to admit air to the lamps within, and did not hide the martyr's body from the sight of the worshipper. In the more ancient *transennae* the interstices were larger that cloths might be passed through them to touch the body; for the corporeal relics were not then generally distributed. On either side of the shrine, steps lead to the platform upon which the altar stands; and to know the use of the altar, we must turn to the episcopal chair behind it, raised by steps above the sedilia, for the priests, diverging from it on both sides. The back of this chair is of white Grecian marble on which the word « Martyr » in large letters is not inappropriately read. The bishop presiding there has passed step by step through the four minor Orders, beginning with the door-keeper; then through the holy orders of subdeacon and deacon, before the sacramental seal of the priesthood imprinted an indelible character for weal or woe upon his soul ; and if in rank and order he now possesses the fulness of the priesthood, and the Orders necessary for the altar can be conferred by him alone , there is one greater still to whom *ad limina apostolorum* he must render an account. Although he has not borne the successive duties of each rank for so long a time as in the ancient discipline of the Church, he began, by the denial of himself, the dedication of his whole will to God. His power and his strength are derived from that altar before him from that Θυσιαστηριον of sacrifice from which they cannot eat who do service in the tabernacle (1). Once he need only have raised his eyes to the silver dove suspended by a chain, which is still preserved, from the ciborium over the altar , to know that *there* was light, and life, and love, that unspeakable Presence, life of the soul, perpetual health of the mind, the bread of angels, eaten by the priest at that table under the sacred veils, carefully reserved that the triumph of Christ might be consummated in that most glorious act when still upon earth He is carried to heal the sick, and give courage to the dying. The ciborium is sustained by four pillars, two of *paonazzetto* and two of *marmo scritto*, precisely such as were found at S. Alexander's and might be seen

---

(1) Hebr. XIII. v. 10.

in the last century in the church of SS. Peter and Marcellinus. Ciampini considered this part known as the Confession so important that he engraved the ciborium of SS. Peter and Marcellinus as well as that of S. Clement. The bishop then was most appropriately placed in that seat where the praetor had decided so many vulgar causes, for between him and the people is no longer the table upon which the death warrant of Christians had been signed, but the altar upon which the Lamb of God who taketh away the sins of the world is immolated. S. John Chrysostom says : « When thou « art going to approach the sacred table, consider « too that the King of all is present there : for, « indeed, he is present really, thoroughly acquainted « with each one's disposition, and seeing who comes « with becoming holiness, who with a wicked con- « science, with impure and foul thoughts, with evil « deeds » (1). And it is precisely because, in the presence of that King, His human court must keep their proper places so as to discharge their limited service, the whole arrangements of His sacred palace have been made ; not at random, but for his intelligent creatures to pay Him suitable honour.

The personality of Christ upon the altar is reflected in the magnificence of that highest place where

---

(1) T. VI. In Illud. Vidi Dom. n. 4. p. 165.

the clergy are found; and the beautiful and elaborate mosaic with the inscription :

« Ecclesiam Christi viti similabimus isti
« Quam lex arentem, sed Crux facit esse virentem »,

« The Church of Christ we liken to that vine
« The law made dry, the cross all green to shine »,

was meant to teach what, long years after, the Council of Trent commanded bishops to teach « that by « means of the history of the mysteries of our re- « demption, portrayed by paintings and other re- « presentations, the people is instructed and confirmed « in remembering and continually revolving in their « mind the articles of faith ». Over the heads of the clergy, and out of their sight, whose minds ought not to be distracted from the altar, and whose eyes, looking beyond the altar, fall upon the people for whose souls they are responsible, that symbolical profusion of coloured shapes was to the people a certain image of heaven and of the connection between the Church on earth and in heaven. In the highest centre is a small cross; and in the circle below it the head of our Saviour with the Gospel, a hint expressed also in the inscription (« *Gloria in* « *excelsis Deo sedenti super thronum, et in terra* « *pax hominibus bonae voluntatis* », « Glory be to « God on high sitting upon his throne, and on

« earth peace to men of good will » into which the circle falls) that the good tidings were to men of good will, and his eyes vigilant to behold and bless them. The emblems of the four Evangelists express the connection between the prophetic vision of Ezechiel in the old law and that of S. John in the new. « The face of a man signifies Mathew who began to write, as it were of a man, the book of the generation of Jesus Christ : then Mark in whom is heard the voice of the lion roaring in the desert, the voice of one crying in the wilderness: the face of the calf which sets forth that Luke began from Zachary the priest : the eagle, John who, hasting to higher things, treats of the Word of God ». And in the Apocalypse (1) there is the same meaning where it is said, « the first living creature like to a lion, and the second like to a calf, the third having the face as it were of a man, the fourth like an eagle in flight. And the four living creatures had each of them six wings, and round about and within they are full of eyes, and they rested not day or night saying : Holy, Holy, Holy, Lord God Almighty who was and who is and who is to come ». The immediate connection between the church in heaven and the things of earth, between our Lord in glory and the diffusion of his Gospel here, is

---

(1) C. 4.

shown in the apostles, and martyr saints who succeed them. On the right is Peter instructing Clement with the inscription: « *Respice promissum, Clemens,* « *a me tibi Christum* », « Clement, behold Christ « promised by me to you ». On the left Paul arguing with the deacon S. Laurence, and the inscription « *De cruce, Laurenti, Paulo familiare* « *docenti* », « Paul. familiarly teaching Laurence « about the Cross ». The latter is evidently an allusion to some tradition connected with the Oratory of S. Laurence *super Clementem* at the Scala Santa ; we regret that we do not know what it is. S. Laurence, broiled alive in 258 by the enraged Praefect to whom he showed the poor as the treasures of the Church, was taught the scriptures and spiritual life by Xyxtus II. His last prayer was for the conversion of the city ; and he asked it for the sake of the two apostles Peter and Paul who had there began to plant the Cross of Christ, and had watered that city with their blood. It is a pleasing thought that the most beautiful lettered pectoral Cross yet discovered, a gold reliquary of the sixth century, with the inscription « The Cross is life to me, death, « o enemy ! to thee », was found in his basilica. The mind of the Christian artist was not satisfied without bringing down the glory of God on high to the predestined places of the earth. And he does it by placing, below S. Peter, Jeremias who mourned over the city that was to be forsaken. The prophet holds in his hand the scroll of Baruch « *Hic est Dominus noster, et non estimabitur alius absque illo* », « This is our Lord and there shall no other be accounted of in comparison of him ». The city of Jerusalem is below him. Under S. Paul, he gives the prophet of the virginal birth of Christ, Isaias, with the inscription « *Vidi Dominum sedentem super solium* », « I saw the Lord sitting upon the throne »; and below him Bethlehem with the child in the arch over its gate. This part of the mosaic has been very little restored, and was probably executed by cardinal Anastasius, in 1108, whose name is on the chair in front of the high altar. That portion of the mosaic which fills the concavity of the arch is the most elegant in Rome, and was probably restored, if not made, by cardinal Cajetan whose name is over the gothic tabernacle. If so, it is of the age of Giotto, a hundred years before Masaccio, and he may have designed it. Giotto designed the *Navicella* over the door of S. Peter's. Cavallini who executed it was his contemporary, if not his pupil, and finished the mosaics on the facade of S. Maria in Trastevere. Gaddo Gaddi, whose son was Giotto's godson and pupil for many years, had a great reputation for mosaics, and was invited to Rome by Clement V. He finished Jacopo da Turitas' mosaics in S. Maria

Maggioré, and executed several relating to our Lady. The repairs in the mosaics of that basilica discovered the name of another artist Philippus Rusutus, A. D. 1317. But, as far as we know, none of these works show the elegant symbolism of the apse of S. Clement's. Giotto painted several frescoes in the Loggia of the Lateran, but the only one remaining is the portrait of cardinal Cajetan's uncle, Boniface VIII, proclaiming the jubilee of 1300, still preserved in that basilica. The concavity is the work of a great artistic mind in its conception, and, as regards execution, we know that Giotto improved the art of working in mosaics; and there is a marked affinity of style to that of the coloured marbles with which he decorated the buildings in his pictures and carried to perfection in his Campanile at Florence. Although the mosaics of S. John in Fonte, at Ravenna, show full-length figures enclosed in arabesque foliage, they have nothing in common with the graceful curves we see here; and the whole concavity, which is the crown of the work, is so superior, in symbolical style, as well as in drawing, to the rest, or any other mosaics in Rome, that it is easier to refer the design to Giotto, than to imagine an unknown artist possessed of similar power. Coming out of the gates of Bethlehem and Jerusalem, we have the usual subject of the twelve apostolic sheep with the mystic lamb, crowned with the

20

nimbus, in their midst. Above them is the following inscription which forms the lower border of the florid arabesques of the concavity :

« Ecclesiam Christi viti similabimus isti
« Quam lex arentem, sed crux facit esse virentem :
« De ligno Christi, Jacobi dens, Ignatiique
« Insupra scripti requiescunt corpore Christi ».

« The Church of Christ we liken to that vine,
« Which, the law parched, the cross makes green to shine ;
« O' th' wood of Christ, of James a tooth, and of Ignace
« In body of that Christ have found a resting place ».

The representation of the Cross excited the devotion of the faithful the more from the knowledge that a particle of the true Cross was before them; and the union of our Lord with his saints, and of His passion with theirs, was more than shadowed by placing a relic of an Apostle, and of the martyr Bishop of Antioch, with the true Cross in the very figure of His body. A broad border, rich with flowers and fruit, goes all round the inner edge of the concavity ; and we recognize in it the grapes, and ears of corn, symbolic of the Eucharistic species. In this border, just over the gate of Bethlehem, is a man with large bunches of grapes ; in the crown of the arch is the Constantinian monogram of Christ, and below it, on the right, a hare among grapes. The meaning of the hare, which is often found in

Christian monuments, is undecided. On a Syracusan lamp, round a jewelled cross, is a border of triangles and leaves, and hares running. In another is one hare, and in another the circular border terminates with a flying dove. It is suggested that the hare represents human nature prone to sin. The vine itself, however, was called *leporaria*, as it were the hare-plant, perhaps from some idea that its leaves had a peculiar attraction for these animals. On the tomb of a child is a hare eating a grape. Here at least, placed in the midst of Eucharistic emblems, the little hare is, more likely, a figure of the soul leaping to its choice food. By this Eucharistic border (if we may so call it) the main subject is framed. At the top, the opening of the heavens is indicated by the waving prismatic circle, and the hand in the wreath in the sky is a common emblem of Almighty power. On either side of it are two lambs. In the centre of his composition, the artist no longer dwells upon apostles and martyrs, but goes straight to the Passion. The Cross let down from the hand of the Almighty roots itself upon the earth in wondrous foliage, spreading, as the mystic vine, in bold and graceful curved lines over the whole field. With that higher instinct, which did not suffer him to represent the naked crucifixion as we have seen it by the naturalist Masaccio, he places, upon the Cross the humanity of our Saviour, decently and devoutly draped. The Virgin Mother and her adopted Son stand beside it, and on its four extremities are twelve spotless white doves, symbols of the Apostles. For the rest, he fills every part among the graceful windings of the vine with an admirable variety of birds and flowers, thus evidently determined to surround the cross with beauty. Where, as he passes under it, he must give other human figures, he makes them mere accessories, distinct, indeed, but not disturbing the luxuriant harmony in which he sets them. A little hart is feeding at the foot of the Cross ; perhaps symbolizing Adam in the garden of Paradise ; or it might be that the artist had in his mind the ending of the Canticles: « Flee away, « O my beloved, and be like to the roe, and to « the young hart upon the mountains of aromatical « spices ». The glad waters are gushing out below from four tongues, symbols of the four rivers which flowed through Paradise, and two thirsty harts, admirably drawn, are drinking from them. That mysterious 47th chapter of Ezechiel is before us. « And he brought me again to the gate of « the house, and behold waters issued out from « under the threshold of the house towards the East: « for the fore-front of the house looked towards « the East : but the waters came down on the « right side of the temple to the south side of the « altar. And he said to me : Surely thou hast

« seen, O son of man. And he said to me these
« waters that issue forth towards the hillocks of
« sand to the East, and go down to the plains
« of the desert, shall go into the sea, and shall
« go out, and the waters shall be healed. And
« every living creature that creepeth whithersoever
« the torrent shall come, shall live: and there shall
« be fishes in abundance after these waters shall come
« thither, and they shall be healed, and all things
« shall live to which the torrent shall come ». The
Christian fishes of the catacombs could have no better
origin than this torrent of healing waters from the
house turned to the East. Whether the artist had
intended to make this allusion, or not, he could not
have expressed more ably, than he has done, his motto,
that the Cross makes the vine dried up by the law
vigorously to bloom : its sap gushes out in living
streams, and the living creatures draw nigh to it
to drink and live. There he has set the pelicans of
the wilderness; and behind them the peacocks of the
catacombs, symbols of immortality on account of their
longevity; and on either hand where the streams are
drunk up by the earth the good shepherd is feeding
his sheep; and the Church, turned away from Jerusalem towards Bethlehem, is doing that office which
the ungrateful city refused at His hands; not indeed gathering the little ones under her wings (for
she is depicted as a woman), but distributing to

her chickens, symbols of her children, the corn of salvation. And, that the shameful circumstances of the passion may not be altogether forgotten in the exuberance of the cross growing lilies and the true vine, nigh Bethlehem the time of night is indicated by the owl, and, in that fatal night, the temptation of the Apostle by the cock below it. But to Jerusalem is turned the lance which, in the hand of a soldier of the Caesar, struck the last blow the faithless people could inflict upon the sacerdotal King. « Before thee I opened the sea : « and thou hast opened my side with a lance ». The subtle delicacy of the artist is astonishing. Of the twelve white birds symbolizing the twelve apostles, the lowest and last, probably symbolizes S. John the Apostle, but, as his martyrdom, though attempted, was not actually effected, the upper half of the dove only appears, and the rest is hid in the verdure of the cross. There are two magpies and various other birds on either side, but we do not know what they symbolize. The serpent is indicated, but it is as a beautiful curve, of crimson and gold, terminated by a flower. In another line of subjects are the four great Doctors of the Church with their names. On the right S. Ambrose and Gregory, on the left S. Jerome and Augustine. S. Clement had been represented with S. Peter already, and there was no occasion to repeat him here : but the miracle of Sisinius is not forgotten. The object which the artist had proposed to himself, to make the cross the mystic vine, and to surround it with the gladness of the vine, the fowls of the air resting in its branches, the living creatures of the earth partaking of its abundance, did not leave space for an elaborate composition of the miracle. The figures are separated but the story is fully told. On the right Sisinius is being led by the boy, and Theodora is behind. The Sacrifice is indicated further on by the detached ecclesiastical figure in a stole with a censer, or perhaps the ciborium enclosing the Host; for in the arabesques at Ravenna a similar object is seen with two deer stooping towards it. On the left Sisinius in full costume, no longer blind, stands turned away with two men behind him. Further on his conversion is finished, for he stands alone making a votive offering of the gospel roll.

On the wall beneath is painted our Saviour, and around Him the twelve apostles separated by palm-branches. The apostles are standing on the bank of a stream in which are seen various fishes swimming. The Saviour is in the attitude of blessing with his right hand, and in his left He holds a scroll on which are written the words « Pacem meam relinquo vobis, « pacem meam do vobis », « My peace I leave you: « my peace I give you ».

We have dwelt too long upon this magnificent mosaic. The brilliancy of the colours, and the minute delicacy of the objects, are set off by its ground of gold. It would be a mistake to suppose that it was only a newer and more excellent developement of mediaeval art ; for the catacombic crypt of Praetextatus with its birds and its flowers, its roses and nests, its grapes, and ears of wheat, its harvest scenes and good shepherds, gives to its altar tomb as elegant and a more concentrated embellishment. There are some who with too fastidious philosophy, and too great a disregard of the mixed nature of man, would soar with the eagle, but not with the steadfast eye of S. John; would have no other vault for their devotions but the myriad constellations of the heavens. But the simple minded faithful cannot attempt such lofty flights. They need the more domestic images of the Church. When they turn from the labours of their daily life to rest the wearied senses, and find some pleasure in the pictures with which men seek to do some honour to God's house, they have beyond it a gratification which is not confined to the philosopher and is enjoyed by the beggar. « When the « Sacrifice is brought forth, when Christ the Lamb « of God is offered, when you hear the signal given, « let us all join in common prayer; then think you « see heaven opened and the angels descending from « above » (S. John Chrysostom).

APPENDIX.

TRANSLATION OF THE RELICS OF SS. CLEMENT AND IGNATIUS.

In the last century, Hannibal Albani, Cardinal Titular of S. Clement's, and nephew of Pope Clement XI, wishing to take relics of S. Ignatius, threw down the high altar, and destroyed the Confession (1) which existed beneath it. He took the leaden reliquary out of the Confession, and had the contents carefully transferred to another; but he did not restore the Confession. On the 22^d of June 1727, the Dominican Pope Orsini, Benedict XIII, preached from the gospel ambo in the choir; then he himself carried the reliquary on his shoulders, in procession assisted by cardinal Albani, and two archbishops, and placed it under the new high altar prepared, by the Cardinal Titular, the year before. Twelve cardinals, four primates, several archbishops, bishops, and prelates, and all the Dominican Friars

---

(1) Confession, in *Church History*, is a place in churches, usually under the high altar, wherein were deposited the relics of the martyrs.

in Rome with the most Rev. Father Thomas Ripoll, General of the Order, walked in the procession.

The excavations of the original basilica of S. Clement discovered, in 1857, by the writer of these pages, and cleared out and restored mostly by public subscription, made it necessary again to take down the high altar. The reliquary was removed on the 3rd of June 1866, and, on tuesday, the 20th of November 1867, was opened, and its contents examined by the proper ecclesiastical authorities. The reliquary contained :

1. Several bones of S. Clement and S. Ignatius.

2. A considerable quantity of earth, or ashes tinged with blood.

3. A glass vase, supposed to be as early as the first century, the inside of which is covered with a deposit of reddish hue.

4. A small phial of very ancient date, also containing coagulated blood.

5. Two crosses, one of wood, the other of metal. The former, at one time, evidently contained some relics.

6. An Agnus Dei made of bees' wax, with the figure of the lamb impressed on either side.

7. A piece of stone, or slate, with the inscription REL . S̄C̄T̄ . XL, relics of the Forty Martyrs.

8. A marble slab, on one side of which are engraved monograms, and on the other inscriptions. We give *fac similes* of both.

FAVS: CEMⱯR:
HE LICTE TI
LEO'I·DOCT'·XIS·ꝐVI·Aꝝ·Ꝑ·EG

The monogram may be read thus :

CHRISTVS . JESVS . DOMINVS

And the first two lines of the inscription, thus :

**FLAVIVS CLEMENS MARTYR
HIC FELICITER EST TVMVLATVS**

The third line is in small characters, and has puzzled the learned to decipher it. Vitry says of it: « It is easier to say how it should not be read, « than how it should be read » (1). Some decipher it thus — **Leo I Doctor Christianitatis anno CDXL assumptus Pontifex Ecclesiae.**

Others explain it — **Leo I Doctor Xystus martyr VI a Sancto Petro Ecclesiae Rector.**

Others — **Leo I Doctor Christi 13 mensis VI ad S. Petrum eumdem gestavit.**

If we were allowed to venture a conjecture, we would say that it should be read — **Leo I Doctor Decembris mense VI anno sui Pontificatus egit.**

---

(1) « Tertia linea facilius est dicere quomodo non sit legenda, « quam quomodo legenda sit ».

The ceremony of examining the relics having been gone through, they were kept under seal in one of the ambries in the sacristy until the high altar was prepared to receive them. In 1868, when the altar was re-erected, Pius IX ordered them to be replaced. The Cardinal Vicar, who has the custody of relics in Rome, directed that they should be transferred to a new copper urn. We felt that, in so ancient a church, ancient forms ought to be restored. To restore the Confession was impossible; but we obtained permission to put back the reliquary in its proper place, where the Confession once was, and where it was found; and as Cardinal Albani had taken away the lattice that was there, and closed all up with a porphyry slab, we had it removed and replaced by a *transenna* of the more appropriate ancient form. The reverence due to relics of martyrs, so early, and so renowned, in the history of the Church, as Clement first Pope of that name, and Ignatius, the Bishop of Antioch: and the recurrence of the feast of S. Ignatius, on the 1st of February, suggested a triduo of devotions to end on that day. His Holiness the Pope granted Indulgences for it.

The Cardinal Vicar came to the church on the 29th of January, and transferred the relics into the new reliquary, on which is the following inscription:

SALBO . BB . D . N . PIO . IX
ET . JVSSV . EJVS . C . CARD . PATRIZI
EPISC . PORT . ET . S . RVF .
RELIQVIAS . IN . THECA . ANTIQVA . DIE . X . JVNII . MDCCCLXVI
SVB . ALTARI . MAJORE . REPERTA
ITERVM . IN . HAC . THECA . REPOSVIT . DIE . XXIX . JANVARII
MDCCCLXVIII

The Cardinal Archbishop of Bologna, the most Rev. Father Jandel, General of the Dominican Order, the Community, and a few others were present at the ceremony of the translation. During the whole of that night the Community kept watch by the relics, and Cardinal Guidi, representing Cardinal De Bonnechose, Archbishop of Rouen, and Titular of S. Clement's, consecrated the high altar the next morning. At 3 o'clock in the afternoon, the procession with the reliquary set out, in the following order, from the altar of the subterranean basilica which was brilliantly illuminated.

The cross and banner of the Order followed by all the Dominican Fathers in Rome, the General coming last next the bier, which was covered with red velvet, and over it a pall of crimson silk and gold, open on one side to show the inscription, and ornamented on the other side with the monogram of Christ, copied from the porphyry cover of

Constantine's sarcophagus at Constantinople. The four bearers, in rich vestiments, were :

The Most Rev. Father Leo Salua O. P.
The Very Rev. Father V. P. O'Doherty O. P.
The Very Rev. Father Paul Stapleton O. P.
The Very Rev. Father Joseph Mullooly O. P.

The following dignitaries of the Church, wearing gold mitres and copes, walked beside the bier:

His Grace, the Most Rev. R. L. E. Antici-Mattei, Patriarch of Constantinople.

His Grace, the Most Rev. P. R. Kenrick, Archbishop of S. Louis.

His Grace, the Most Rev. F. X. De Merode, Archbishop of Melitene.

His Grace, the Most Rev. P. De Villanova Castellacci, Archbishop of Petra.

After the bier, came in cappa magna:

His Eminence Cardinal De Reisach.
His Eminence Cardinal Barnabò.
His Eminence Cardinal Pitra.
His Eminence Cardinal Bilio.
His Eminence Cardinal Mertel.
His Eminence Cardinal Guidi.

The Procession was closed by

His Grace, the Most Rev. P. Brunoni, Archbishop of Taron.

The Right Rev. J. A. Goold, Bishop of Melbourne.

The Right Rev. F. Marinelli, Bishop of Porphyrus; and several other Prelates, whose names we cannot recal to mind.

The Swiss Guard of the Pope walked beside the bier, and a Company of Zouaves kept the line of the Procession. It was followed by a great number of the Regular and Secular Clergy, who, accompanied by an extraordinary crowd of people, formed, as it were, a supplementary procession; and all seemed to profit by the following invitations addressed to them from the doors of the church of S..Clement:

1.

QVI . TRIDVANIS . SVPPLICATIONIBVS
SANCTORVM . CORPORA
IN . HAC . BASALICA . QVIESCENTIA
VENERATVRI . CONFLVITIS
FIDEM . AVGETE . PETITE . ET . ACCIPIETIS

2.

HEIC . VBI
APOSTOLORVM . CHRISTI . ET . SVMMORVM . PONTIFICVM
ENIXAE . AD . DEVM . PRECES . OLIM . ASCENDEBANT
CONVENIENTES . EX . OMNIBVS . MVNDI . PLAGIS . FIDELES
SANCTORVM . IN . AEDE . D . CLEMENTIS . QVIESCENTIVM
SACRAS . EXVVIAS . VENERATVRI
SCINDANT . CORDA . SPEM . AVGEANT . EXAVDIENTVR

The quiet kneeling reverence with which the reliquary was welcomed, as it moved above the cortege of Prelates towards the Coliseum, was most impressive. It was a picture of old Christian Rome to see that simple chest, containing nothing but the bones of men who had died for Christ, rising over the flashing steel, and plumed helmets glistening in the sun, and the crimson habits of the Princes of the Church, seventeen hundred years and more after the martyrs had passed through the waves of the Euxine sea, and the jaws of the lions of the Caesars, slowly nearing, with no sound but the Litanies of the Saints, the lofty ruins of the Flavian Amphitheatre, and descending into its midst. There in the centre, by the plain wooden cross, but not on the arena, where S. Ignatius, Trajan's victim, was given to the lions ; for time has heaped up mouldering decay, age after age, upon it, as if to hide, from human eyes, the hellish rage and cruelty of which men are capable who hold imperial power, and has draped with moss, and grass-green shrubs, and gay flowers, the tiers of seats up to which the conquered gladiator cast an imploring look for life, and where that ferocious race made the silent sign that they might enjoy the sight of the blood gushing from his heart ; there the Procession made a pause. Doubtless angels looked down from the battlements of heaven upon the scene, and *there* too the hymns of martyrs ceased, when *here* the Magnificat Antiphon rose upon the still air : « Hic est vere « Martyr, qui pro Christi nomine sanguinem suum « fudit, qui minas judicum non timuit, nec terre- « nae dignitatis gloriam quaesivit, sed ad coelestia « regna pervenit » ; and the clear voice of the Cardinal Archbishop of Bologna put up the prayer for all. « Look down upon our weakness, Omni- « potent God, and because the weight of our own « actions is heavy on us, may the intercession of « Thy blessed Martyr and Pontiff Ignatius pro- « tect us. » So it passed through the theatre of pagan diversions, and, returning by the Lateran road, entered, through the great door, the church of S. Clement, amid the hearty « Te Deum laudamus: « Te Dominum confitemur » : and proceeding at once into the choir, the relics of the Martyrs were laid in the Confession, and the marble *transenna* fixed before them.

Every day of the triduo there was a high mass, and vespers, in Gregorian chant, a sermon and benediction. The Most Rev. Father De Ferrari O. P. preached, on the first day, the panegyric of S. Cle- ment. He dwelt on the genealogy, conversion, learning, piety, exile, and martyrdom of the saint; and on the discovery of his relics by S. Cyril who brought them back to Rome and deposited them in the church built on his paternal house, and dedicated to his memory. On the second day, the Very Rev. Father Caprì O. P. treated of the martyrdom of the Consul Flavius Clement, of the holy life and saintly death of the cripple Servulus, who used to beg alms in the porch of our basilica, and of the missionary labours, and zeal of SS. Cyril and Methodius, the Apostles of Sclavonia. And on the third day Cardinal Guidi O. P. eulogized the virtues of S. Ignatius, Bishop of Antioch, one of the most illustrious and heroic martyrs of the early Church. His Eminence pointed to the Roman empire in its luxurious and cruel capitals of the West and East, Rome and Antioch, Rome filled with idols, Antioch pervaded by Judaism, though with a large Christian population: the Caesars vainly drowning S. Peter and S. Paul in their own blood, vainly bandying from East to West, and *vice versa*, their successors Clement and Ignatius, proving the unity of the Church in their very act, vainly sacrificing these and thousands of other lives, for apostolic blood watered the tree of faith, and on every side fresh heroes bore the Cross and conquered. He spoke of the spirit of Judaism never spent, and at work now in modern Europe. He called upon the Romans especially, again to kindle the fire of faith, again to rally by the shrines of the martyr saints: and gravely warned them if they failed. Then pointing at how faith, far from being extinguished, was lighted anew by the violence of the world; how the meek and suffering were the chosen champions of Christ, he asked to whom, in this our day, had God given these precious relics? To the poor and humble Dominican Friars of Ireland. To the children of that long suffering race whose faith no persecution of government could crush, nor any repentance of rulers adequately reward. There, beneath the altar, in that little chest, was their consolation, their hope, and their reward. And so as the evening drew in, and the lamps and candles in the old church grew brighter, again the Te Deum pealed, and a man, who has had no small part in the Pontificate of Pius IX, once a soldier, now an archbishop, Monsignor De Merode, slowly approached the altar and lifted up in benediction the Body of the Lord before which every Catholic head and heart must bow.

THE END.

INDEX.

A

Adelmus - 10.

Adrian I - 122. 123.

Aglae - 117.

Alaric - marches against Rome - is deterred from entering - marches again in 408 - returns the third time and enters it by the Salarian gate - XL.

Alexander I. P. and M. - Eventius and Theodulus interred on the Nomentan way, by Severina - V - Basilica of Alexander discovered on the Nomentan way in 1854 - XLIV - relics of in a sumptuous crypt, in the church of S. Sabina on the Aventine - *ib.*

Alexander Natalis - 37 note - 67. 68.

Alexius S. - painting of in S. Clement's - 170 - convent of on the Aventine - 171 - account of his life - 172. 176.

Alfred, the great, of England - 89.

Ambrose S. recovers the relics of SS. Gervasius and Protasius - 97. 265. 267. 276.

Anacletus P. - 19. 20. 21. 25. 26. 34.

Anastasius S. - 48. 122.

Andrew S. Ap. interred by Maximilla - V.

Anicetus P. - 18. 19. 26.

« Apostolic Constitutions » - 27. 28. - not by S. Clement - 29.

« Aromatibus sepelivit » explained - XV.

Art Christian - XXVIII - Eusebius quoted on drinking fountains - XXIX - restoration of after Constantine gave peace to the Church - XXXVII - bronze medallion of SS. Peter and Paul found in S. Domitilla's cemetery - good style of - *ib.* - painting of the martyrdom of S. Euphemia V. and M. of Chalcedon - XXX - Prudentius describes a painting of the martyr S. Cassian - XXXI - Eusebius quoted on early Christian art - XXVIII - on tablet of Constantine - *ib.* - after the peace of the Church, revived in the basilicas - XLII - votive paintings in the subterranean church of S. Clement, bolder in composition than those found in the catacombs - *ib.* - a link of ancient Christian art with the early Italian school - *ib.*

Assemanni, Simon - 52 note.

Assemanni, Louis - 52.

Asterius S. Bp of Amasea, quoted - IX. XV note - XXIX - describes a painting of S. Euphemia V. and M. of Chalcedon - XXX - also the festivals of the martyrs - XXXIII. XLIX.

Atina, a city near the Pontine marshes - 56.

Audisius - 9.

Augustine S. - 11.

Auphidianus puts the Christians of Cherson to various kinds of torture and death - 85.

Aurelia Marciana - IV.

Aurelius M. Syntomus - epitaph - IV.

Aymon - 32.

B

Baillet - 6. 9 note.

Baronius - 36. 49. 67. 68. 106. 153. 192.

Basil S. (379) praise of the martyrs - XXXV note. 52. 271.

Basilicas - 25 in Rome under Pope Cornelius (A. D. 251) - 252 - each title had two priests under Pope Damasus - XXIII note - on the destruction of the suburban cemeteries bodies of martyrs transferred to the city - XXIV - in the third century Rome had 46 churches - Christian burials take place in about the middle of 5th century - XXXIX - of Alexander P. and M. discovered on the Nomentan way in 1854 - XLIV - meaning and purpose of basilica - 109 - basilicas of Pagan Rome - 110 - Christian basilicas - *ib.* - some of those of Pagan Rome converted into Christian churches - 111 - design of - *ib.* - modern of S. Clement - *ib.* - ancient of - *see Clement's.*

Bassenius - 68.

Belisarius compels Ricimer, the Goth, to evacuate Rome - XL - expels Totila from that city - XLI.

Bellarminus - 68.

Bembo, cardinal - 167.

Bencini - 48.

Beno de Rapiza and his wife Mary - 164. 206. 207.

Berengarius - 231.

Bessarion - 51.

Besson, Father - his paintings in S. Sisto - 256.

Bianchi - 34.

Blaze S. patron of the wool combers of Norwich - 177 -

relic of, in S. Maria in Via Lata - 178 - another in his church in the Via Giulia - *ib*.

Boigoris, king of the Bulgarians - 92 - his conversion to Christianity - *ib*. - sends letters and ambassadors to Pope Nicholas I - 93 - abdicates in 880, embraces the monastic state - *ib*. 152. 214.

Boldetti - 48.

Bollandists - 36.

Boniface S. - 117.

Bosio, quoted - XLV.

Brun Le - 52.

Burial of the Christian dead - *see Dead*.

Burius - 35. 67. 68.

Butler, Alban - 20 note - 29. 37. 66.

Bzovius - 67.

C

Calendar Liberian - 34.

Calmet - 9 note.

Callixtus S. - inscription found in church of - cemetery of on the Appian way - XXXIX.

Cantu, Cesàre - 168.

Carmen against Marcian - 34.

Carthage - V - Council of - 119.

Catacombs, a name for some time exclusively applied to the crypts at S. Sebastian's - *see Cemeteries*.

Catharine S. of Alexandria - 135 - her body translated to Mount Sinai in Arabia - 135 - some of her relics at Rouen - 136 - painting of her martyrdom - *ib*. 143.

Cave - 9 note.

Cecily S. - relics of found by Paschal I - 98.
Celestine P. - 182. 183.
Celestius, condemned by Pope Zosimus - 121. 139. 178. 181.
Ceillier - 8.
Cella, or cella memoria, explained - VII - *memories* after persecution become basilicas - XIV. 115. 116.
Cemeteries, Christian, why constructed - XIII - no Pagans or heretics interred in them - XIX - Mithric tombs occasionally found in - *ib*. - Pope Zephyrinus sets Callixtus over them - XXIII note - cemeteries and lands confiscated under Diocletian - XXIII - forty six priests attached to, in 251. 252 - jurisdiction of priests and Popes over - XXIV note - suburban, when ruined by barbarians, remains of the martyrs removed from, into the city - XXIII - Pope John III (560. 573) restores them, has them furnished with lights, the holy sacrifice offered up there on every sunday - XXIV - habitual practice of Sergius I of the VIII century, whilst a simple priest, of celebrating in, recorded - *ib*. - Gregory III (731. 741) on the principal feasts of the martyrs provides for the offering of the holy mass in - XXIV - at the instance of the Benedictine Abbot, Gueranger, Pius IX revives the old custom of celebrating the holy sacrifice at the grave of S. Cecily - XXV - Prudentius (A. D. 405) quoted on the cemetery of S. Cyriaca - XXVI - the Christian cemeteries profusely painted - *ib*. - varied and beautiful representations of our Saviour, his blessed Mother and the saints - of the miracles of the Old and New Testament - many typical of the holy Eucharist and the other Sacraments - in fresco and on glass, found in - *ib*. - des-

truction of those above ground in Africa under Diocletian - XXXVII - subterranean - fall into disuse - XXXVIII - Melchiades last buried in - after the death of Julian the Apostate, use of visibly declines - XXXIX - first public invasion of by Valerian (A. D. 257) lasts three years - *ib.* - Gallienus orders the holy places to be restored to the bishops - *ib.* - again destroyed by Astolphus and the Lombards in 760 - restorations of by Adrian I and Leo III - XLII - bodies of S. Cecily and other martyrs removed from by Paschal I in 817 - *ib.* - others again by Sergius II and Leo IV - last restorations of by Nicholas I - *ib.* - Six of the Apostolic age reckoned by Bosio - XLV - bodies of SS. Peter and Paul, for nineteen months, rested in - *ib.* - cemetery of Alexandria - 133. 134.

Cerdon - 40.
Cerinthus - 39 note 140. 179.
Cesarotti - 9 note.
Christopher S. - 251.
Chrysanthus and Daria - 118.
Chrysogonus S. M. - 82 note.
Chrysostom S. - 52. 99. 203. 277. 292.
Churches - use of - XX. XXI - *see Cella and Basilica.*
Ciacconius - 2. 3. 12. 37. 53.
Ciampini - 118. 214. 282. 286. 287. 292.
Cicero - XXXVI.
Classical learning insufficient to elucidate Christian ruins - X.
Clement of Alexandria - 13.
Clement, Marcus Aricinus, twice consul - 6 - put to death under Diocletian - *ib.*
Clement S. Pope and M. - origin of his family according

to Zazera, Hesychius Salonitanus, and other writers - 5 - the « Recognitions » falsely attributed to - *ib*. - translated into Latin by Rufinus - *ib*. - born probably of an older son of Titus Flavius Sabinus, many years prefect of Rome - 6 - according to Tillemont, Ceillier and others of Greek or Jewish extraction - *ib*. - this opinion controverted - 7 - was a Roman noble citizen - *ib*. - his father called Faustinus or Faustinianus - *ib*. - his mother Matidia or Macidiana - 8 - was born on 1 of July, Sext. Elius and C. S. Saturninus consuls - *ib*. - had two brothers - *ib*. - converted by S. Peter - *ib*. - was companion and fellow-labourer of S. Paul - *ib*. - mentioned in Epistle of S. Paul to the Philippians - IV. 3. 9. - was not a Canon Regular, nor a Carmelite, nor first Bishop of Velletri, nor of Cagliari in Sardinia, nor of Sardis in Lydia - these opinions refuted - 19. 11 - is baptized and ordained deacon by S. Peter - 12 - converts many souls to Christ by precept and example - *ib*. - ordained priest, raised to the episcopal dignity and appointed co-adjutor in the Apostolic ministry - 13 - by his zeal and earnestness in the ministry he earns for himself the glorious title of apostle - *ib*. - not Bishop of Metz, as asserted by some writers - *ib*. - in this instance mistaken for his uncle - 14 - noted for purity of mind and chastity of body - 14. 15. 16 - letter to James, Bishop of Jerusalem - 16 note. 20. 27. 28. 30. 35 - was he the immediate successor of Peter ? - 16. and following pages - opinions of ancient writers on this subject - *ib*. - of the moderns - 27 - succeeds Linus and Cletus in the line of Popes - 33. and following pages -

the Ebionite and Marcotian heresies condemned by - 37. and following pages - divides the city into seven districts, and places over them as many ecclesiastical notaries, to collect the Acts of the Martyrs - 46. 47 - considered to be the founder of the Prothonotaries, called *Participantes* - *ib.* - styled by many writers the author of the Roman Martyrology - 48 - leaves in writing the form of offering the holy sacrifice of the mass, as delivered to him by the apostles - 49 - his care for the liturgy of the church - 50 - zeal for the diffusion of the Gospel - 54 - sends missionaries to France, Spain and elsewhere - S. Denys, the Areopagite, to Paris - S. Photinus to Lyons - S. Paul to Narbonne - S. Gratian to Tours - S. Julian to Mans - S. Austronomius to Clermont - S. Trophimus to Arles - S. Martial to Limoges - S. Ursinius, S. Nicotius, S. Saturninus to other parts of France - 54. 55 - consecrates Eugenius first bishop of Toledo in the 2 year of his Pontificate - 55 - his epistle on the occasion of the schism at Corinth - 56. 57 - its authenticity - 64 - second epistle to the Corinthians - 65 - two others to virgins - *ib.* - other works attributed to - 66 - is accused and cited before Mamertinus, the prefect - 81 - banished to Cherson - 83 - finds two thousand Christians condemned to forced labor in the marble quarries there - 84 - cheers and consoles them with the hope of the life to come - *ib.* - provides them with water in a miraculous manner - *ib.* - merciful effect of this miracle on the Pagan people - 85 - they destroy their temples and erect 75 Christian churches on their ruins - *ib.* - he inspires and animates the martyrs to suffer, as it becomes Christians to suffer - is himself cast into the sea, with an anchor made fast to his neck, by order of the prefect Auphidianus - 86 - the Christians implore of God the recovery of his body - *ib.* - miraculous result of their pleading - *ib.* - the receding of the waters - the marble temple - the finding of his body - and the instrument of his martyrdom - annual recurrence of the reflux of the sea, for two centuries, on the anniversary of the Saint's martyrdom - *ib.* - remains discovered by S. Cyril - 87. 95 - brought to Rome and honorably placed in the basilica of his name at the foot of the Caelian Hill - 103 - oratory of - 112 - memoria of - 119. 149 - basilica of erected about the beginning of fourth century - *ib.*

Clement S. - subterranean basilica of - votive paintings discovered in - bolder in composition than those found in the catacombs - XLIII - a link of ancient Christian art with the early Italian school - *ib.* - basilica built upon his own house - XLVII - style of its decorations - XLVIII - its frescoes the earliest Christian compositions now left to us - *ib.* - peculiarity in their arrangement - *ib.* - homily of S. Gregory the Great on S. Servulus in - 122 - restored by Adrian I - 122. 123. 131 - donations of Leo III to - 123 - ruin of accounted for - 125 - all records of it disappear, or are forgotten 126 - discovery of - 127 - architect employed in its restorations, Cavaliere Fontana - 128 - inscription facing entrance to - 129 - description of - 130 - paintings in - the martyrdom of S. Catharine of Alexandria - 136 - the Council for condemnation of Celestius - 138 - the Madonna niche - 142 - fragmentary figure of our Saviour - 147 - crucifixion of

S. Peter - baptism by S. Cyril - and other remnants - 150 - Libertinus - 154 - two anecdotes of the subject of this painting - 154. 155 - installation of S. Clement by S. Peter - 160 - S. Clement saying mass - 161 - miracle of Sisinius - 162. 163 - S. Antoninus - Daniel in the lions' den - 168. 169 - S. Alexius - 170. and following pages - S. Egidius and S. Blaze - 175. 177 - S. Prosper of Aquitaine - 178 - Crucifixion - 184 - the Marys at the sepulchre - 185 - descent into Limbo - 186 - marriage-feast at Cana - 187 - Assumption of our blessed Lady - 189 - miracle at the tomb of S. Clement - 203 - translation of relics from the Vatican to S. Clement's - 208 - our Saviour blessing according to the Greek rite - 211 - head of a female - 214 - head of a man - 215 - our Saviour releasing Adam from Limbo - 215 - Sarcophagi, and monumental and lapidary inscriptions found in - 218. and following pages - fragment of altar to Mithras - 222 - Conclave held here in 1199 - its titular Cardinal, Raynenius elected Pope - 240.

Clement S. - modern basilica of - the most perfect model of early Christian basilicas - 126 - preliminary remarks on - 223 - was erected before 1299 - restored by Clement XI in 1715 - 242 - inscription - *ib.* - *paintings* on walls of nave, executed in the last century - 243 - death of S. Servulus, by Chiari, described - 244 - condemnation of S. Ignatius, by Piastrini - 245 - his parting with S. Polycarp, by Triga - 246 - his devouring by the lions, by Ghezzi of Ascoli - 246 - S. Clement giving the veil to Flavia Domitilla, by Sebastian Conca of Gaeta - 248 - the same causing water to flow from the rock, by Grechino - *ib.* - S. Clement cast into the sea, by Odasi of Rome - *ib.* - translation of relics of S. Clement, by Chiari - 249 - on the ceiling of nave, the saint's entrance to glory, by the same artist - *ib.* - on the end wall of nave, SS. Cyril and Methodius, in episcopal robes, of the Greek rite - 250 - the chapel of the Crucifixion and S. Catharine of Alexandria, painted by Masaccio, described - 250. and following pages - ancient inscription outside this chapel - 254 - chapel of S. Dominic - 255 - the altar-piece by Roncalli - the paintings on side walls by S. Conca, or Ignatius Hugford - 256 - chapel of Blessed Sacrament - 259 - vaulted with glazed terra-cotta sunk in panels - *ib.* - statue of S. John the Baptist, by Simon di Donatello - *ib.* - the cinque-cento monument of cardinal Roverella, and that of his nephew, Francis Brusati, described - 259. 260 - chapel of our Lady of the Rosary - altar-piece, by Conca - monument of cardinal Venerio of Recanati, outside it, described - 260. 261 - porch, quadriportico and vestibule - discipline of the church therein - 261. and following pages - interior described - 274. and following pages - monogram - 280 - ambones, choir, and apsidal mosaic - 285. 286. and following pages.

Clement, Titus Flavius Sabinus, many years prefect of Rome - 6 - is banished by Diocletian - 45.

Cletus S. - 16. 18. 21. 23. 25. 26. 32. 33. 34 - suffers martyrdom (A. D. 92. 93) - interred in the Vatican - 37.

Column, Antonine - 87 - Trajan - *ib.*

Collyridian, heretics - 191.

Confession - public - prohibited - 269.

Constantine - 138.

Cornelius S. Pope - Cereale and Salustia with twenty others interred by Lucina, in a crypt on her farm, on the Appian way - VI - under Pontificate of Cornelius (A. D. 251. 252) 46 priests in Rome connected with parishes and cemeteries, and only 25 basilicas - XXIII note.

Coteler - 36 works of S. Clement collected and published by - Paris 1672 - 67.

Coustant, Peter - 32. 40.

Cyprian S. quoted - XIX.

Cyril of Alexandria S. - 277.

Cyril Lucarius - 57.

Cyril S. Constantine of Thessalonica - discovers the relics of S. Clement - 87. 95 to 97. 102 - carries them with him on his missions - 103 - apostle of the Chazari - 91 - converts that nation - *ib*. - on his second mission to the Bulgarians, is attended by his brother Methodius - 92 - conversion of Boigoris - *ib*. - they pass into Moravia and baptize king Rastices and most of his people - *ib*. - Cyril first Bishop of the Moravians - 94 - apostle of the Sclavonians - *ib*. - Sclavonian alphabet invented by - *ib*. - with his brother, they translate the liturgy and mass into that language - *ib*. - comes to Rome on the invitation of Nicholas I - carries the relics of S. Clement with him - 94. 103 - dies in Rome - *ib*. - is interred in the Vatican - translated to the church of S. Clement - 105 - condemnation of Nestorian heresy by - 147 - painting of - 152. 208. 209 to 214.

D

Damascene, S. John - 68.

Damasus S. - XL. XLIV - his church - XLVIII.

Dead - the Christian - burial of, a sacred duty - XVII - S. Ambrose quoted on this point - XVIII - prayer for - *ib.* - liturgies of the second half of fifth century record burial of - in the basilicas - XXXIX - burial of, usual in Rome in sixth century - *ib.* - custom of burial nigh to the martyrs' tombs, revived by P. Damasus - from 370 to 372. XL.

Diocletian - his persecution - XXIII - sacred pictures destroyed during - XXVII - burns and ravages the holy places in 303 - XXXIX. 133. 137. 138.

Domitian - beheads his cousin-german, the consul Flavius Clement - 45 - banishes his own sister, Flavia Domitilla, the wife of Flavius Clement, to the island Pandatereia - *ib.* - he exiles his niece, Flavia Domitilla, for having embraced the Christian faith, to the island of Ponza - *ib.* - his persecution - *ib.*

Domitilla - inscription from cemetery of - XXIV note.

Donatists - 177.

Dubravius - 93. 106.

Dydimus - 133.

E

Ebion - 140 - Ebionites - 37. 38 - excommunicated by the African Bishop S. Victor - 141. 179.

Eleutherius - 19.

Ennodius of Pavia - 284.

Ephraim S. Bishop of Cherson - 86.
Epiphanius S. Bishop of Salamis - 8. 25 - quoted - 27. 35. 37. 38 - notes - 67.
Epitaph of M. A. Syntomus and Aurelia Marciana - IV.
Eugenius, emperor - 133.
Eulogia - 134.
Euphemia S. of Chalcedon - description of a painting of - by S. Asterius Bp of Amasea - XXX. 143. 146 - church of at Rome - *ib*.
Euphimianus - 171. 174.
Eusebius, quoted on early Christian art - XXVIII - on tablet of Constantine - *ib*. 8. 20. 25. 35. 41 44. 203.
Eutychian P. and M. interred in the cemetery of Callixtus three hundred and sixty two martyrs himself; buried there - VII note.
Eutychian heresy, condemned - 146. 147.
Evaristus - 19. 26.
Evodius, Bishop of Uzalis - 102.

F

Fabian, P. (A. D. 236. 250) appoints seven deacons in charge of the poor of the several districts of the city, and ordains as many subdeacons to collect the Acts of the Martyrs - XXIII note.
Fontana Cavaliere - 128.
Fountains, Christian - XVIII.

G

Gallandius - 20. 67.

Galerius - 137. 138.

Gallicciolli - 6.

Gallienus, orders the holy places to be restored to the bishops - XXXIX.

Gamaliel - 99.

Gaudentius Bp of Brescia - 30.

Genseric the Vandal (A. D. 460) destroys Rome and its suburbs, excepting the three principal basilicas - XL.

Germanus Bp of Auxerre, legate of Pope Celestine to Britain - 141. 182.

Gervasius and Protasius MM. - relics of - 98.

Gnostics - 40.

Gracchus - 150.

Grafiti - 146. 195.

Grancolas - 52 note.

Gregory S. the Great, quoted - XI note - his letter to the hermit of Ravenna, quoted by Adrian I when writing to Charlemagne on holy images - XXXI. 127. 154. 244.

Gregory III - *see Cemeteries*.

Gregory S. of Nissa - 395 - his description of a Christian shrine - XXXI. and following pages. 102. 187.

Gregory of Tours - 86.

Gregory VII - 125. 126. 131. 226.

Gueranger, Benedictine Abbot - *see Cemeteries*.

Guiscard, Robert - 238.

H

Hammond, Henry - 36.
Henry IV of Germany - 226. and following pages.
Heinschenius - 10. 33. 107.
Hilaria - relict of Claudius M. - 118.
Hilary S. quoted - XX. 276.
Honoratus - 154.
Honorius emperor - 142.
Horace - 10. 14.
Hyginus - 19. 26. 40. 41.

I

Iconoclastic Mania - LI.
Ignatius S. Bp of Antioch - part of « letter to Philadelphians » attributed to - 15. 74 - condemned to the wild beasts by Trajan - 75 - conducted to Rome - *ib*. - his interview with S. Polycarp at Smyrna - his letters to various churches - *ib* - his letter to the faithful at Rome quoted - 75 to 80 - devoured by lions in the Coliseum - 80 - his relics borne with religious veneration through all the cities between Rome and Antioch and deposided there - *ib* - translated to the church of S. Clement - Rome - (A. D. 637) - 81.
Innocent I - 24 note - declares the Roman liturgy of Apostolic origin - 52.
Ireneus of Lyons on S. Polycarp - 17 - made Bishop (A. D. 177) - quoted - 18. 19. 21. 25. 27. 35. 40. 41. 140.
Isidore Mercator - 31. 32. 34.

J

Jerome S. - IX. XXVII. 8. 27. 35. 56. 66. 127. 264.
John III - *see Cemeteries*.
John VIII - 94.
Justa, a pious and religious matron, inters the body of the martyr Restitutus on her farm, on the Nomentan way - VI.

K

Kerostata - 163.

L

Labbè - 31.
Ladvocat - 9 note.
Lanfranc - 232.
Leibnitz - quoted - 155.
Leo the Great prohibits public Confession - 169.
Leo III - 123.
Leo IV - 123. 124.
Leo emperor (A. D. 813.) - LI.
Licinius - 138.
Lucian priest finds the relics of S. Stephen protomartyr - 98.
Lucina, two ladies of the name - their devotedness to the burying of the martyrs - V. VI.
Lupus Bp of Troyes - 182.

M

Mabillon - 52. 153. 192.
Mai Cardinal 55.
Marcellus P. (A. D. 308. 310) sets apart within the city, twenty five titular churches for Pagan converts, and

burial of the martyrs - XXIII - invites Priscilla to erect another on the Salarian way - *ib.*

Marcotian heresies - 39.

Mark (A. D. 336) buried in cemetery of Balbina - XXXVIII.

Mark and his followers at Lyons - 41. 43.

Mark the Manichean - 43.

Martini - 9. 192.

Martyrology, an Epitome of the Acts of the Martyrs - 48 - see *S. Clement.*

Martyrs - honor paid to - and why - XXI - praised - XXIV - festivals of - XXXIII - shrine of, described by S. Gregory of Nyssa - *ib.* - praised by S. Basil - XXXV note.

Mary S. of Egypt - 263.

Masaccio (Tommaso Guidi) - 136. 250.

Maurist Fathers - 55.

Maximinus - XX. 136. 138.

Memoria - 116. 118.

Mercurius Cardinal, afterwards John II - 281.

Methodius S. brother of S. Cyril of Thessalonica, assists in the conversion of the Bulgarians - 92 - his painting of the last judgement - *ib.* - Borivorius, duke of Bohemia, baptized by - 94 - builds several churches at Prague - *ib.* - Apostle of the Sclavonians - *ib.* - assists his brother Cyril to translate the liturgy and mass into their language - *ib.* - obtains leave of John VII to celebrate mass in the Sclavonian language - 95. 106 - comes to Rome under Nicholas I - *ib.* - after S. Cyril's death becomes Archbishop of Moravia - 95. 106 - his archiepiscopal See of Moravia is exempted from the jurisdiction of Saltzburg by John VIII - 106 - dies in Rome and is buried in church of S. Clement - *ib.* - portion

of his relics sent to collegiate church at Brunne in Moravia - 107. 209. 213. 214.
Mithras - 133. 140 - worship of, proscribed in Rome - 150 - broken altar dedicated to, described - *ib*.
Monogram - 120.
Muratori - 34. 52. 233. 234.

N

Narses, after the defeat of Totila, marches upon Rome, which the Goths surrender to him - XLI.
Nestorian heresy condemned - 147.
Nibby - 127.
Nilus S. - his advice to a friend, who was about building a church - XXXII.
Nimbus, square - signification of - 195.

O

Oldoinus - 9. 10. 13. 53. 55.
Optatus, Bishop of Milevis, in Numidia - 25. 26.
Origen - 14 note.
Orsi - 34.

P

Pacian S. - 264. 286.
Pagi - 33. 67. 193.
Panciroli - 107. 127.
Paschal I discovers the relics of S. Cecily - 98.
Paul, the deacon - 13.
Paulinus S. of Nola, quoted - XXXII. 101. 198. 268.
Pearson, John - 36.

Pelagius - 141. 147. 178. 180. 181.
Peregrina, mother of S. Andrew Corsini - 90.
Peter S. comes to Rome and fixes his See there - 2 - his preaching - 4 - who his immediate successor - 16 - consecrates Linus of Volterra, Cletus, and Clement of Rome - *ib*. - memoria of - *ib*.
Peter and Paul SS. - traditional likeness of - XXXI - earliest medallion of - XXXVII.
Peter de Natalibus - 86.
Phara - 10.
Photius - 11.
Pin du - 226.
Pius I - 19. 26.
Polycarp - 19. 23.
Pompeia Graecina - VI.
Praedestinatus - 39.
Primus and Felicianus MM. - 117 - basilica of - *ib*.
Priscilla - cemetery of, on Salarian way - XXIII - Sylvester (A. D. 314. 336) buried in - XXXVIII.
Proclus P. of Constantinople - 49. 51. 52.
Prosper S. of Aquitaine, secretary to Leo the Great - 183.
Prudentius - *see Cemeteries* - an incident on his way to Rome - XXXI.
Pudentiana S. - church of - remains of several martyrs and sponges impregnated in their blood, found in - V.

R

Rabanus Maurus of Mentz - 30. 31. 32.
Raphael of Volterra - 11 note.
Rastices duke of Moravia - 92. 93.

Relics of saints and martyrs - veneration and love of the church for - XVI. LII.

Religious system cannot be constructed from the catacombs alone - XLII.

Renaudot, Eusebius - 52 note.

Ricimer, the Goth, towards the close of the V century besieges and destroys Rome - XL.

Rohrbacher - 9 note.

Rondinini - 9. 10. 14 note. 29. 35. 47. 55. 127. 162.

Rossi, Commendatore de - XIX. XXVII. XXXI. XXXIX. 5. 6. 12 note. 153. 215.

Rufinus - « the Recognitions » translated into Latin by - 5. 13 note. 26. 31.

S

Sardes, Bishop of - his answer to the Iconoclastic emperor, Leo - LI.

Schulting, Cornelius - 51.

Sebaste, in Armenia, forty martyrs of - 176. 197.

Semipelagians - 176. 183.

Sergius I - *see Cemeteries.*

Servilius, Troilus - 117 - memoria of - *ib.*

Servius - 67.

Servulus S. - 122.

Severina, wife of count Aurelian - V.

Simon S. of Jerusalem - of more than a hundred years - tortured and crucified - 73.

Sirletti Cardinal - 10.

Sisinius - 162 - conversion of - 166 - embraces the Christian faith and seals it with his blood - 163. 303.

Sisto S. - his church - paintings in chapter room by Father Besson, a French Dominican - 256 - subjects of explained - 256. 257.

Sixtus I - 19. 26.

Sixtus V increases the number of Prothonotaries from seven to twelve - and confers additional privileges on - 47.

Solinina, a Christian, mother of emp. Gallienus - XXXIX.

Soter - 19.

Sozomen - 268. 269.

Spelman, sir Henry - 89.

Stredowski - 94.

Stephen S. protomartyr - 98 - miracles wrought at finding of his body - 100.

Subiaco - 154.

Sylvester (A. D. 314. 336) buried in cemetery of Priscilla - XXXVIII.

Symmachus - 127.

Symphorosa S. and her seven children suffer martyrdom under the emperor Adrian (A. D. 120) - V.

T

Telesphorus - 19. 26.

Tertullian - XXVII note. 4. 19 - quoted - 20. 22. 23. 24. 27. 40. 266.

Thecla, an Egyptian woman, transcription of S. Clement's letter to the Corinthians by - 57.

Theodora, mother of the emperor Michael III - 91. 162. 303.

Theodoret - 198.

Theodosius emp. - 133. 142.

Theodosius, two of this name - their errors - 141.

Tillemont - 6. 7. 36.

Tomb, pagan, description of - III - Christian, adaptation of - IV.

Totila takes Fiesole and lays siege to Rome in 545 - XL - enters it by treason, April 546 - XLI - drives the people into the Campagna - *ib.*- expelled by Belisarius - *ib.* - returns again, but is routed with much slaughter - *ib.* - attacks the city a third time, in 549 enters by the gate Asinaria - keeps possession of it till 552 - slain in the engagement with Narses in the passes of the Appenines - XLI. 154.

Tullius Servius - 149.

Turrianus - 67.

U

Ughelli - 11.

Ugone - 127.

Urban VIII revises and approves the Sclavonian Missal of SS. Cyril and Methodius - 94.

Usher - 49. 51. 52.

Uzales, Bishop of - 262.

V

Valentinian - 40. 41.

Valerian (A. D. 257) invades the cemeteries - XXXIX.

Vendolinus, Godfrey - 13. 33.

Venema, Henry - 66.

Victorinus - 286.

Vossius, Isaac - 13.

W

Waterworth - 52.
Westein - 65.
Whiston - 67.

Y

Young, Patrick - 55 - translation of S. Clement's letter to the Christians at Corinth by - 57.

Z

Zachary P. (A. D. 202. 218) sets Callixtus over the cemeteries - XXIII note.
Zosimus P. S. - condemnation of Celestius by - 121. 139. 142. 181. 285.

The right of Translation is reserved.

ERRATA		CORRIGE
	page	
dependants	I.	dependents.
Eutichyan	VII note	Eutychian.
there	ib.	three.
superstion	VIII.	superstition.
paralitic	X.	paralytic.
eat	XIII.	ate.
Tobit	XVIII.	Tobias.
Priscilla	XXIII.	Priscilla
sucking up his		soaking up his
blood on	XXVI.	blood from.
Dyonisius	XXXIX	Dionysius.
irresistably	3.	irresistibly.
unroll	49.	unrol.
dust	74.	durst.
Pylicarp	75.	Polycarp.
least	ib.	lest.
Behemiae	95 note.	Bohemiae.
censo	171.	censer.
travels	194.	travails.
Zozomen	268-9.	Sozomen.

NIHIL OBSTAT
Fr. Thomas Burke O. P. R. O.
Fr. Ph. V. O'Doherty O. P. R. O.

IMPRIMATUR
Fr. Marianus Spada O. P. S. P. A. Magister

IMPRIMATUR
Joseph Angelini Archiep. Corinth. Vicesg.

BX 1004 .M84 1869 SMC
Mullooly, Joseph,
Saint Clement, pope and
martyr, and his basilica in
47235130

ImTheStory.com

Personalized Classic Books in many genre's

Unique gift for kids, partners, friends, colleagues

Customize:
- Character Names
- Upload your own front/back cover images (optional)
- Inscribe a personal message/dedication on the inside page (optional)

Customize many titles Including
- Alice in Wonderland
- Romeo and Juliet
- The Wizard of Oz
- A Christmas Carol
- Dracula
- Dr. Jekyll & Mr. Hyde
- And more...

CPSIA information can be obtained
at www.ICGtesting.com
Printed in the USA
BVHW081502270519
549348BV00014B/693/P